International Jobs

Where They Are ☆ How to Get Them

ERIC KOCHER

International Jobs

Where They Are ☆ How to Get Them

A
Handbook for
Over 500 Career Opportunities
Around the World

Addison-Wesley Publishing Company

Reading, Massachusetts · Menlo Park, California
London · Amsterdam · Sydney · Don Mills, Ontario

The letters that appear on pages 37 and 38 are reprinted from A TREASURY OF THE WORLD'S GREAT LETTERS, FROM ANCIENT DAYS TO OUR OWN TIME, ed. M. Lincoln Schuster, copyright © 1940, 1968 by Simon & Schuster, New York. Reprinted by permission of Simon & Schuster, a Division of Gulf & Western Corporation.

The author is indebted to all organizations whose annual reports and informational material were used to describe their functions in Part II.

Library of Congress Cataloging in Publication Data

Kocher, Eric, 1912-
    International jobs.

    Bibliography: p.
    Includes index.
    1. Vocational guidance. 2. Americans in foreign
countries--Employment. I. Title.
HF5381.K596   331.7'02   79-50800
ISBN 0-201-03898-6
ISBN 0-201-03899-4 pbk.

*To all students everywhere—and their parents—who
cast a longing eye on international work;
and
To Peggy, who was once a student herself and still has that glint in her eye.*

Acknowledgments

This handbook would not have been written without the contribution of students. In a sense they have written it for me, because the problems they have posed in their search for an international career—and the various courses of action we have discussed—provide the material that appears in the following pages.

An older group, Foreign Service Officers leaving the Department of State for other international jobs, must also be thanked. Many of the job leads developed in my work with this group have found their way into this Handbook.

Special thanks must go to a number of my recent colleagues at the School of International Affairs of Columbia University, especially Deans Harvey Picker, Ainslie Embree, Robert Randle, and Steven Noble for their helpful suggestions on the manuscript. I am indebted particularly to the latter's assistant, Pearl Brown, who knows the field of international job opportunities as few others do.

Thanks also to a group of students for their special assistance: Jane Weeks, my research assistant, who tracked down crucial information on the functions and addresses of organizations with international interests; Howard Lew, whose special art was to transform an illegible handwritten paper into an exemplary typed manuscript; and finally to Inna Efimov, who meticulously and imaginatively prepared the manuscript for submittal to publishers.

International Jobs—Where They Are, How to Get Them is being used by the Council for Intercultural Studies and Programs as the handbook for its International Careers Advisory Service, for which Eric Kocher is the Senior Consultant. For more information, write to:

Council for Intercultural Studies and Programs
60 East 42nd St.
New York, NY 10017

Contents

Introduction

Introduction

This handbook is for everyone interested in an international career, whether an undergraduate at college or a graduate student. If you are already at work full-time but wish to explore opportunities in the international field, it will also help you in shifting jobs and/or careers.

The purpose of this handbook is to broaden your knowledge of international career opportunities so that you can find the job you want. Its contents are divided into two parts: Part I is concerned with career planning and job strategy; Part II, with the international job market.

In Part I, we take up job-hunting problems chronologically as you will probably experience them. First you have to plan your career in the international field (Chapter One). Then you will want to tailor your curriculum to one or more possible careers (Chapter Two). If you are a student looking for summer work overseas—or if you are the spouse of an American working abroad who decides to get a job—you will need information on work permits and any special problems related to work in a foreign country (Chapter Three). On any job hunt—whether for summer or full-time employment—you must present yourself in the strongest and most favorable light using three main tools: job letters, résumés, and interviews (Chapter Four).

Even with the most effective job strategy in the world, you will not get far unless you know your target. This subject—the available job opportunities in each international field—is so crucial it constitutes a special section of the handbook, Part II.

The handbook recognizes that some of you may know specifically what kind of international career you want; others may not yet have defined your goal any more closely than "doing something international."

No matter which group you are in, the following breakdown of international career opportunities, which is the focus of Part II, will be of interest to you:

Federal Government (Chapter Five)
United Nations (Chapter Six)
Nonprofit Organizations (Chapter Seven)
Business and Banks (Chapter Eight)
Journalism, Broadcasting, and Publishing (Chapter Nine)
Teaching (Chapter Ten)
Law (Chapter Eleven)

The names and addresses of organizations in each field are listed, as well as a brief description of their functions. Further, the handbook lists the qualifications for each type of job.

If you know which career or careers interest you, you will want to look closely at the detailed opportunities available in these fields. If you are not attracted to any particular career, you may wish to browse through Chapters Five through Eleven. Perhaps exposure to the organizations and jobs in each international field may dissipate the uncertainty and inspire you to experiment with one particular career.

PART I

International Career Planning and Job Strategy

First Questions

Despite an occasional longing for isolationism, the United States seems firmly committed to internationalism. This orientation is shared by government and private sector alike. As a result, job opportunities in the international field cover a broad spectrum. The range encompasses most well-known occupations: federal government, business, communications, banking, nonprofit organizations and foundations, and of course the whole United Nations system.

This diversity of occupations affords unparalleled opportunities for those of you who know what you want to do in the international framework and who prepare yourselves accordingly. A career decision, however, needs focusing and definition if you want it to work for you, "Doing something international" is usually only the first stage in a decision. Your goals must be further narrowed to help you compete effectively with others who are also entering the international market.

Do you want to be a Foreign Service officer working in one of the embassies of the Department of State? Do you wish to be an intelligence analyst for the federal government? Or a branch bank manager in some remote—or cosmopolitan—part of the globe? How about a UN employee working on developmental problems of Third World countries? Or a foreign correspondent in Rome, Paris, London—or Ougadougou or Tegucigalpa—for one of the press services?

All of these are acceptable and reasonable career goals. But don't be so rigidly committed to one that everything else is excluded. If, for example, you want to work in the UN Development Programme, don't overlook similar job opportunities in the Agency for International Development (AID) or development work in foundations. If your aim is to be a *New York Times* correspondent in Moscow, consider also working as an overseas press officer for the federal government's International Communication Agency.

The first question, then, is, "What is it I really want to do in the international field?" Your answer will probably be narrower than "doing something international" but broader than "the UNDP office in Bangladesh." If you are really lucky, you may be able to achieve a very specific objective such as the latter, but the odds are against you so it is generally preferable to keep yourself flexible—within limits. As you go through this handbook you will find that a career objective need not be nailed down to one specific job. There are related jobs that will use your background just as fully and probably give you equal satisfaction.

After you have decided what it is you really want to do in the international field, you will come upon another major question needing equal attention: "How available are jobs in the field or fields I have chosen?" Then further questions will have to be looked at: "How do I prepare myself so that my academic credentials are strong enough to attract employers? What limiting factors (such as location and salary) exist in my job search? Are there special considerations—because of the international aspect—that enter into my job strategy?" These are some of the questions that will be discussed in this handbook.

What Exactly Is an International Job?

"International" does not necessarily mean "abroad." You can have an international career working in the international division of a corporation in New York and seldom if ever go overseas. You can work in the Department of State in Washington and spend your whole career on foreign policy problems without leaving the country. The usual international career, however, consists of varying degrees of work at headquarters and in the field.

What Do You Want to Do?

A specific job objective (or objectives) is the foundation on which the edifice of job-hunting techniques is built. If you don't know what you're looking for, the search becomes aimless, each action taken by itself without relation to a central focus.

Still, there are no absolute truths in career guidance and exceptions to the above do exist. None of the international careers available may attract you sufficiently to orient your curriculum toward such an objective, narrow or broad. Accordingly, you may decide—either consciously or through failure to make a choice—to "hang loose" and "see what comes up." In other words, you stick with "doing something international," which is usually only the first step in a career decision.

International drifting does not necessarily mean disaster or an unsatisfactory professional life. It *does* mean that the initial job hunt may be more difficult; it can also mean that the level you reach on the organizational ladder may not be as high as that of some of your colleagues. If you are prepared to accept these risks because of your own emotional predispositions, don't allow yourself to be pushed into a career in which you have little interest.

What if You Don't Know What You Want to Do?

If you don't know what you want to do but prefer not to drift, you will be seeking two kinds of knowledge. One is self-knowledge, an awareness of your skills, capabilities, and emotional needs; the other is knowledge about the world of work.

Self-knowledge lies beyond the scope of this handbook and may be explored through psychological and testing centers as well as self-evaluation. Knowledge of the kind of international work available is more tangible. A large part of this handbook is concerned with providing information on this subject. But you will also want to inform yourself about various international careers in a number of other ways.

Available Literature

There are many books and brochures giving information on international careers. The UN organizations, the various federal agencies, nonprofit organizations—all have informational literature available for the asking. Banks and businesses have annual reports and recruiting brochures, also readily available. Glamorized as much of this material may be, it will give you helpful information on organizational functions, availability of jobs, and career development.

Especially useful is the *Encyclopedia of Careers and Vocational Guidance.** It is in two parts: *Planning Your Career* (volume one) and *Careers and Occupations* (volume two). If, for example, you wish to explore a vague attraction for banking without much knowledge of the field, go through the material on banking in these volumes. In the first volume you will find information on the nature of banking, opportunities in the field, educational preparation for a career, and areas of employment. Volume two discusses specific bank jobs, such as the functions of a lending officer or the meaning of credit analysis. Each job category lists information on qualifications needed, methods of entering the field, advancement opportunities, employment outlook, earnings, and conditions of work. By going over this material and visualizing yourself in a number of roles, you will make progress in determining their suitability for you and yours for them. The various Departments of Labor in the federal and state governments also have much useful reference material on occupations and job functions. Much of this material will round out your knowledge and clarify questions arising from your study of the two-volume *Encyclopedia.*

If you are interested in federal government work, be sure to get *Guide to Federal Career Literature* put out by the US Civil Service Commission. This lists the brochures used in nationwide recruiting by each federal agency. For example, under Department of State we find two brochures listed, *Examination for Foreign Service Officer Careers* and *The Foreign Service of the Seventies,* both of which can be obtained easily from that Department. Order the *Guide to Federal Career Literature* from the US Civil Service Commission, Washington, DC 20415 or from the Government Printing Office, Washington, DC 20402 (price: $1.05). Also, directories of businesses and banks (see the bibliographies) are available in your city or college library.

Friends, Relatives, and Alumni

It is said that 85 percent of all jobs are obtained through contacts. Even if the correct figure is only 60 or 70 percent, that percentage is still too high for you to ignore this most important source of jobs. Have you friends or relatives working in organizations with international interests? If so, go see

---

* (Garden City, NY: Doubleday, 1967, revised edition, 1975-76).

them. Get names of alumni in specific international occupations from your school and ask them about their work. Knowledgeable people are better sources of career information than printed material, which sometimes raises more questions than it answers. Talk to your contacts at length. Find out how they prepared for their careers, how they obtained their jobs, what their career development has been. In particular, get information on what they do on a daily basis. A detailed description of their functions may provoke boredom, curiosity, or enthusiasm in you; whatever the reaction, this information provides one more indication of your suitability for that field of work.

The Outlook for Each Occupation

If you have read the available literature on one or more careers and talked to friends, relatives, and alumni, you should by now have a great deal of useful information. You may be quite turned off by one or more of these careers—or perhaps your interest has grown and you are eager for further exploration.

Suppose you are favorably disposed toward one of these international occupations. What sort of future does it have? Is it a growing industry or a shrinking one? What will it look like in the year 1984 or 2001? The *Occupational Outlook Handbook** is helpful in answering these questions. If you consult the *Handbook*, you will find, for example, that the number of bank jobs (not necessarily international) is expected to increase rapidly through the 1980s.

Substantial increases in employment are also expected in the fields of population, ecology, conservation, energy, pollution control, service industries (such as leisure activities and hospital care), and manufacturing (rubber, plastic products, and furniture, for instance). Concerning federal government employment, the numbers of professional and administrative personnel will probably increase in the next decade, whereas employment in clerical jobs will most likely decrease.

Experiment: Summer Jobs

Expose yourself whenever possible to various kinds of international work. One way is to look for summer and part-time jobs.

There are more summer jobs in the federal government than elsewhere because the government has a policy of attracting young talent. Therefore, each agency is encouraged to provide a certain number of jobs for beginning professionals during the summer.

These jobs are listed in *Summer Jobs—Opportunities in the Federal Government*, a brochure available in December or January of each year. Go

---

* (Washington, DC: US Department of Labor, 1978–79 edition).

through the job listings and you will find many opportunities for those with a background in economics (sometimes international economics), public administration, and business administration. This booklet can also usually be found in a college placement office or at the local office of the US Civil Service Commission. Get it as soon as it is issued because deadlines for submitting applications are sometimes as early as the end of January.

Summer exposure to government work is not only remunerative, it also provides illumination on the pressures, peculiarities, and pleasures of a government career. In almost all cases, Standard Form 171, Personal Qualifications Statement, and Form 226, List of College Courses, available in college placement offices or at the local US Civil Service office, are needed to apply for these summer jobs. Exams are usually not required, although a high rating on the Professional and Administrative Career Exam (PACE) or a place on the Mid-Level Civil Service roster will be helpful. (These exams are discussed in Chapter Five.)

If your career aims lie in nongovernment directions, you may have a harder time getting a paid summer job with international content. Some years ago many large businesses and banks with international interests had regular summer programs that employed graduate students working toward these careers. Now, however, the size of these programs has been whittled down to the selection of a very few highly qualified and talented students.

Another drawback: If you are specializing in international business or banking within your MA in international relations you will find yourself competing with MBA students for the few summer jobs available. The MBAs may have the edge in getting business jobs because they will have had more technical business courses and need less training to become productive in a short-term assignment. On the other hand, you may have the edge in getting the bank jobs, because as the international earnings of banks increase vis-à-vis their domestic earnings, these organizations turn to schools of international affairs for their young professionals. More on this later.

The experience of summer work abroad can be one of the strongest items on your résumé; it is also one of the most difficult to get. Hardly any organizations—whether they are business, banks, nonprofit organizations, government, or the United Nations—will pay your transportation abroad for a job lasting only two or three months. In addition, there is the considerable problem of work permits (see Chapter Three). If you can get overseas on your own, however, your chances improve considerably. Contact the foreign branches of American or international organizations for possible short-term work; these include US embassies and consulates, UN offices, businesses, and local Citibank and other bank branches in whatever country you happen to be.

Finally, the Council on International Educational Exchange (777 UN Plaza, New York, NY 10017) publishes a fact sheet on employment abroad that discusses opportunities for short-term unskilled jobs, primarily in Europe.

Experiment: Internships

If you can't find a paid job, a useful alternative is to volunteer as an intern and accumulate experience that will help you get the paid job you want later.

In fact, internship and paid summer work can sometimes be the same, since a stipend may occasionally come with the internship.

Here are some organizations that usually use interns each summer, and sometimes during the academic semester as well. Where a stipend is paid, that fact will be noted.

United Nations

Secretariat Send UN P-11 Form (obtainable from college placement offices or from the UN Office of Personnel), giving an indication of several types of work in which you are interested and qualified, e.g., international economics, Middle East research, social studies, or youth programs. Look at Chapter Six for additional information. Write to:

> Office of Personnel Services
> United Nations Secretariat
> United Nations
> New York, NY   10017

UN Office of Public Information This office has two internships each summer, one in New York and one in Geneva. A general international background suffices. Chapter Six has additional information. Write to:

> United Nations Office of Public Information
> United Nations Secretariat
> United Nations
> New York, NY   10017

UN Development Programme Internships exist both at headquarters in New York and in field offices overseas. A background in economics, economic development, and/or developing areas is needed. Write to:

> Recruitment Office
> Division of Personnel
> United Nations Development Programme
> 1 UN Plaza
> New York, NY   10017

Federal Government

Department of State Internships are available both in headquarters in Washington as well as in various embassies abroad. Applications (a résumé and a statement of motivation) must be sent to the Executive Office of the geographic Bureau for which you have qualifications, for example, the Bureau of African Affairs, Bureau of East Asian and Pacific Affairs, or Bureau of European Affairs. A stipend is usually available only in US embassies in Africa. In all cases, you are responsible for your own transportation abroad.

Banks

Citibank Internships both in New York and in various branches abroad are available. A stipend is paid if you are lucky enough to get an assignment overseas. Obviously, you should have an accounting and finance background, although economics may be used as a substitute if you can show motivation for a banking career. Write to:

> Internships
> Citibank
> 399 Park Ave.
> New York, NY   10043

European American Bank Here again, internships may be in New York or in an affiliated bank abroad, for instance, Deutsches Bank or Société Générale of Brussels or Paris. In addition to a banking or economics background, the language of the country of assignment is required. Stipends are sometimes paid for overseas work. Write to:

> Internships
> European American Bank
> 10 Hanover Square
> New York, NY   10005

Business

Mobil Oil Internships both in New York and overseas (Paris, London, Rome) have been available. A small stipend is given. Language of the country of assignment is desirable, along with a marketing background. Write to:

> Mobil Oil
> 150 East 42nd St.
> New York, NY   10017

Pan American Airways Internships have been available for those with a marketing background and aviation interests. Those with a Latin American background should apply to the Latin American Division; those with an Asian studies background, to the Asia–Pacific Division; and those with a European background, to the Atlantic Division. The beautiful part of these internships is that the lucky successful candidate in the past has received free transportation plus a good stipend. Write to:

Pan American Airways
Pan Am Building
New York, NY   10036

Communications

Newsweek For those with a journalism background plus some area knowledge and research interests, this is a good place to try. Write to:

International Division
Newsweek
444 Madison Ave.
New York, NY   10022

Associated Press Again, this is for those with a journalism background and motivation for a journalism career. Write to:

Associated Press
50 Rockefeller Plaza
New York, NY   10020

United Press International UPI usually requires a journalism background, also. Write to:

United Press International
220 East 42nd St.
New York, NY   10017

Experiment: Academic Work

You can also expose yourself to an occupation through academic work. If, for example, you have been looking into a journalism career but are still plagued with uncertainties, take a course or two in international communications. It won't be long before you get an idea of your competence in the field as well as another indication of how comfortable you might feel as a practicing journalist.

If you decide that taking a course for credit is too much of an investment in time because of your career uncertainties, the next best thing is to audit a course. Listen to the lectures and class discussions. Auditing won't be as helpful as doing all the class work but it will take a minimum of time while throwing some light on your interest in the subject matter.

Experiment: Visit Job Sites

Another way to savor a career—albeit superfically—is to visit the job site. If, for example, you think you might be interested in a banking career, visit a bank just to sense what goes on. Enter without any thought of depositing or withdrawing money. Observe the comings and goings of people, the faces of tellers, the activities of all those enterprising people sitting behind the Vice-President signs on their desks. Get the "mood" of the place. Is this the right atmosphere for making your own special impact on the professional world, whether your aims are for money, prestige, self-expression, security, helping people, or a combination of all of these and more?

Unfortunately, this type of impression-and-information gathering cannot always be practiced. In the foreign-oriented agencies of the federal government—e.g., the Department of State or the CIA—you will probably find yourself in deep trouble if you tell the guards at the entrance that you "just want to look around."

College Placement Offices

If still in school, you should consult your placement office during each stage leading to your career decision. A knowledgeable placement officer can be enormously helpful in expanding your job horizons. He or she will not make a career decision for you but can act as a sounding board for your questions and doubts.

Mobility Between Careers

Even after informing yourself thoroughly about a career, you may still hesitate to make a decision. You're pretty sure but not absolutely sure. Further, you fear that any decision will commit you to a specific career for the rest of your life.

Recognize that there will almost always be a degree of uncertainty in any career choice you make. It is the rare individual who will be absolutely certain. It is only when you are actually at work that you will really know the atmosphere, the people, the details of the job, and all those other fine, intangible points that sometimes make the difference between liking and not liking the work.

When you have reached the stage of 80 or 90 percent certainty, perhaps it is time to relax. No choice is irrevocable or totally binding. If you start in on an international banking career, for example, and later wish to slip over into government, the skills and experience you have learned will strengthen your credentials for work with the Treasury Department, the Export-Import Bank, and other government agencies dealing with matters of international finance.

If, to take an outside example, you should decide to switch from banking to a career in the theatre, you'll have less immediate mobility. The choice of quite a different career may mean returning to school or otherwise gaining credentials to make you attractive to an employer in that field.

Fortunately, mobility between careers these days is higher—and more acceptable—than it was some years ago. Employers are now usually more tolerant of individuals who move from one career to another. Instead of change being viewed as the action of an insecure or even neurotic individual, it is often considered as adding richness and depth to an applicant's background and personality.

Are Languages Important?

It depends. For the Foreign Service of the Department of State, no—initially. You can be hired without any foreign language capability, but you will be placed immediately in a rigorous language training program. For the United Nations, French and Spanish are important but even more important are economics, economic development, and area studies. For businesses dealing with China and Russia, knowledge of these languages is highly desirable, but even more desirable is a background in technical business subjects: accounting, finance, marketing. Language, then, is an extra added attraction—one more arrow for your job-hunting bow—but it's not usually what you get hired for.

BA? MA? PhD?

Two of the most-asked questions are, "How far will a BA get me?" and "Do I need a PhD?"

A BA won't get you very far but it's not worthless. In some careers, such as Foreign Service of the Department of State, no degree at all is needed. If you can pass the written Foreign Service exam through your own accumulated knowledge, you have the same chance of eventual entry as the PhD. In government jobs depending on a Civil Service rating (see Chapter Five), a BA will qualify you for some lower-level jobs. The same applies to business and banking. In some small nonprofit organizations a BA is quite adequate, and if you apply with a PhD you may well be told that you are overqualified.

As for the second question—"Do I need a PhD?"—the answer again must be hedged. In essence, the value of the doctorate depends on the kind of job you are seeking.

If you are after a teaching job at any level over junior or community college, the PhD is necessary. If you wish to go into profound research (e.g., in international relations, regional studies, or international economics), the PhD will be exceedingly helpful. If you are after a career in international banking, business, or journalism, the PhD is either irrelevant or may even be considered a liability—unless you have a persuasive answer to the question, "Why did you take a doctorate instead of courses in accounting, finance, marketing, or journalism?" The old "egg head" aspersion is liable to be encountered by a PhD trying to break into these fields—plus honest doubts about your motivation for this kind of career.

A further warning: Don't take the PhD just because the extra two or three years will postpone the fears and frustrations of job hunting. The economic climate some years from now may be better—or worse. So why postpone the inevitable unless the extra degree will help you toward your international job objective? In other words, know your motivation for taking a PhD. Know how you will use it and what it will do for you.

In general, an MA is an optimum degree for most international jobs.

Should I Go to a School of International Affairs?

If the optimum degree is an MA in international affairs, the optimum way of getting it is through a school of international affairs. There are several that deserve your particular attention: Columbia University's School of International Affairs, New York City; Georgetown University's School of Foreign Service, Washington DC; Johns Hopkins' School of Advanced International Studies, Washington, DC; Princeton University's Woodrow Wilson School of Public and International Affairs, Princeton, N.J.; and Tufts University's Fletcher School of Law and Diplomacy, Medford, MA.

A degree from any of these schools will bring you closer to the international job you want. The help given is not only through their excellent international curricula but also through the prestige enjoyed by each school in organizations with international jobs.

Some or all of the following career-oriented programs are offered in these schools:

Career Conversations Representatives of various international organizations come to the campus each week to discuss careers in their fields.

Career Workshop Material covered includes available job opportunities in the international field, academic and professional qualifications for entry jobs in each occupation, and job strategy, including résumés and interviewing techniques.

Career Day Alumni representing each major international occupation visit the campus for in-depth discussions of careers in each international field.

Trip to Washington An annual trip to Washington for those interested in exploring a career with the federal government.

Field Work An internship with an international organization. Students taking field work perform a substantive project of value to the organization. Reimbursement is usually not received, but academic credit may be given toward the degree. Time spent on the job may vary from one or two days a week during the academic semester to five days a week during the summer. Field work programs abroad during the summer may be available at US embassies, at UNESCO headquarters, in field offices of the UN Development Programme, and in foreign branches of banks, businesses, and the wire services.

In Chapter Two we will assume that you are now finishing your academic work and are unsure how and where to use the skills you have acquired. What international jobs are available for someone with your background? Suppose, say, that you have a major in international economics, Russian studies, or even in that most amorphous of specializations, foreign policy. Who will find your credentials of particular interest? Where do you apply?

CHAPTER TWO

Making Your Academic Studies Work for You

So far we have discussed the problems inherent in planning an international career. Now it is time to focus in more detail on the vital connection between your academic work and the attainment of your career goals.

Career Objectives and Academic Courses

In planning your curriculum, you should ideally work backwards from your career objective. Your starting point should be: "What do I want to do *after* I have my (graduate or undergraduate) degree?" Try to answer this question before you finish—and preferably before you *start*—your international studies.

Once you know what you want to do with your degree, the other necessary decisions fall into place: first, the choice of a major or specialization within international affairs; and then the selection of courses within this concentration. By knowing the result of your academic work, you will be able to choose the best courses to reach your goal.

For example:

If your career objective is	*Your specialization should be*
International banking	International finance and banking
International business	International business
International communications (journalism, broadcasting, publishing)	International media and communications
US government Foreign affairs agencies (State Department, AID, ICA, etc.)	International economics, economic development or world resources, area studies, foreign policy
International divisions of domestic agencies (Departments of Commerce, Labor, HEW, etc.)	International economics
UN agencies	International economics, economic development, world resources, preferably combined with area studies and French or Spanish
Nonprofit organizations	International economics, economic development, world resources, or area studies, depending on the nature and orientation of the organization

In some cases, the choice of a specialization is an obvious one. If you eventually want to be a foreign correspondent, you will take a specialization in international media and communications. If you want a career in international banking, you will take courses in international finance and banking; and if you want your future to be in international business, you will specialize either in that or in international marketing or international finance, depending on which track you wish to follow.

However, if you wish to enter the Foreign Service of the State Department, your choice of specialization is less obvious. You can approach your goal either through area studies or international economics, or a generalized background in international affairs and foreign policy. This plan works also with the other career objectives listed.

The above progression—starting with a career choice and working backwards to specialization and courses—represents the ideal. Further, it avoids the fatal embarrassment of deciding during your last semester before graduation that you want to go, say, into international journalism only to discover that you have never taken any of the required courses for jobs in that field.

A General vs. Specialized Background

But suppose, despite all logic, you have worked forward. You have taken international courses in college or grad school without knowing what kind of work you want. Graduation comes along and anxiety, if not actual panic, takes over. You still don't know what you want to do. What organizations will find your academic work attractive? Where do you apply for a job?

Let us take three types of academic backgrounds in international affairs—(1) a major in international economics, (2) a major in area studies (Chinese, Russian, Middle Eastern, African, Latin American, and so on), and (3) a generalized background of international courses without specific focus—and trace their acceptability in the federal government, the UN structure, in nonprofit organizations, business and banks, and in the media organizations.

International Economics

This is one of the most valuable and job-worthy majors or specializations that you can offer. There are more jobs available for economists, particularly in the US government, than for those with most other international skills. International problems, which were at one time considered purely political, now are seen as having important economic components. Accordingly, job opportunities for those with an economic background extend to almost all international occupations.

US Government Both the foreign-oriented and the domestic agencies of the government value those with an economic major or specialization (see Chapter Five).

UN Organizations Most UN vacancies require economic skills. Try particularly the United Nations Secretariat, the Development Programme, the Population Fund, the International Children's Emergency Fund (UNICEF), and the United Nations Institute for Training and Research (see Chapter Six).

Nonprofit Organizations Many of these, except for those oriented toward academic exchanges or cultural matters, need economic-minded individuals (see Chapter Seven).

Businesses and Banks Even though most corporations are seeking skills in finance, accounting, and marketing, some of them find economics an acceptable substitute (see Chapter Eight).

Media Writing and reporting skills are of paramount importance in these organizations, but even here a knowledge of economics that can be expressed in simple popular language can be put to good use (see Chapter Nine).

Area Studies

You may have taken Russian, Chinese, or other area studies with the thought of teaching after getting a graduate degree. When faced with the difficulty of finding a teaching job, you have perhaps decided to explore research or nonteaching jobs. Where then can you put your area specialization to good use?

If you have taken mostly political courses in your area, you may find yourself at a disadvantage on the job market; the purely political problem is a rarity. Accordingly, you may be required to show some expertise in economics, marketing, or journalism, depending on the kind of job for which you are applying. This means that with an appropriate second major or subspecialization you will increase your chances of being tapped for a vacancy.

US Government Area studies with a political orientation will limit your attractiveness. Try the Department of State, the Central Intelligence Agency, the National Security Agency, or the Library of Congress. With economics, however, your chances improve, and you can get a favorable reception in a broad range of agencies, both foreign-oriented and domestic (see Chapter Five).

United Nations If you have area studies without economics, your main chance is to apply to the UN Secretariat, where some political research is undertaken. Area studies with economics, however, will give you a hearing in many other UN organizations (see Chapter Six).

Nonprofit Organizations A politically oriented area background will be best received in those organizations geared to that area, such as the Center for Inter-American Relations (for those with a Latin American background), or the Citizens Exchange Corps (for those with Russian studies). Again, your chances increase if you add a subspecialization or minor to your concentration,—economics, administration, or cultural studies, for example (see Chapter Seven).

Businesses and Banks Sole emphasis on the political side of area studies will not get you very far. Finance, marketing, and accounting are still considered the optimum background for an applicant, although exceptions occasionally occur. An export–import firm about to start trade with China may find political knowledge of China plus fluency in the language of sufficient importance to overcome deficiencies on the business side. The same consideration may apply in the case of a bank starting a branch in Moscow or a Japanese bank opening a branch in New York. But these are rare opportunities. It would be wise to broaden your background with economics, marketing, finance, and accounting if you hope for serious consideration in these organizations (see Chapter Eight).

Media The political specialist with an area background should look to research periodicals, such as *Time, Newsweek,* and *Facts on File.* Otherwise, an area knowledge without journalism studies will not get you far. A rare exception may be the sudden need of a wire service for an area and language specialist in one of its overseas offices (see Chapter Nine).

If I Have Two Specializations, Should Both Be Played Up in Applications?

This depends on the job for which you are applying. In some cases, your chances increase because of the two specializations offered. In other cases, only one background is relevant. If, for example, you have a dual background in Latin American studies and economics, both count heavily if you apply to the Agency for International Development. If, however, you apply for a job in the Center for Inter-American Relations, your Latin American background is probably going to be all important and economics of little relevance. In still other cases, it may be that your economics will be the more attractive specialization and your Latin American studies of subsidiary or no importance. In other words, know the type of job for which you are applying, so that the appropriate part of your background can be emphasized on your résumé and in your interview.

Note If you were not born in the United States, you probably do not have to prove your credentials as an expert in the part of the world from which you come. Therefore, unless you have overriding reasons for taking an academic major in the area of your birth, it would be helpful to have some specialization in which your credentials must be proved, such as business, economics, or journalism.

Generalized International Background

You are in the danger zone if you have no specific major or concentration in the international field. Most organizations with international interests have become more specialized over the years, and they now look for specific skills when they recruit new employees.

What do you do if you have taken a hodgepodge of international courses? You have no area specialization; you have insufficient economics to claim a concentration; you have no marketing, accounting, finance, and certainly no journalism. Your chances are distinctly limited, but they are not nonexistent. Try the following fields:

US Government Even though most government agencies have a constant need for economists or area-trained people, openings do exist occasionally for administrators and those classed loosely as "foreign affairs/international relations specialists" (see Chapter Five).

Nonprofit Organizations Unless these organizations have area interests (for example, the Asia Society) or are into development (the Ford Foundation or the Overseas Development Council), they sometimes prefer to fill vacancies with people who have a generalized international background (see Chapter Seven).

Myths and Realities

The relationship of academic work to career goals is full of myths that, unfortunately, most students do not uncover until it is too late. So perhaps the best way to summarize this chapter is to list some of these myths—and their corresponding realities.

Myth	*Reality*
Courses on the United Nations and international organizations are helpful in getting a UN job.	The United Nations primarily wants economics, economic development, area studies, and languages.
An economics specialty is necessary for a business or banking job.	Only in rare cases. Normally business employers want an international business major; banks want finance and banking majors.
Students aiming for a career in international business or international banking will get jobs in those fields if they take courses in economics of the firm, business in a changing economy, statistics, industrial management, and industrial relations, instead of marketing, finance, or accounting courses.	Business employers usually look for marketing and accounting; banks usually require accounting and finance.

Myth	*Reality*
Foreign-born students should specialize in studies of the area from which they come; i.e., African students should major in African studies as a help on the job hunt.	Employers assume that the foreign-born have intimate knowledge of their part of the world; academic studies in that area are therefore usually not needed.
General courses in foreign policy are helpful on the job hunt.	Except for the Foreign Service and some nonprofit organizations, these courses rarely help.

CHAPTER THREE

How to Get a Job When You Live Overseas

Getting a job in the United States is plagued with well-known difficulties. Getting a job overseas is plagued with the same difficulties plus a few more unique to the foreign milieu. For one thing, in these days of increasing unemployment and nationalism, most countries—including the United States—insist that their nationals receive priority in the local job market. This means that a foreigner usually must have a work permit, which is not easy to get. Often the foreigner has to find a job before the permit is issued. The employer in turn is given the sometimes difficult task of showing that the job opening cannot be filled satisfactorily by a native of that country. Long-winded forms of justification must often be completed by the employer, who will clearly not relish the bother unless the foreigner to be employed has qualifications vastly superior to the local competition.

Start the Hunt at Home

How then can you maximize your chances for getting a job when overseas? One way is to start the job hunt *before* you leave the United States. If you are able to find a job abroad while you are still here, it sometimes simplifies the problem of legalizing your work status. With a job promise under your belt you may receive a work permit or at least diminish the procedural hassles in getting yourself legalized.

Immediately, however, you run up against a new set of difficulties. Before you are offered a job, you usually must have an interview. If you're in the United States, how do you arrange this interview with an employer who may be twelve thousand miles away? Sometimes, foreign employers may be visiting the United States and interviews can be arranged, but this is a rare opportunity. Usually there is no touring representative of the company at hand and the only way to get an interview is to pack your bags and travel overseas.

Fortunately, there is sometimes a small loophole out of this almost impossible situation. In countries that have close economic ties with the United States, many important jobs—and even some that are less important—require a knowledge of English. This is especially true of Japan. As a result, there are many language schools in that country filled with Japanese from all walks of life learning English. This in turn has created a demand for English language teachers. Japanese journals in America often carry ads for this type of work. The qualified applicant can write to several of these Japanese schools and might perhaps be offered a job without an interview. Once the job is obtained, a work visa is readily forthcoming from the Japanese Embassy in Washington or the Japanese Consulate General in New York.

This is an exceptional situation, admittedly. But you will probably have to search out many exceptional situations before you land a job overseas.

Another unusual way to minimize permit problems is to get a job with a foreign organization in New York, such as a British bank. If, after working there a while, you ask for a transfer to England, your supervisor may be able to arrange it; if not, perhaps you can at least get introductions to officers at headquarters in London.

Also before you leave the United States, explore possibilities with the headquarters of American banks and businesses that have a branch in the country you expect to visit. You won't have your transportation paid—and you won't be sure of a job—but you may be able to carry with you an introduction from headquarters to the branch manager in the country where you will be going.

To get lists of American companies with foreign branches, go to the reference desk of any large library and ask for the *Directory of American Firms Operating in Foreign Countries,* compiled by Juvenal Angel and published by Simon & Schuster.

Another interesting prospect exists for those of you who have a journalism background and are interested in writing. Arrange, if you can, to submit articles from abroad to the wire services—Associated Press, United Press International, North American Newspaper Alliance—or to large metropolitan or small-town dailies in the United States. There will be no guarantee that your articles will be accepted, but if they are, you will be paid. Another advantage to being a "stringer" is that you will not be hamstrung by permit problems.

Actions Abroad

Suppose that you find yourself abroad—perhaps as the spouse of someone working for an American firm—and then decide you want to work. Immediately you come up against a Catch 22: You won't be able to get a job unless you have a work visa, but in some cases (again let us use the example of Japan) you won't be able to get the visa unless you apply for it *outside* Japan. This results in a rather ludicrous series of events. First you have to latch on to a job in Japan; then you must leave the country for, say, Korea, where you will apply for a work visa from the Japanese Embassy; and finally, when you get it, you return to Japan endowed with the legal wherewithal for work. The procedure is the same whether your employer is Japanese or American, a bank or a language school. There is an exception, however: If you are a student in Japan and you want to work part-time, permission can be obtained from the Japanese authorities without leaving the country.

Americans abroad often take jobs illegally, hoping that the authorities will not catch up with them. This may work if employers cooperate in the conspiracy and if the job is temporary or part-time. Most governments find it hard to police work laws when abuses are both widespread and muted.

Procedures: Two Cases

Since the employment situation varies from one country to another, we will examine the policies of other nations, primarily England and France. Both are meccas for tourists and students, some of whom, infatuated with the foreign ambience, impulsively decide to take a year off, stay abroad, and, of course, work.

Nonstudents

A work permit is required in England and, as might be expected, is extremely difficult for nonstudent foreigners to obtain. You have to be outside England to get it, and the proposed employer has to prove to the government that no British citizen has the appropriate qualifications for the job under consideration. If, for example, the job requires excellence in Urdu, Arabic, Chinese, Japanese, Russian, Serbo-Croatian, and Malay, and you happen to be fluent in all six languages, it may not be hard to beat the British competition and get the work permit and the job. However, if you apply for ordinary clerical work in an office, neither will probably be forthcoming.

If you are not a student, getting a work permit and a job in France has been termed impossible in official government quarters. Even though nothing is really impossible, getting legal jobs for nonstudent foreigners comes perilously close to it. Chances are you will be in France under a tourist visa, and work permits are not issued for that category. The sole possibility seems to be a black-market job (some part-time or casual work for which the employer is willing not only to hire you but also to conceal your presence from the authorities). An American we know, unable to find work legally, learned that a chateau on the outskirts of Paris was about to be renovated by its owners. He persuaded them to hire him both for his skills in carpentry and for his willingness to teach them English.

There are always jobs to be found—in France and elsewhere—by those with initiative and without preconceived ideas of the level or type of work they are willing to accept. But if you have trouble, don't go rushing to the nearest American Embassy or Consulate General with your work permit problems. The most they can do is direct you to the appropriate foreign authorities or, in some cases, inform you of regulations and procedures for obtaining the permit.

Students

The prospects for students are brighter, especially in England, Ireland, France, and New Zealand. In these four countries the Council on International Educational Exchange (CIEE) in New York can be of help. For a fee of $35 (for Ireland the cost is only $20) you can get a permit allowing you to work. In France the permit is good for a summer; in the other countries, up to six months any time during the year. No guarantee of a job goes with the permit, but quite obviously, with a permit in hand you have a better chance of connecting with a job.

For additional information on job opportunities in other countries, you may find it useful to consult the *Whole World Handbook,* which can be obtained from the CIEE for $3.95. Write to:

> Council on International Educational Exchange
> 777 UN Plaza
> New York, NY   10017

Since the difficulties and procedures for getting permits to work abroad vary among nations, get detailed information on the problems you will face before you leave the United States—from the particular embassies (in Washington) or consulates (usually in New York) of the countries where you want to work. If you are a student, be sure to mention that fact, since you will probably find fewer obstacles in your path toward summer or part-time employment.

Special Situations

International Association of Economic and Management Students (AIESEC)

This association offers a worldwide program of work traineeships. Students are placed in positions in industry abroad, usually for the summer. They receive a stipend to cover living and incidental expenses. Over 3,500 students are placed annually in traineeships in fifty-five participating countries. Write to:

> International Association of
> Economic and Management Students
> 622 Third Ave.
> New York, NY   10017

International Association for the Exchange of Students for Technical Experience/United States (IAESTE/US)

This organization has a program for students of engineering, architecture, mathematics, and the sciences to obtain on-the-job training with employers in forty-six countries. Traineeships usually last from two to three months during the summer. Some longer-term placements are possible by special arrangement. Trainees receive a maintenance allowance and pay their own costs of travel. Write to:

> International Association for the Exchange of Students
> for Technical Experience/United States
> American City Building
> Columbia, MD   21044

Central Placement Office of the Federal Republic of Germany

The **Zentralstelle für Arbeitsvermittung** (ZAV) in Frankfurt has a special job placement service—without charge—for students of several countries, including the United States. Most of the jobs are available only to women, but a limited number of opportunities exist for men. Jobs are usually for the summer, last a minimum of two months, and ordinarily are in hotels and restaurants. Write to:

> Zentralstelle für Arbeitsvermittung
> Feuerbachstrasse 42
> 6 Frankfurt am Main 1
> Federal Republic of Germany

CHAPTER FOUR

Attack and Counterattack: Getting the Job

Now that you have identified an international career that interests you, and (if still in school) tailored your curriculum to help achieve this goal, you come to the two final stages of the job search.

The Final Stages

The first stage is uncovering the many kinds of international opportunities available. These opportunities are so diverse and numerous that Part II of this handbook is given over entirely to listing the organizations where jobs may be available, as well as the necessary qualifications.

The second of these stages is planning your campaign. Until now you have been preparing yourself—through self-analysis, studies, research—for the attack. At this point the tempo increases considerably. Now you must use all the training and knowledge you have accumulated to impress a number of employers with your qualifications so that you get the job you want.

No matter what career you have in mind—banking, law, the Foreign Service—the strategy you use to reach your goal consists of three simple tools: (1) a letter of application, (2) one or more résumés, and (3) a few techniques for the interview. These three—letter, résumé, and interviewing techniques—are common to all job strategies, whether your goal is domestic or international. You will almost never get a job without an interview, and you will ordinarily not get an interview without first submitting a letter and résumé. The trick, then, is to make your letter interesting enough to lead to a reading of your résumé, which in turn should be impressive enough to lead to an interview.

Many books, some of them listed in the bibliography, have been written on letters, résumés, and interviewing techniques. Here we shall dwell primarily on those aspects of strategy that are different for the international arena.

Before you start sending out résumés and letters, you will have to make three fundamental decisions:

**1. Do You Want to Work Abroad or
at International Headquarters in the United States?**
The decision may be based on personal desire or on family considerations, but the question will have to be faced and the answer known before you start the job hunt. If, for example, you have a spouse who is unwilling to live abroad, you may have to eliminate the Foreign Service and some Citibank jobs from your goals—unless you are prepared for a separation or divorce. Likewise, if you have an ailing parent, you may have to adjust your target to family needs.

2. When Should You Start Looking for Work?
The lead time for international jobs is often longer than for other types of work. In government jobs the time between initial application and a job

offer may be as long as eighteen months because the security check itself may take up to six months. Jobs in the UN system may take up to a year because of the many levels of approval needed. In a business where hiring is decentralized, approval may have to be obtained from a branch office in the country where you will be working.

For government and UN jobs, then, begin the application process at least a year before you want to start working. With other types of international work, count on a lead time of four or five months.

3. To Whom Should Letters and Résumés be Sent?

If you have no contact in an organization, you may automatically assume that you should apply to the Personnel Section (often called Human Resources Section). It's an easy solution, but resist it. *It is preferable to apply to the head of the section in which you want to work.* If the organization has an International Division, sending your letter and résumé to the head of that division will net you an advantage because your international training will be more highly valued and understood when examined by someone knowledgeable in the field. Of course, it takes time to research the organization and to determine if there is an International Division, and if so, the name and title of the person in charge. But sometimes the effort pays off.

A student with a major in Asian studies and international economics once sent his résumé to the Personnel Section of a large corporation. Personnel rejected him offhand. Undeterred, he applied directly to the Asian Department of the corporation and had no difficulty in making contact with a high official of that department. An interview followed. A month later a job developed and he was subsequently hired. Admittedly, this type of success story does not always happen, but it does happen frequently enough to warrant the extra research required to identify those involved in the international work of an organization.

The following is a rough guide to optimum contact points in each of the international occupations covered in this Handbook:

Government

Foreign-oriented agencies: Personnel Section (these agencies have exams and panels to screen applicants, so there is little point in trying to bypass Personnel)

Domestic-oriented agencies: International Division (Civil Service rating needed)

UN Agencies

Heads of divisions in which you are interested; otherwise, Personnel Section

Nonprofit Organizations

Large foundations: International Division

Small foundations: President or Chief Executive Officer

Businesses
>Large businesses and multinationals: International Division
>Small businesses, including export-import: President
>>or Chief Executive Officer

Banks
>International Division, if there is one; otherwise, Personnel Section

Communications
>International Division, if there is one; otherwise, Publisher, Marketing
>>Chief, or Personnel Section

Letters

Four examples of letters used in the application process follow:

1. Letter in response to a job vacancy notice, at school or in the classified ads.
2. Letter for foreign nationals and Americans with regional specializations.
3. Letter when you don't know whether any job exists.
4. Follow-up letter (after the interview).

These are sample letters. They are not meant to be followed slavishly, and in fact you would be doing yourself a disservice if you did so. They are included here only to expose you to various styles of letter writing and to set your mind working on constructing the kind of letter you think will present your credentials in the strongest and most favorable light. Above all, letters should reflect your personality and style.

However, there are certain characteristics of letters that seem to have a positive impact on many employers:

a. Keep the letter brief—no longer than one page.
b. Emphasize achievements and accomplishments rather than duties.
c. Start with the most impressive achievement in your background.
d. Refer to your résumé (which should be attached).
e. Request an interview.
f. Make it easy for the employer by pointing out those parts of your background that are pertinent to the job for which you are applying.
g. Above all, write the letter from the employer's point of view: not "I want to do so and so," but "I have certain qualifications that will help you. . . ."

1. Letter in Response to a Job Vacancy Notice, at School or in the Classified Ads

33 Loudoun Street
Yonkers, NY 10705
April 13, 1979

Mr. Thomas Sawyer
Continental Can Company
1211 Avenue of the Americas
New York, NY 10017

Dear Mr. Sawyer:

Your recent contact with Columbia University

[or]

Your recent ad in *The New York Times*
about a job opening suggests that research on the Middle East is
an increasingly important concern of Continental Can Company.

As the attached résumé indicates, I have been specializing in Middle East research for the last few years. Among subjects I have researched are:

1. the effect of the Arab boycott on US policy;
2. Jordan's relations with Syria, Egypt, and Israel;
3. the internationalization of Jerusalem; and
4. divisive forces in OPEC.

Readers of my reports have commended me for new insights into these subjects. In all cases, I have used original sources through my reading knowledge of Arabic and Hebrew.

I expect to be graduating from Columbia University in December 1979 with the degree of Master of International Affairs and a specialization in Middle East studies.

At your convenience, I would enjoy meeting with you to review my background in relation to your research needs.

Sincerely,

Jeanette Gomez

2. Letter for Foreign Nationals or Americans with Regional Specializations

1834 Beacon St.
Brookline, MA 02146
11 May 1978

Mrs. Alma Potter
Director, Market Analysis
Doyle, Johnson, and O'Reilly
Prudential Center
Boston, MA 02199

Dear Mrs. Potter:

As a native of Venezuela, I have unique knowledge of Latin America and its potential as a market for American products.

If your company intends to expand its markets in Latin America and needs someone with a specialized knowledge of the area, you may be interested in the details of my background:

1. I have a resident visa and can stay in the United States for an unlimited time.
2. I am fluent in the two languages of Latin America—Spanish and Portuguese.
3. I graduated from the University of Caracas with a major in International Relations, where I ranked in the top 5 percent of my class. I subsequently obtained an MBA from New York University.
4. I worked for two years as an Assistant Economist with the Ministry of Economic Affairs in Caracas.
5. I was elected leader of a delegation of Venezuelan exchange students. In the United States I lived for two years with different American families.

I should be glad to discuss with you my potential usefulness to your organization in the specialized markets of Latin America.

Sincerely,

Jorge Cabezudo

3. Letter When You Don't Know Whether Any Job Exists

Sample Opening Paragraphs

Where You Have a Contact

1. I'm acquainted with your friend George Smith, who has phoned about me. He suggested that I meet with you briefly to get your advice on possible employment opportunities.

2. Several months ago, a group of us from the Sloan School visited the Department of Commerce and were impressed with your emphasis on the need for economics in the federal government.

Where You Have No Contact

1. As a researcher in Middle East problems, I have concentrated on bringing new insights into Arab–Israeli relations.

   You may be looking for someone with specialized research skills. If so, you may be interested in some of the analyses I have made:

2. As a summer employee of the Coca-Cola Company, I helped influence the expansion plans of that organization in the Latin American area.

   You may be looking for a trainee in your marketing department. If so, you may be interested in some of the other things I have done:

4. Follow-Up Letter
(After the Interview)

927 Follen #4
Seabrook, Texas 77012
August 17, 1978

Mr. George A. Sims
Research Coordinator
Cooper Industries
First City National Bank Building
Houston, Texas 77002

Dear Mr. Sims:

Thank you for the opportunity of meeting you yesterday to discuss a research opening with Cooper Industries.

In talking over your research needs, I was struck by the increasing importance of an in-depth knowledge of the Middle East, not only to your organization, but to the people of this country. With this in mind, it may be useful to recapitulate some of my research work in the field:

1. Effect of the Arab boycott on US policy
2. Libya's relations with Syria, Egypt, and Israel
3. Divisive forces in OPEC
4. Effect of a possible oil find in Jordan on US policy

My background in research has, I believe, given me the necessary skills to make an effective contribution to the work of your corporation. The job opportunity we discussed sounds extremely rewarding.

Sincerely,

Lawrence Golden

To conclude this section, here are two fascinating letters that were actually used in applying for jobs. The first was written by Franz Schubert when he applied for the post of Assistant Conductor at the Imperial Court of Vienna in 1826. The second letter is a petition from Leonardo da Vinci to the Duke of Milan, written in 1482, for a job that seems to have been a combination of chief engineer, Minister of Defense, and artist in residence.

Your Majesty!
Most gracious Emperor!

With the deepest submission the undersigned humbly begs Your Majesty graciously to bestow upon him the vacant position of Vice-Kapellmeister to the Court, and supports his application with the following qualifications:

1) *The undersigned was born in Vienna, is the son of a school teacher, and is 29 years of age.*

2) *He enjoyed the privilege of being for five years a Court Chorister at the Imperial and Royal College School.*

3) *He received a complete course of instruction in composition from the late Chief Kapellmeister to the Court, Herr Anton Salieri, and is fully qualified, therefore, to fill any post as Kapellmeister.*

4) *His name is well known, not only in Vienna but throughout Germany, as a composer of songs and instrumental music.*

5) *He has also written and arranged five Masses for both smaller and larger orchestras, and these have already been performed in various churches in Vienna.*

6) *Finally, he is at the present time without employment, and hopes in the security of a permanent position to be able to realize at last those high musical aspirations which he has ever kept before him.*

Should Your Majesty be graciously pleased to grant this request, the undersigned would strive to the utmost to give full satisfaction. Your Majesty's most obedient humble servant,

Having, most illustrious lord, seen and considered the experiments of all those who pose as masters in the art of inventing instruments of war, and finding that their inventions differ in no way from those in common use, I am emboldened, without prejudice to anyone, to solicit an appointment of acquainting your Excellency with certain of my secrets.

1. *I can construct bridges which are very light and strong and very portable, with which to pursue and defeat the enemy; and others more solid, which resist fire or assault, yet are easily removed and placed in position; and I can also burn and destroy those of the enemy.*

2. *In case of a siege I can cut off water from the trenches and make pontoons and scaling ladders and other similar contrivances.*

3. *If by reason of the elevation or the strength of its position a place cannot be bombarded, I can demolish every fortress if its foundations have not been set on stone.*

4. *I can also make a kind of cannon which is light and easy of transport, with which to hurl small stones like hail, and of which the smoke causes great terror to the enemy, so that they will suffer heavy loss and confusion.*

5. *I can noiselessly construct to any prescribed point subterranean passages either straight or winding, passing if necessary underneath trenches or a river.*

6. *I can make armoured wagons carrying artillery, which shall break through the most serried ranks of the enemy, and so open a safe passage for his infantry.*

7. *If occasion should arise, I can construct cannon and mortars and light ordinance in shape both ornamental and useful and different from those in common use.*

8. *When it is impossible to use cannon I can supply in their stead catapults, mangonels, trabocchi, and other instruments of admirable efficiency not in general use—In short, as the occasion requires I can supply infinite means of attack and defense.*

9. *And if the fight should take place upon the sea, I can construct many engines most suitable either for attack or defense and ships which can resist the fire of the heaviest cannon, and powders or weapons.*

10. *In time of peace, I believe that I can give you as complete satisfaction as anyone else in the construction of buildings both public and private, and in conducting water from one place to another.*

> *I can further execute sculpture in marble, bronze, clay, also in painting I can do as much as anyone else, whoever he may be.*
>
> *Moreover, I would undertake the commission of the bronze horse, which shall endue with immortal glory and eternal honour the auspicious memory of your father and of the illustrious house of Sforza.*
>
> *And if any of the aforesaid things should seem to anyone impossible or impracticable, I offer myself as ready to make trial of them in your park or in whatever place shall please your Excellency, to whom I commend myself with all possible humility.*

As you might suspect, Leonardo, with his emphasis on achievements and his eye on the Duke's needs, got the job. Schubert's letter—bland and unexciting—was not even acknowledged by his most gracious Emperor.

Résumés

Accompanying your letter of application is usually a résumé. The two are closely related. You may have one letter of application to be used in all employment situations, or you may have several letters, depending on your résumé. The kind of résumé used depends in turn on the number of your career objectives and how closely defined they are.

How does your strategy change if, for example, you have one job objective, three objectives, or no objective at all? If you know you are going into international banking and that's all that concerns you, your job strategy is relatively simple. Not only is your target well-defined and easily identifiable, but the search itself will be facilitated. You will ordinarily have one résumé that has a job objective of "international banking" or something similar. You need then have only one letter of application, which will also be geared to banking. The two together—letter and résumé—will suffice very well if your objective stays in the international banking world.

Suppose, however, you have had a specialization in international economics and there are three kinds of jobs you would like to explore: research with the government or a nonprofit organization; banking; and writing economic articles for a newspaper. With three such varying objectives you would probably do well to have three résumés, each with a different focus. The three objectives might be stated roughly as follows: (1) "economic research"; (2) "international banking"; and (3) "economic writing in the communications field." Each résumé would be constructed differently to emphasize those parts of your education and experience that are pertinent to the job for which you are applying. Sending a résumé with the second objective to a nonprofit organization, or a résumé with the third objective to a bank or research organization would all but destroy your chances of getting an interview. Accordingly, these three résumés should be matched with three different letters, each geared to the specific objective mentioned in the accompanying resume.

Now let us examine your job strategy if you have no job objective whatever. You have taken many courses in international affairs but have majored in nothing more specific than world affairs or foreign policy. In other words, through inability or unwillingness you have not narrowed your career objective beyond "something international." Since it would be rather foolhardy to mention "something international" as an objective on your résumé, what do you do?

In one sense your job is easier; in another sense, harder. You will probably end up with one résumé, a rather bland one, since it lacks a job objective and, therefore, a particular target. If you send out this résumé, you will have to write a special letter adapted to the particular job for which you are applying. In other words, a "something international" background often means one résumé and innumerable letters. Again, there is nothing wrong with this once you are aware of the results of the choices you make all along the job-hunting route.

On the following pages you will find examples of five different types of résumés to fit varying situations. Analyze each one and you will notice certain key questions about the motivation and background of the applicant.

JAMES SMITHEY
817 West End Ave.
New York, NY 10025
(480-2234)

OBJECTIVE

Research with specialized knowledge of Latin American area

HIGHLIGHTS OF EXPERIENCE

Research

At IBM, helped make estimates of IBM business in Ecuador for 1978–88. These estimates influenced expansion plans of IBM in that country.

At Center of Inter-American Relations, evaluated coverage of Latin American countries in American press. Procedures I recommended to increase coverage were accepted.

Latin America

At Institute of Latin American Affairs at Columbia University, specialized in political and economic problems of area.
At University of Texas:
–spent junior year abroad at University of Santiago, Chile
–as President of Latin American Club, arranged Conferences on United Nations and international problems

EMPLOYMENT CHRONOLOGY

Spring 1978 IBM World Trade, New York. Research Intern
1975–77 International Student Services, New York. Program Officer
Summer 1974 Center of Inter-American Relations, New York. Program Assistant

EDUCATION

1979 – Master of International Affairs (MIA), School of International Affairs, Columbia University
 Specialization: Latin American Studies.
 Was commended for writing paper giving new insights into effect of Castro on eight Latin American countries.

1975 – BA, University of Texas

ACTIVITIES

<u>Memberships</u>: Student representative on Committee on Instruction, School of International Affairs
Recommendation that field work program be expanded was accepted.

<u>Languages</u>:   Spanish (excellent); Portuguese (good)

PERSONAL

Born: Akron, Ohio, November 5, 1951
Health: Excellent

<u>References</u>: Available on request

Résumé #1
With the Education and Experience to Support Your Career Objective, Version A

James Smithey did not go into Latin American work after getting his BA, even though as an undergrad he had done several things in that field. An employer now will ask: "Why did you go to graduate school? Weren't you able to get what you want with a BA, or is your Latin American job objective one that you only recently decided on?"

Pedro Vasquez
1020 Amsterdam Avenue
New York, NY 10025
(212) 963-1071

OBJECTIVE   Career in International Banking

EDUCATION   Master of International Affairs, School of
                       International Affairs, Columbia University   1979

                         Specializations:
                           International Finance and Banking
                             (Courses taken at Columbia School of
                             Business)
                           Latin American Studies

                     Financed tuition and expenses through work as
                       security guard

                     BA, University of Wisconsin   1977
                       Major: Political Science

WORK   Bank of America, New York, Intern, Trainee
EXPERIENCE   Program   Jan.–May 1979
                         (Developed internship myself without aid from
                         School of International Affairs)

                     CITICORP, New York. Intern.   Sept.–Dec. 1978
                       Worked on Sovereign Risk analysis for Latin
                       American area. As a result of my analysis,
                       CITICORP was able to increase profits in Peru
                       and Venezuela.

                     Summer Employment: Warehouseman, shipping
                       clerk, house painter

MEMBERSHIPS   School of International Affairs
& ACTIVITIES   Study Group on Professionalism
                         Represented School on Committee composed of
                         representatives of Columbia, Princeton, Johns
                         Hopkins, Georgetown, and Tufts. My recom-
                         mendation that curriculum of schools of inter-
                         national affairs be more heavily oriented toward
                         job market was accepted.
                       International Fellows Program

HONORS & AWARDS	Dean's List of Honor Students, University of Wisconsin
LANGUAGES	Spanish (excellent), Portuguese (fair)
TRAVEL	Argentina, Brazil, Chile, Paraguay, Colombia, Spain, England, France, Scotland, Italy, and continental United States
PERSONAL	Born: December 29, 1954 Health: Excellent Single
REFERENCES	Available on request

Résumé #2
With the Education and Experience to Support Your Career Objective, Version B

This is a straightforward résumé that does not pose any particular problems of why, when, or where.

H. Ramanathan
1312 Netherland Avenue
Riverdale, NY 10471
(212) 980-4623

PERSONAL	Married, 1 Child Excellent Health US Citizen
JOB OBJECTIVE	Product Management in Company with International Interests
EDUCATION	COLUMBIA UNIVERSITY – School of International Affairs Master of International Affairs degree 1979 Concentration in International Marketing – top 10% of class (Courses taken at Columbia School of Business) Business Manager, *Journal of International Affairs* Increased subscriptions by 20% Financed 100% of education costs through loans and work UNIVERSITY OF OKLAHOMA Bachelor of Arts degree 1975 Major in History Treasurer, Student Association; Varsity Soccer Member: AIESEC; College Band Financed 40% of expenses through part-time work
WORK EXPERIENCE	CORNING GLASS WORKS, CORNING, NEW YORK 1975–1977 <u>Marketing Analyst</u> Recommended product line modifications that increased profits of reporting units by 15% annually. Changed procedures so that subsidi- aries were able to accelerate marketing reports to head office in half usual time. GULF OIL COMPANY, HOUSTON, TEXAS 1975 <u>Summer Sales Trainee</u> Sold 175% of quota and, as a result, received special commendation and monetary award

OTHER SUMMER AND PART-TIME JOBS
Waiter, bank clerk, bookkeeper, taxi driver

INTERESTS   Playwriting (one-act play produced at University of
Oklahoma), Swimming, Tennis, Stamp Collecting

LANGUAGES   Hindi (fluent), French (good), Spanish (good)

REFERENCES   Available on request

Résumé #3
With the Education and Experience to Support Your Career Objective, Version C

Ramanathan went into business but apparently decided he was not getting as far or going as fast as he wanted. Question: With all the glowing accounts of his performance at Corning Glass Works and Gulf Oil, why didn't he make it? Why did he have to go to graduate school?

Trudy Schmidt
1415 Nostrand Avenue
Brooklyn, NY 10411
(212) 423-3406

<u>Objective:</u>	Career in Travel Industry

<u>Qualifications:</u>   Extensive foreign travel:
        Four European trips since 1971
    Residence abroad:
        Six months in West Germany
    Languages: German, French
    Have facility for getting along with people and help-
       ing them with travel problems as needed

<u>Skills:</u>

Escorting, Hosting — Have frequently invited foreigners to meet Americans in my home. Have also escorted foreign friends throughout New York state.

Planning, Administration — Planned European trip for four friends and myself. Based on success of this trip, was asked following year by parents of one of my friends to plan European trip for them.

Learning — Lived in Hamburg with family that knew no English. My German, at first mediocre, soon became fluent.

Negotiation — In Berlin, bargained with shopkeepers until I succeeded in obtaining complete glass menagerie at reasonable prices.

Friendliness — Frequently have met Europeans at public places, e.g., restaurants, theatres, opera, and several times was invited to their homes.

<u>Education:</u>	Duke University, BA in History	1975
	In top 10% of class	

<u>Employment:</u>	Research Associate, March of Dimes, New York	1976–79
	Research Assistant, Conference Board, New York	1975–76

Other: Waitress at summer resort hotel (Wyoming)
Taxi driver (through experimentation learned routes and hours that produced most business)

Personal: Born: 1952
Single
Health: Excellent

References: Available on request

Résumé #4
Without the Education and Experience to Support Your Career Objective

Trudy Schmidt wants a job in the travel industry, but as far as education and experience are concerned, there is little to recommend her. She therefore turns to another type of résumé, one that draws on the skills she has used in private life.

William Brown
29 Loudoun Street
Yonkers, New York 10705
(914) 963-1070

EDUCATION

Master of International Affairs, School of International Affairs, Columbia University

Degree expected: May 1979

Specialization:
East Asian Studies

University of Taipei, Taiwan   1976–1977
Courses taken in Chinese language, culture, history, and Buddhism
Lived with Taiwanese family and received room and board in exchange for tutoring family in English

BA, University of Wisconsin   1976
Major: History
Financed tuition and expenses through summer work and position as Head Resident, graduate residence hall, University of Wisconsin

WORK
EXPERIENCE

Foreign Policy Association, New York: Intern
Jan.–May 1979
Helped evaluate *Great Decisions* program

US Embassy, Singapore: Intern   Summer 1978
Won transportation award from School of International Affairs
Commended by Ambassador for new insights revealed by my study on Singapore-Malaysian cultural relations

Other Summer Employment:
Warehouseman, shipping clerk, house painter, taxi driver

MEMBERSHIPS
& ACTIVITIES

School of International Affairs
Committee on Instruction
Recommendation that new International Energy course be added to School's curriculum was accepted
University of Wisconsin Football Team

HONORS & AWARDS	Phi Beta Kappa, University of Wisconsin Dean's List of Honor Students, University of Wisconsin
LANGUAGES	Modern Mandarin Chinese (excellent), Classical Chinese (excellent)
TRAVEL	Taiwan, Western Europe, continental United States
PERSONAL	Born: December 29, 1954 Health: Excellent Married
REFERENCES	Available on request

Résumé #5
Without a Specific Career Objective

Bill Brown has progressed from an objective of "something international" to "something Chinese," but what? Since he does not know, he ends up with this bland curriculum vitae, which would probably have to be accompanied by a different letter for each job lead he explores.

In all of these résumés you will find certain characteristics that often make a positive impact on employers:

1. *They are all one page long.* Since the purpose of a résumé is to get an interview, don't overload it with details. Include just enough information on each item to hook the employer so that, out of the many applicants for the job, you will be among the favored few to be interviewed.

2. *They emphasize achievements and accomplishments rather than duties.* Not "Subscription manager of the *Journal*," but "As subscription manager of the *Journal*, increased circulation by 60%." Not "Conducted Career Workshop," but "Organized Career Workshop that helped students get jobs they wanted."

3. *They utilize an outline format.*

4. *They usually show a job objective.* If you decide to include your objective, word it simply. Not "Want position of responsibility that will utilize my background and experience," but "International banking" or "Research with emphasis on the Middle East." Everyone wants a position of responsibility and to utilize his or her background and experience. Why make the employer wade through all these useless words?

5. *They facilitate evaluation by the prospective employer.* This is particularly true of Version A, which extracts those parts of education and experience most pertinent to the job applied for.

6. *They list the most important things first.* If experience is most impressive, it should come first; if education, it should come first.

7. *They show dates on the same vertical line.*

8. *They list education and experience chronologically, working backwards from the most recent.*

9. *They mention summer employment.* Even manual work has features in common with professional jobs: discipline, punctuality, ability to work with people. All types of summer work will strengthen your qualifications on the job hunt.

10. *They are phrased from the employer's point of view.* Keep in mind: "Are the words I'm using getting across to the employer the ways I can help do the job he or she is supposed to do?"

11. *They do not give references.* No names or addresses should be listed. Some organizations may contact references if listed, and ask for letters of recommendation even if there is no job opening in sight. This means you will soon wear out the people whose recommendations you want. Give the names and addresses of your references only when an employer is seriously negotiating with you about a job you know actually exists.

There is no perfect résumé any more than there is one perfect way to Tao. This means that you should expose yourself to a variety of formats, then make your own decision on the style that presents your credentials in the strongest, most favorable light.

Interviewing Techniques

We now come to the last stage of the job hunt—and perhaps the most important. You may have been brilliant all along the way: the self-knowledge you have poured into the job hunt; your early decision of a career objective and the superb choice of majors and courses to support this objective; the extensive research you have undertaken to identify your targets; the hours you've sweated over your letter(s) and résumé(s). All this effort has borne fruit. You have impressed an employer who has the exact job you are after and you have been asked to come in for an interview. This is the moment that counts. The whole job-hunting structure you have diligently built up over the years has brought you within calling distance of the job you want. If you blow the interview, however, the job will slip down the drain.

How can you take steps to avoid this disaster?

Interviewing for a job is essentially a game of skill and wits. It is as much an art as a science. Much of the result will depend on the chemical reaction between personalities and there's not much you can do about that. Further, much of the result will be based on psychological and mood factors, for instance, the employer's frame of mind—and yours, for that matter. These factors also may be outside your control.

But even if interviewing is as much an art as a science, there are still certain tips that may be helpful. Twelve of these that seem to have stood the test of time follow.

Twelve Interviewing Tips

1. *Know the company.* Read all available literature on it. Consult annual reports, brochures, and the directories listed in the bibliographies. This knowledge will increase your confidence during the interview.

2. *Prepare questions you wish to ask the interviewer.* These should be based on your research of the organization's functions, plans, and problems. Don't ask obvious questions such as "Did you make a profit last year?"

3. *Know the points about yourself you wish to make.* The insertion of this material into the discussion is a skill that comes with practice. Don't wait until the last moment, when you are at the door saying goodbye, to suddenly blurt out, "By the way, I forgot to mention that I'm President of the Student Association. Oh yes, I'm also. . . ."

4. *Evaluate your strengths and weaknesses before the interview.* You may be asked about them. Sometimes a weakness can be presented as a strength, e.g., highly demanding of yourself and other people.

5. *Expect the unexpected.* Some interviewers may insist on doing all the talking; others may lean back, close their eyes, and murmur, "What are all the things I should know about you?" leaving you an open field for the next twenty-five minutes. Fortunately, most interviews approximate conversations, with questions and answers on both sides.

6. *Be familiar with the parts of an interview.* Most are roughly divided into five parts:

   (a) Amenities and platitudes ("How are you?" "What a lovely view from your window," "Smoke if you wish.");

   (b) Discussion of your qualifications, background, and career plans ("Why do you want an international career?" "How far along in your career do you expect to be in ten years?");

   (c) Discussion of requirements of the job opening;

   (d) Attempt to relate (b) to (c); and

   (e) Summation and final instructions ("Fill out this form," "Call me in two weeks.").

   The order may vary. Sometimes (c) precedes (b). Sometimes (d) may not be voiced; if it isn't, the attempt to relate your qualifications to the requirements of the job will certainly be churning around the interviewer's mind.

7. *Keep this question in mind throughout the interview: Why would someone want to hire me for this job?* Remember the employer's point of view and base your case on how you can be useful to the employer. The latter will be less interested in whether the job gives you an emotional thrill or advances your career objectives.

8. *Be prepared to explain your motivation.* "Why do you want to work in international economics?" or "Why are you applying to our particular firm?" are common types of questions. If you are honestly enthusiastic about the job, don't hesitate to express your enthusiasm. Everyone likes to feel popular.

9. *Don't raise questions about salary, vacations, or pensions during your first interview.* If asked about salary, indicate that it is negotiable. If pressured to name a specific figure (an unfair tactic but all too common), know the salary range of the type of job for which you are applying and set your figure accordingly.

10. *Always tell the truth.* As someone once said, "You will have less to remember."

11. *Stress accomplishments and achievements, rather than duties and responsibilities, in any past employment.* ("As circulation manager of school magazine, I increased subscriptions by 50%.") You are not being immodest. You are making it easier for the employer, who, when faced with a hundred résumés, has time for only six or eight interviews and wishes to see only the outstanding applicants.

12. *Keep the initiative, if possible, for future contacts.* ("Shall I call you in two weeks to see how my candidacy is coming along?") Certainly don't sit by the phone waiting for employers to call, unless they have specifically stated they will contact you within a definite time frame. Be pleasantly surprised if they do contact you at the appointed time. If they don't, give them a few days leeway, then phone to determine the status of your candidacy and express continuing enthusiasm for the job.

Above all be yourself—not what you think the employer wants, and certainly not a stereotype. Let the interview reflect your personality just as your letters and résumés have. If in a banking interview you find yourself giving an interpretation of what you think a banker should be, you might want to consider if banking is really the career you're after. And if you are taking the oral exam for the Foreign Service, you don't have to pretend to agree with all aspects of US policy. If, for example, you disagree with US policy toward Cuba, give reasons for your disagreement ("I understand the reasons why the State Department has recommended so and so, but I wonder whether certain factors were given adequate weight."). In all probability, the oral panel has become fed up with the platitudes they've heard from other candidates and will respect a fresh and original point of view, once your reasoning indicates you are not living on cloud nine.

Some organizations—particularly businesses and banks—have special forms on which an interviewer evaluates each candidate. Here are two examples.

Bank A rates candidates on the following factors:

1. Introductory Material
   Oral communication skill
   Self-confidence
   Appearance
   Social effectiveness

2. Education
   Ability to reason logically
   Level of overall academic accomplishment
   Ability to apply academic background
   Apparent maturity of judgment

3. Work Experience
   Apparent motivation to succeed
   Significance of summer work to career goal
   Prior leadership roles
   Ability to work with others

4. Self-Direction
   Overall management potential
   Maturity of career objectives
   Commitment to banking

Bank B rates candidates on the following factors:

1. Interpersonal/Social Skills
   Ease in working with clients and associates
   Effectiveness of communication skills
   Ability to develop and maintain client confidence

2. Judgment/Analytical Skills
> Ability to reason logically
> Planning and organizational skills
> Affinity for numbers

3. Motivation/Internal Drive
> Realism of career objectives
> Achievement orientation
> Commitment to banking

Every factor in each bank's assessment is given a numerical rating. The ratings are added and candidates with a high total are invited back for further interviews. Below a certain numerical level, no invitation to return is tendered.

You may well wonder how some of the above factors are evaluated, such as Achievement Orientation or Overall Management Potential. Obviously, personal impressions and vibes play a large part in some evaluations.

Most importantly, you should note that academic standing is one factor among many in Bank A's assessment; in Bank B's, grades are not directly evaluated at all, although they are taken into consideration under Judgment/Analytical Skills and Motivation/Internal Drive.

Many organizations look for the "rounded individual," one who preferably has a number of extra-curricular interests, social presence, and at least average intelligence.

Academic standing and grades are more important if the job under discussion is in research, requiring intellectual capacities. Other jobs may put a premium on social effectiveness or leadership abilities.

The first interviews may well be grueling, but as you gain experience the encounter with employers should resemble a game: you will be trying to impress the interviewer that you are the right person for the job; the interviewer will be trying to assess your qualifications and personality in relation to the job available. Even if it's not ping pong, it can still be fun.

Good luck!

PART II

The International Job Market

CHAPTER FIVE

The Federal Government

Most of you considering an international career with the federal government focus promptly on the Foreign Service of the Department of State. True, the Department, as it is popularly known, is the focal point of foreign policy and a primary source of jobs for those with international training, but other government agencies also offer opportunities for an international career. Many of these agencies are in the executive branch; some are in the legislative.

Executive Branch: Foreign-Oriented Agencies

The main foreign-oriented agencies of this branch of interest to those with an international background are the Department of State, the International Communication Agency, the Agency for International Development, the National Security Agency, the Central Intelligence Agency, the Defense Intelligence Agency, the Arms Control and Disarmament Agency, the Peace Corps, the Office of the Special Representative for Trade Negotiations, the Overseas Private Investment Corporation, the Export–Import Bank, the US International Trade Commission, and the Inter-American Foundation. For each one, we will look at the type of jobs available, procedures for applying, and optimum academic preparation.

Foreign Service of the Department of State

It is a good time to enter the Foreign Service. Hundreds of years ago the Republic of Venice threatened with death any Venetians who had relations with foreign diplomats. More recently, in the early 1950s, ambassadors who predicted bad news, such as a communist victory in China, were thrown out of the Service, similar to the old custom of beheading messengers bearing bad tidings. Also until recently, Foreign Service Officers (FSOs) had to have a private income to survive financially. None of this is now true. FSOs are encouraged to have contacts with foreign diplomats; they are not beheaded for accurately reporting developments of potential damage to the United States; and they now receive entertainment allowances—and sometimes hardship and cost-of-living allowances as well—in addition to a very fair salary, so that their economic survival is no longer at stake.

Foreign Service jobs exist both in the Department of State in Washington and in US embassies and consulates abroad. Some 3,600 FSOs serve the Department in more than 260 embassies and consulates in over 130 nations. What do they do?

Political officers cover political developments in their country of assignment, analyzing their significance to the United States. They convey US government views on political issues to foreign governments, negotiate agreements, and maintain contact with foreign officials, political and economic leaders, diplomats of other countries, and other influential foreign nationals.

In Washington, political officers analyze reports from overseas, prepare guidance for embassies, and brief senior State Department officials. They also work closely with other US government agencies and with foreign embassies in Washington.

Economic/commercial officers in US embassies and consulates analyze and report on economic trends and events that affect US interests. They gather and interpret economic data, present US economic positions to foreign officials, and negotiate agreements. They also promote US exports and aid American investors abroad. They work closely with the Department of Commerce and American businesses. They often alert US companies to trade and investment opportunities.

In Washington, economic/commercial officers analyze reports from the field, help set US economic policy in trade, monetary, energy, economic development, aviation, transportation, and maritime matters.

Administrative officers abroad manage the support operations of US embassies and consulates. They are responsible for budget and fiscal planning, maintenance of vehicles and other property, procurement of supplies, negotiating leases for housing, general financial functions, and travel arrangements for officers and their dependents.

In Washington, the administrative officer is involved in a variety of functions: coordination of Presidential and Vice-Presidential overseas trips, escorting and making arrangements for Congressional travel, developing computer techniques for information and communications systems, preparing budget submissions to Congress, preparing emergency evacuation plans, and setting policy for administrative offices overseas.

Consular officers abroad have more contact with foreign citizens than do other embassy officers. They grant visas to foreigners visiting or immigrating to the United States; they issue passports and handle questions concerning US citizenship; they help Americans abroad in serious accidents or emergencies; they try to ensure that Americans in foreign jails are fairly treated; and they issue birth certificates to Americans born abroad, register absentee voters, and take testimony for US courts.

Background Desired

Every scrap of knowledge may be helpful in passing the written exam (see How to Apply). Accordingly, there can be no specific guidance on the curriculum you should take, since almost any course at a school of international affairs will be useful. Certainly you should know basic economic theory and its application to current economic woes; US foreign policy, history, and geography; and cultural and international affairs.

Answer the sample questions in the Foreign Service exam booklet (see next sections) containing the application form for the written exam. The results, which you can score yourself, will show you your areas of weakness and strength. Gaps in your knowledge can be filled by taking the appropriate courses or by working on your own. If, for example, you are weak on cultural matters, you should read the art, book, and theatre sections of any of the weekly newsmagazines or the Sunday *New York Times.* At a minimum, you should be able to identify major American names and their contribution in each cultural field. If you are weak in economics or US history, read a basic text in these subjects. If you know little of the functions of US embassies and can't describe what a consular officer does, glance through some of the reference books listed in the exam booklet.

How to Apply

The Foreign Service written exam is given annually in December, and applications for it must be submitted in October. The exam varies slightly from year to year, but is usually a multiple choice test with questions covering English expression, general knowledge (these questions range from international relations, current events, economics, US history, and geography, to US art, literature, and culture), and functional knowledge (these questions test an applicant's knowledge of the four principal areas of work in US embassies: political, economic/commercial, administrative, and consular). All facets of US foreign policy, customs, and culture are stressed, since FSOs need a solid background in Americana to be effective US representatives abroad.

A booklet describing the work of the Foreign Service and listing sample exam questions is available generally in August of each year. It can usually be picked up in college placement offices. Otherwise, write to:

> Board of Examiners
> Department of State
> Washington, DC 20520

Exam Questions

Test your skills on these sample questions:

1. The most effective power of the US Congress in influencing executive action in foreign policy making is its
   A. role in the treaty-making process.
   B. exclusive authority to declare war.
   C. control over the appropriation process.
   D. role in confirming presidential appointments.
   E. authority to regulate the nation's armed forces.

2. Which of the following has the greatest proportion of its foreign trade with the United States?
   A. Australia
   B. West Germany
   C. Japan
   D. Great Britain
   E. Canada

3. If each of the following groups of artists could collaborate on a work, which group would most probably create an American folk

opera based upon themes drawn from the early history of the nation?

    A. Leonard Bernstein, Jack Kerouac, Pearl Primus

    B. Aaron Copland, Carl Sandburg, Agnes de Mille

    C. Paul Hindemith, Henry Miller, Anthony Tudor

    D. Gian-Carlo Menotti, Tennessee Williams, Martha Graham

    E. Lukas Foss, Ernest Hemingway, George Balanchine

4. Which of the following has *not* been a major cause of large-scale immigration to the United States?

    A. Religious persecution

    B. Marriages of US servicemen abroad to foreign nationals

    C. War and civil disorders

    D. Famine

    E. Economic opportunity in this country

Each year 14,000 to 15,000 eager applicants take the Foreign Service written exam and answer questions such as those above. About 2,000 pass and are eligible to take the "personal assessment" exam. Eventually, 100 to 200 are taken into the Service.

Timing

The length of time between applying to the Foreign Service and—if you're lucky—getting a job offer is at least nine or ten months and frequently longer. The timing may seem inordinately long but is more readily understood in light of the detailed steps required: applications are due in October; the written exam is held in December; papers are graded and results sent to applicants by the end of January or the beginning of February; if you pass the written, a "personal assessment" exam (a day-long assessment replacing the previous one-hour oral exam) is scheduled during the spring or early summer; if you pass the "personal assessment," a security check is instituted, which takes from four to six months and sometimes longer if you have lived abroad; and you are given a medical exam.

At the end of this lengthy process, a panel will give you a rating based on your scores on the written and assessment exams, on written essays, if any, and occasionally on other tests you may be asked to take. Your name is then placed on a roster, according to the grade you have received. If you get a low grade, your name will be near the bottom of the list and you may never be called. If you have not been given an offer within a year and a half, your chances get progressively slimmer, as new applicants with higher scores from the following year's exam are placed above your name on the roster.

The extraordinary length of time of the whole process means that many students who apply may graduate well before the final verdict is in. Therefore, even if the Foreign Service is your primary career objective, keep your lines open to other careers. You may well find you have to take a temporary job in an unrelated field while waiting for the hoped-for bid from the Department of State.

Must You Take the Exam?

Practically all the professional jobs in the Department of State and in US embassies are staffed with FSOs who have successfully gone through the endlessly protracted written–oral–security check–medical exam route. Exceptions are:

Technical Jobs Lawyers, trained economists, and others with desired technical skills may be brought in from the outside. Also, those with media experience may be considered for jobs in the Office of Media Services.

Researchers Very occasionally the Bureau of Intelligence and Research may be unable to obtain an FSO with particular skills to staff a research vacancy. In this case, it may be authorized to recruit from outside.

Interpreters and Translators People with these skills may be hired for full- or part-time work.

Visa Personnel, Clerks, and Secretaries These are low-level jobs with limited career potential.

Minorities The Department, similar to many other government agencies, has a program to encourage minority employment. If interested and qualified, write to:

> Office of Equal Employment Opportunity
> Department of State
> Washington, DC 20520

Languages

Contrary to popular belief, knowledge of a foreign language is not essential to get into the Foreign Service. If you don't have a second language under your belt, however, you will be assigned promptly to language training and won't be promoted or assigned overseas until you have competence in at least one foreign language.

There is a reverse twist to the language question. If you have language competence in Arabic, for example, you may assume you'll spend all or most of your career in the Middle East. Not so. The Department will try to use your language skills but it will not guarantee that all your assignments—or even a majority of them—will be in a specific country or area. In fact, you may on occasion be assigned to a non-Arabic-speaking area solely to expand your knowledge of the world and the variety of its foreign policy problems.

First Assignment

If you are lucky, your first assignment may be a rotational one at an embassy. You will then spend six months in each of the four sections of the embassy: **Political, Economic, Administrative,** and **Consular.** At the end of your two-year tour of duty you will have learned a great deal about the operations and functions of all parts of an embassy.

Another first assignment might place you for your full tour of duty in a specific section of an embassy or consulate general—or perhaps in Washington, assisting a country desk officer. During your career you will bounce many times between Washington and abroad. In general, you should expect about half of your career to be spent overseas.

Newly appointed junior officers are hired at the level of Class 8 (about $12,500 to 15,000 per year—generally without a college degree or with a BA and little or no experience) or Class 7 ($14,500 to $17,500—generally with a graduate degree and/or significant experience). Salaries have a habit of moving upwards, so it would be wise to check the latest figures.

International Communication Agency (ICA)

The ICA has taken over the functions previously carried out by the US Information Agency (USIA) and the Bureau of Educational and Cultural Affairs of the Department of State. The ICA combines the emphasis on media communication of the former with the emphasis on human communication of the latter. It is very much concerned with image-building.

Washington headquarters has four **Associate Directorates**, each performing certain functions:

Broadcasting (Voice of America) sets VOA policy for programs in each regional area.

Programs assists in formulating ICA policy consistent with US foreign policy and interests. This Associate Directorate is also responsible for policy liaison with the White House and the State Department and gives policy guidance to the Agency media. It does research on media reaction and the effectiveness of Agency libraries and also recruits speakers for overseas programs.

Educational and Cultural Affairs is responsible for academic exchange programs and supervises the Board of Foreign Scholarships. Cultural presentations for overseas audiences, logistic support for libraries, English-teaching programs abroad, programs for visitors from overseas, and book programs all come within the purview of this associate directorate.

Management handles administrative, personnel, and comptroller services.

In conjunction with the State Department, ICA headquarters defines policy for disseminating the American image abroad. ICA Washington also administers its overseas offices. Each office in the field usually has at least a press officer, a cultural affairs officer, and a librarian. If you are a *press officer,* you will be responsible for trying to get an objective reporting of US events in the press of the country of assignment, a particularly thankless job in a communist or unfriendly country. Further, you may write the ambassador's speeches, issue press releases, and arrange press conferences for the ambassador or for visiting US officials.

The *cultural affairs officer* in a typical week may arrange for the visit of an American orchestra or dance group, organize lectures and seminars on American topics, and perhaps plan for student exchanges. The *librarian* is in charge of the American library, generally located in the center of the city and usually more visible than other US establishments, which explains why it is sometimes the focus of anti-American demonstrations. Whether you are a press officer, a cultural affairs officer, or a librarian, you will spend a major part of your career overseas.

Background Desired

The same qualifications previously required for USIA are needed for ICA, journalism or cultural studies in particular. Area studies, languages, foreign policy, international relations, and administration (for the Management Associate Directorate) are also helpful. The desirable background for a VOA intern includes academic work or experience in broadcasting and/or journalism and international affairs.

How to Apply

For most non-VOA jobs in Washington and for overseas jobs, the timing and procedure are much the same as for the Foreign Service exam. Get the FSO exam booklet in August or September so that you can submit your application before the October deadline; you will take the major part of the FSO exam as well as a separate section specifically for ICA work. This booklet should be available at college placement offices. If not, write to:

> International Communication Agency
> 1776 Pennsylvania Ave. NW
> Washington, DC 20547

As with the Foreign Service, the length of time between applying and getting an offer is unbearably long. The advice remains the same: Explore other career opportunities and keep your options open in case you don't pull through.

Procedures are different for VOA. Each year the Broadcasting Associate Directorate chooses about six interns, usually obtained by recruiting on selected campuses. Successful candidates spend about a year in on-the-job training, developing their skills in voicing, directing, producing, and writing. During the year they rotate among the most important VOA divisions: **English, News and Current Affairs,** and a regional area. At the end of the year, each intern receives a definite assignment. For VOA work, write to:

> Voice of America
> International Communication Agency
> 330 Independence Ave. SW
> Washington, DC 20547

ICA also has positions for guides who accompany exhibits to the USSR and Eastern Europe for six-month periods. Fluency in the language is required as well as a more than average knowledge of the American scene—political, economic, social, and cultural. As a guide at an exhibit in Russia, you are expected to have the answers for any question on America that may be posed by Russian visitors. Write to:

> International Communication Agency
> 1776 Pennsylvania Ave. NW
> Washington, DC   20547

Since the ICA is a comparatively small agency, fewer positions are available each year than in the Foreign Service. If you are motivated for ICA work, however, don't be deterred. Any job that is worthwhile will be highly competitive.

Agency for International Development (AID)

AID administers the entire US economic aid program to developing countries. It dispenses two different types of aid:

Grants, which support specific development projects in the poorest countries. Grants also provide emergency aid in case of natural disasters. Technical assistance is sometimes offered to speed the solution of complex development problems.

Loans, which provide financing for programs that focus on key sectors of a country's economy, for example, agriculture, health, education, and rural development. These loans are interest-bearing and repayable in dollars.

AID is one of the most controversial programs of the US government. For many years its future was in doubt. Now, however, the principle of assisting poorer nations seems to have been accepted by most members of Congress, and even though the size of each year's program usually provokes controversy, AID has stabilized its recruitment of new young personnel on a regular annual basis. The result is the **International Development Intern Program.** IDIP is a two-year career program that leads to positions of responsibility in AID headquarters and in its missions in the developing countries of Asia, Africa, Latin America, and the Near East.

Background Desired

AID positions are quite varied and, therefore, need different curricular training. The following is a list of some target jobs:

Program officers advise the Mission Director on policy, planning, and evaluation of AID programs. This is the main generalist job in AID on an entering professional level and the one most applicable to students with an international affairs background. International relations, economics, political science, or area studies in Third World countries are appropriate background studies.

Agricultural economists analyze production, distribution, and consumption of food products; identify problem areas; and study methods of increasing and conserving food. Agricultural economics is essential to obtain this job.

Capital development officers determine feasibility of projects proposed by a developing country and help prepare necessary financial statements. Economics and/or finance are necessary prerequisites.

Economists study economic conditions in countries applying for US assistance. International economics is naturally a basic requirement.

Education advisers advise on the planning of educational programs on all levels. Applicants should have a background in educational administration.

Population officers assist in managing family planning programs and projects. World resources, population, or health studies would facilitate obtaining this job.

Foreign language proficiency is required in many positions. The preferred languages are French and Spanish, although this depends on the country of assignment.

How to Apply

There is no written examination for the IDI program of AID. Applicants should send a résumé to:

> Intern Recruitment
> Recruitment Branch
> Office of Personnel and Manpower
> Agency for International Development
> Washington, DC   20523

An application packet with information on the IDI program is sent to each applicant considered eligible for the program. This set of applications, in turn, must be returned by a specific date. Interviews with applicants are scheduled during the spring.

As with the Foreign Service exam of the Department of State, there is a long wait between application and eventual appointment. For example, applications for the annual fall class must generally be received in AID Washington no later than November of the preceding year. In some years there may also be a spring class. In any case, early career planning is particularly required for AID applicants.

Similar to the Foreign Service, you will spend a major part of your career overseas.

Interns are appointed Foreign Service Reserve Limited Officers and salary is determined by level of education and work experience. A grade of Foreign Service Reserve Limited Seven (FSRL-7), currently paying $11,500 to $16,000, is usually assigned to new interns with an MA.

National Security Agency (NSA)

NSA is responsible for all US communications security. It also develops and analyzes foreign intelligence information considered crucial to national security.

Background Desired
NSA puts a premium on people with a technical background that can be applied to cryptographic work and people with proficiency in certain exotic languages, particularly Russian, Chinese, Japanese, Arabic, and East Central European. An ability to translate from original sources, rather than conversational ability, is required.

How to Apply
Applicants must take an aptitude test, called a Professional Qualifications Test, which measures ability to reason as well as to understand and use verbal and quantitative materials. This test is given usually in November of each year.

The first step in applying for an NSA job is to obtain a Professional Qualification Test booklet early in the fall. If it is not available locally, write to:

> College Recruitment Program
> National Security Agency
> Attn: M321
> Fort Meade, MD   20755

This booklet contains a registration form that should be filled out and sent to the Educational Testing Service (ETS), which administers the test. ETS will then send you an admission ticket indicating where the exam is to be taken. If you pass the exam, an interview will subsequently be arranged on a local campus with an NSA recruiter or panel. Again, there is a premium on time because of the spread between application and possible appointment, so apply early.

Most NSA jobs are in the United States, although occasional travel abroad may be required.

Central Intelligence Agency (CIA)

The CIA is perhaps the most important government agency providing intelligence information in the formulation of foreign policy. Although the cloak-and-dagger operations of the Agency, as it is known in Washington, appeal to the movie-going public because of their melodramatic content, the bulk of CIA work has to do with intelligence-gathering and analysis. The gathering is done primarily in the field; the analysis, at headquarters in Langley, Virginia.

Background Desired

Each year the size and emphasis of the CIA recruitment program vary. Mainly, however, the Agency is interested in graduate students specializing in the following regions of the world: Russia, East Central Europe, East Asia (particularly Japan and China), and the Middle East. Africa seems to be assuming increasing importance to the Agency, but so far Latin America has received lower priority than other areas. Ability to translate original material in the language of these areas, rather than conversational ability, is stressed. Another basic skill of value to the Agency is international economics, used in the collection, research, and measurement of data relating to the economic performance of foreign countries.

A PhD with the above background may have an edge over an MA in international affairs, because of the Agency's stress on analytical ability and research capabilities, but many appropriately qualified students at the masters level have been accepted by the Agency.

How to Apply

Write to: Central Intelligence Agency
              Washington, DC   20505

If you are in New York and wish to explore career possibilities, consult the Agency's regional representative, who has an office in the Federal Building, 26 Federal Plaza, New York, NY 10007, (212) 264-3316.

It should be noted that students who hope to visit Moscow at any time in their career for non-CIA research or study often decide not to work for the CIA because of the belief—usually justified—that the USSR will find out about their CIA affiliation and deny their request for a visa.

Defense Intelligence Agency (DIA)

Still another intelligence agency exists in the DIA, which is the intelligence arm of the Department of Defense. The DIA is oriented toward military intelligence and points to its past role in disclosing missiles in Cuba and the North Vietnamese infiltration into South Vietnam as examples of its achievements. Less glamorous aspects of its work include analysis of military capabilities of various countries, transportation intelligence, photo interpretations, and economic analysis of foreign military production and expenditures. To perform these functions, skilled personnel are needed, and each year a few graduate students are hired.

Most DIA jobs are in the United States, although occasional travel abroad may be involved.

Background Desired

Political science, international relations, area studies, and economics are the optimum courses to take for generalist research jobs. For technical or scientific jobs, a background in engineering, computer science, math, communications, physics, or statistics is valued.

How to Apply
Write to: Defense Intelligence Agency
            1201-1301 South Fern St.
            Arlington, VA   22202

Arms Control and Disarmament Agency (ACDA)

The ACDA is a semiautonomous agency operating under general policy guidance of the Department of State. It recommends to the President, the Secretary of State, and Congress policy on arms control and disarmament. It also assesses the effects of these recommendations on US national security and on our economy.

Background Desired
The ACDA uses specialists knowledgeable in foreign policy, international organizations, weapons technology, military strategy, and economics. Academic courses on national security, disarmament, military technology, and Russian studies will be very helpful, as well. Personnel working in the international relations field are often FSOs on loan from the Department of State. Military personnel are also borrowed from the Department of Defense.

How to Apply
There are three ways of getting into the ACDA:

1. Become a Foreign Service Officer through the normal written-oral exam channel, and if accepted, request an assignment with ACDA.
2. Obtain a Civil Service rating (types of ratings and application procedures are discussed in the section on domestic-oriented agencies of the government).
3. Try for a direct appointment—but this really works only for those with considerable experience in the disarmament or related fields.

Most ACDA jobs are in Washington.
For those of you without much experience in this specialized field, your best chance of getting into the organization is through the Foreign Service channel, but you may write to:

Arms Control and Disarmament Agency
320 21st St. NW
Washington, DC   20451

Peace Corps

The Peace Corps has been a part of ACTION since 1971 but still operates independently in its specialized task of training people of developing nations. Although in recent years the program has been reduced in size, positions are available in many fields.

Background Desired

BA generalists as well as graduate students in economics, agriculture, engineering, the health professions, and in many other areas are encouraged to apply for field positions. Expenses are paid but the salary is minimal. Clearly, only those with a service ideal should apply.

Occasional positions may also be available in Washington headquarters. Here policy is set up, personnel are processed, and work in the field is supervised. Those with administrative interests, finance background, or economics qualifications are needed.

How to Apply

Write to: ACTION
Peace Corps
812 Connecticut Ave. NW
Washington, DC   20525

Office of the Special Representative for Trade Negotiations

The Special Trade Representative is the chief US representative in all trade negotiations and reports directly to the President and Congress. The Office of the Special Representative for Trade Negotiations was established to help the STR carry out these functions. Negotiators, analysts, and support staff all work in the office on policy making and negotiations. Staffs are maintained both in Washington and Geneva.

Background Desired

A high degree of skill in economics, with an emphasis on trade and negotiations, is required of applicants for the occasional job opening that develops in this office. A PhD in economics or trade is preferred.

How to Apply

Write to: Office of the Special Representative
for Trade Negotiations
1800 G St. NW
Washington, DC   20506

Overseas Private Investment Corporation (OPIC)

OPIC is an executive agency that fosters economic development and progress in the developing countries of Latin America, Asia, Africa, and Europe. It does this by providing US investors with political risk insurance and financial assistance to support their investments in these countries. The investors may be large or small, corporate or individual.

OPIC programs cover new projects or the expansion of existing ones. All projects supported by OPIC must assist in the economic or social development of the country and "must be consistent with the economic and foreign policy interests of the US."

At the same time, OPIC operations help the US balance of payments through the profits they return to this country and the new jobs and exports they create. OPIC offers US investors assistance in finding investment opportunities and loans and loan guarantees to help finance projects. It reduces the need for government-to-government lending programs by involving the US private sector in establishing capital-generating capacity and industrial capacity in developing countries.

OPIC insurance is of particular importance in protecting investments against: (a) the inability to convert into US dollars any local currency received by investors as profit; (b) the loss of investments from nationalization or confiscation of facilities; (c) war, revolution, or insurrection.

Background Desired
Since many OPIC functions revolve around insurance and finance, a background in either or both fields is essential. Economics, economic development, Third World area studies, banking, and statistics are also helpful. A Civil Service rating is required (see the Domestic-Oriented Agencies section for more on this).

How to Apply
Write to: Overseas Private Investment Corporation
1129 20th St. NW
Washington, DC   20527

Export–Import Bank (Eximbank)

The Export–Import Bank helps to finance and facilitate exports of US goods and services. Although about 85 percent of US manufactured exports go forward without the bank's support, many exports cannot be financed by the private sector alone. Eximbank, accordingly, plays a limited but critical role in the US export effort. Specifically, it assumes commercial and political risks unable to be undertaken by private financial institutions and assists US exporters to meet the competition of officially supported foreign export credit.

Background Desired

The personnel of Eximbank have degrees in economics, finance, banking, business, and accounting. These skills—preferably a minimum of two or three—are required for the few jobs available.

How to Apply

Write to: Export–Import Bank
     811 Vermont Ave. NW
     Washington, DC 20571

US International Trade Commission

This organization is concerned with international trade and tariff matters. Specifically, it analyzes the effects of imported products on US industries.

  The commission has an East–West monitoring system that checks imports into the United States from countries without a market economy and, in particular, investigates whether increased imports of articles produced in communist countries are causing market disruptions in the United States.

Background Desired

The commission states that it is primarily interested in applicants with the following specializations: international economics, international trade, marketing, international law, and communist studies. A Civil Service rating is required.

How to Apply

Applicants should send a completed Personal Qualifications Statement (Government Form SF-171) to:

     Personnel Division
     Office of Administration
     US International Trade Commission
     701 E St. NW
     Washington, DC 20436

Inter-American Foundation (IAF)

Even though the IAF is a foundation it is still a federal government agency. It was established by Congress in 1969 as a means of channeling US resources to the impoverished nations of Latin America and the Caribbean. The IAF supports developmental self-help efforts on the part of the people of these areas. It has arranged with the Inter-American Development Bank to channel some of its resources to foundation projects. Projects funded by IAF include a wide variety of activities, such as workers' self-managed enterprises, credit and production cooperatives, self-help housing, agricultural extension services, legal aid clinics, a bank run by and for workers, peasant associations, and informal education.

Background Desired

The variety of activities of the IAF define the skills needed by this agency: economics, economic development, Latin American studies, finance, agriculture, labor, cooperatives, banking, housing, law, industrial management, statistics, labor relations, and a fluency in Spanish and Portuguese. Obviously, no one applicant is going to have that complete a background. The more of these skills you have to offer, however, the better your chances. A Civil Service rating is required.

How to Apply

Write to: Inter-American Foundation
              1515 Wilson Blvd.
              Rosslyn, VA   22209

Executive Branch: Domestic-Oriented Agencies

Most students specializing in international affairs think almost entirely of the foreign-oriented agencies of the US government as sources of appropriate jobs. Don't forget the so-called domestic agencies, however. They also have positions of potential interest for you.

All the large government agencies, such as the Department of Labor, Department of Agriculture, Department of Energy, Department of Commerce, and many others, have international divisions with jobs for those with an international background. Unlike the foreign-oriented agencies, many of which have their own procedures for establishing your qualifications, the domestic agencies have one system of testing and entry: Civil Service. It is the rare job in these domestic agencies that is exempt from Civil Service requirements.

Civil Service Ratings

All Civil Service jobs are ranked according to a "General Schedule" (GS) rating. Within each Civil Service grade there are ten steps, each corresponding to a certain salary. Although you are usually hired at the beginning salary of each grade, an unusually strong background may get you started at a higher step. A BA or three years of "responsible" experience will qualify you for GS-5 jobs (starting salary about $10,000); one year of graduate study or four years of "responsible" experience, for a GS-7 rating (starting salary about $12,500).

Most mid-level jobs are listed as Grades 9 through 12. GS-9 pays a beginning salary of over $15,000; GS-12, about $22,000. Applicants with two years of graduate work or five years of "responsible" experience are eligible for a GS-9; applicants with two years of graduate work plus one year of "responsible" experience or six years of experience are eligible for a GS-11 or 12. Again, an unusually strong background may get you started at a salary higher than the beginning of each grade. Check salary levels to see if they are still current when you apply.

As a student of international affairs, you should take two Civil Service exams to give you the optimum ammunition for your assault on the federal bureaucracy: the Professional and Administrative Career Examination (PACE) and the Mid-Level Exam.

PACE

The PACE exam, originally given once a month, is currently given two or three times a year; there is less need now to add additional names to a roster already overlong. Contact your nearest Civil Service office for information on dates when the exam is to be held. Also ask for applications to take the exam. Addresses of all the Regional Civil Service Offices can be found on page 77.

Using multiple choice questions, PACE tests the following abilities of a candidate:

1. Basic comprehension and vocabulary.
2. Ability to discover underlying relationships or analogies and problem solving.
3. Ability to analyze facts, discover their implications, and reason from general principles (inferential reasoning).
4. Ability to solve quantitative problems: algebra and perhaps simple geometry and trigonometry.

There is not much you can do to prepare yourself for this type of exam. If you are weak in algebra, however, it would be wise to get a simple math text and go over some of the equations. No oral exam is given.

You will be given scores for each type of ability tested. At the same time, new jobs opening up will be identified with one or more of the test batteries mentioned above. A job requiring particular emphasis on mathematic ability, for example, will use candidates who have the highest rating in the quantitative problem test battery.

If you were in the top 10 percent of your graduating class or had a 3.5 or better average, you must still take the written exam. However, you will be given additional points for the excellence of your academic career. Veterans also get 5 or 10 extra points added to their scores.

In order to be considered for available jobs, you ordinarily have to score in the high 90s. For graduate students, this may not be as difficult as it seems, since PACE is geared to the BA level. If you pass PACE you are eligible for jobs as *passport examiner, management analyst, immigration inspector, financial institution examiner, social insurance representative, criminal investigator,* and a whole host of low-level economic and administrative jobs in executive branch agencies of the government.

The Mid-Level Exam

"Exam" in this case refers to an evaluation by Civil Service of your qualifications and background. You do not have to take a written or oral exam. You *do* have to submit the Personal Qualifications Statement (Standard Form 171) plus the List of College Courses and Certificate of Scholastic Achievement (Form 226).

The Mid-Level Exam has been decentralized in recent years. Civil Service headquarters in Washington handles job vacancies in the headquarters of all federal agencies; regional Civil Service offices handle all government jobs in particular areas. Accordingly, if you are looking for Mid-Level jobs in New York as well as Washington, you will have to apply at the Civil Service offices of both cities. If you want to apply for a Mid-Level rating for Washington jobs, write to:

> Job Information Center
> US Civil Service Commission
> 1900 E St. NW
> Washington, DC   20415

and ask for a Mid-Level packet, which includes an application form, categories of jobs for which you may apply, and other useful information. Fill out these forms and return them to Washington.

Those who obtain a Mid-Level rating can expect consideration for the following types of jobs: *international economist, economist, intelligence analyst, public information officer* (radio, TV, motion pictures), *foreign affairs/international relations specialist, writer/editor, and administrative officer.*

You may wonder if some of the jobs listed for the Mid-Level rating as well as for PACE need the international background that you've accumulated over the years. Some of them do; others may not, at least initially. If you are offered a job in the noninternational operations of a government agency, you may wish to consider it with the thought that, once on the inside, you will have priority for job openings in the international division of that agency.

If you do land an international job in any of these domestic-oriented agencies, you will work in Washington with perhaps an occasional trip overseas.

The Evaluation Process

The information on your background and qualifications submitted with your application is entered into a computer record. The notice you receive from Civil Service when this process is complete implies neither eligibility nor any specific rating. It indicates merely that your background data have been recorded and will be analyzed when job vacancies for which you seem to qualify arise.

When a federal agency has a job vacancy, it presents Civil Service with a job description and a list of skills and abilities needed. Based on this description, Civil Service chooses the occupational code or codes most applicable and pulls out the applications of individuals whose qualifications seem to match the requirements of the job. Presumably, many candidates will be evaluated at this time and each one is given a rating for the specific job under consideration. The names of the three individuals with the highest ratings are then submitted to the agency for its decision.

Special Tips

All of this may sound as if you should wait by the phone to be summoned for a job interview once your papers are submitted to Civil Service, but don't. You increase your chances immeasurably by taking certain actions.

While your papers are being processed in Civil Service, consult the *US Government Manual*, which can be obtained at large libraries or ordered from the Government Printing Office, Washington, DC 20402 for $6.50. This manual describes the mission of each executive branch office, department, and independent agency, complete with organization charts. Information is available on the chain of command in these offices, including names and titles of top-level people. It also discusses agencies in the legislative and judicial branches.

This volume should enable you to identify those agencies for which you would like to work, as well as the sections within each agency that particularly interest you. The manual will also give you the names of the individuals in charge of those sections. College placement offices can be helpful as well in providing you with contacts in some government agencies.

Since most government agencies do not recruit on campus and jobs are not obtained without interviews, students will have to conduct a mail campaign to lay the groundwork for face-to-face meetings in Washington. Your communication with an agency should consist of a covering letter and a résumé or Form 171. Keep the letter brief. Send it to the director of the international division or other office to which you are applying.

A less effective alternative is to send your letter to the agency personnel officer. This should only be done if you are unable to identify the offices for which you wish to work. Letters to office directors are more likely to receive individualized attention, although in some cases your letter may be sent by the office director to the personnel office. You can send letters to several offices within the same agency.

An effective time for starting your mail campaign will be several weeks before a planned visit to Washington. Mention the approximate date of your trip and indicate that you will phone the office director or other recipient of the letter for an appointment before or on arrival.

Phone for an appointment at the time indicated. You may find to your annoyance that the person to whom you have written does not remember hearing from you or may even have misplaced your letter. Often enough, however, you will find the recipient of your letter aware of your application and willing to meet with you. If you do get an appointment, find out if any PACE or Mid-Level vacancies exist or are anticipated. If you impress the employer, he or she may ask Civil Service to submit your name for consideration when vacancies arise. If you are lucky, you may even have the job description rephrased to include specifics of your background and qualifications, thus giving you an edge over your competition.

Check the various addresses of the offices you will be visiting on a map of downtown Washington before making appointments. Knowledge of agency locations and careful planning can double the number of people you can see in a day.

Avoid scheduling your trip to Washington during major holiday periods. It is preferable to go during the middle of the week. This increases the likelihood of the top management people being there.

Caution: The first question you are likely to be asked is: "Do you have a Civil Service rating?" If you reply in the negative, you will probably be asked to return when you have the necessary qualifications. Therefore, do not descend on Washington unless you are well on the way toward a Civil Service rating.

US Civil Service Commission Regional Offices

Atlanta Region

1340 Spring St. NW
Atlanta, GA   30309
(Alabama, Kentucky, North Carolina, Florida, Mississippi, South Carolina, Georgia, Tennessee)

Boston Region

John W. McCormack Post Office
and Courthouse
Boston, MA   02109
(Connecticut, Maine, Massachusetts, New Hampshire, Rhode Island, Vermont)

Chicago Region

John C. Kluczynski Building
29th Floor
230 Dearborn St., Chicago, IL   60604
(Illinois, Indiana, Michigan, Minnesota, Ohio, Wisconsin)

Dallas Region

1100 Commerce St.
Dallas, TX   75242
(Arkansas, Louisiana, New Mexico, Oklahoma, Texas)

Denver Region

Building 20, Denver Federal Center
Denver, CO   80225
(Colorado, Utah, North Dakota, Montana, South Dakota, Wyoming)

New York Region

New Federal Building
26 Federal Plaza
New York, NY   10007
(New Jersey, New York, Puerto Rico, Virgin Islands)

Philadelphia Region
William J. Green, Jr., Federal Building
600 Arch Street
Philadelphia, PA   19106
(Delaware, Maryland, Pennsylvania,
Virginia, West Virginia)

St. Louis Region
1256 Federal Building
1520 Market Street
St. Louis, MO   63103
(Iowa, Missouri, Kansas, Nebraska)

San Francisco Region
Federal Building
Box 36010, 450 Golden Gate Ave.
San Francisco, CA   94102
(California, Arizona, Hawaii, Nevada
Pacific Ocean Area)

Seattle Region
Federal Building, 26th Floor
915 Second Ave.
Seattle, WA   98174
(Alaska, Idaho, Oregon, Washington)

Types of Jobs

A degree in international affairs will probably qualify you for one or more of
the following mid-level jobs, each one represented by a specific occupational
code:

Economist or international economist
Research into economic problems, analysis and interpretation of economic
data, and preparation of reports on economic facts, activities, and trends.

REQUIREMENTS Twenty-one semester hours in economics plus three
semester hours in statistics, accounting, or calculus. Both undergraduate
and graduate courses are accepted. Almost any course with the words "economic" or "economy" in the title is liable to be acceptable. If in doubt, list
the course and add a few lines to explain its economic content. Courses to be
considered for this rating are negotiable with Civil Service.

Foreign affairs analyst
Research on subjects related to foreign affairs. (This rating is not used by
the Department of State or any of the foreign-oriented agencies, but the
Treasury Department and Department of Commerce, for example, might
use it for some jobs relating to their international activities.)

REQUIREMENTS Twenty-four semester hours in one of the social sciences,
including international relations, political science, economics, and international law.

International relations officer
Work on the formulation and implementation of US foreign policy in the
conduct of its relations with other governments. This rating is also used for
jobs in domestic-oriented agencies.

REQUIREMENTS Same as for foreign affairs analyst.

Intelligence research specialist

Research in military science, international relations, and related fields. Interpretation of relevant facts to help in the formulation and implementation of US foreign policy.

REQUIREMENTS   A blend of academic work and professional experience depending on the grade for which applied. Academic work should focus on subjects concerning foreign policy, military technology, and general international relations.

There are hundreds of federal government agencies, some small, some large. Only the largest ones—those with jobs of interest to people specializing in international affairs—will be covered in this section. To help you zero in on the appropriate targets to match your qualifications, consult the Civil Service brochure, *Federal Recruiting*, which is issued annually. This is a synopsis of federal career information. It summarizes existing position vacancies, with grades, for each government agency.

Department of Agriculture

The **Foreign Agricultural Service (FAS)** of the Department of Agriculture is an export promotion agency for US agriculture. It improves access to foreign markets for US farm products through representations to foreign governments and through participation in trade negotiations. The FAS also appraises overseas marketing opportunities and makes this information available to the US agricultural trade.

Of particular interest to students of international affairs is the global operation of FAS. It maintains an overseas network of *agricultural attachés* who report and analyze world agricultural production, trade, and policies affecting US agriculture. These attachés are stationed at sixty-five key posts, usually embassies, covering more than 100 countries.

Background Desired

As might be expected, a Mid-Level Civil Service rating is almost always a prerequisite for these jobs. If interested, take courses in international economics or agricultural economics.

How to Apply

Qualified applicants should submit an SF-171, a notice of your eligibility received from Civil Service, and college transcripts. Write to:

Director, Personnel Division
Foreign Agricultural Service
US Department of Agriculture
Washington, DC   20250

Department of Commerce

This department with its wide variety of programs offers some unusual opportunities for those with an international background. **The Domestic and International Business Administration** (DIBA) promotes the growth of US industry and commerce, foreign as well as domestic. It is particularly concerned with the stimulation and expansion of US exports. Within DIBA there are two bureaus that are of special interest.

The **Bureau of International Commerce** (BIC) helps US businesses sell their goods abroad by providing commercial and marketing information on prospective exports and potential customers. Among BIC's many publications is a series entitled *Foreign Economic Trends and Their Implications for the United States,* with issues on many countries of commercial interest to US exporters.

The **Bureau of East-West Trade** (BEWT) coordinates policies and programs regarding trade promotion and other commercial relations with Russia and the socialist nations. BEWT also turns out analyses of problems inherent in East-West trade, and studies the market potential for US trade with socialist countries. Some of the positions in BEWT are *international economist, international trade specialist, trade assistant,* and *plans and exhibits officer.*

Another part of the Department of Commerce that deserves your attention is the **Maritime Administration**. It administers programs to aid in the development and promotion of the US merchant marine. It also operates the subsidy program under which the United States pays the difference between certain costs of building and operating ships under the US flag versus similar costs under foreign flags.

Also part of the Department of Commerce is the **US Travel Service** (USTS). This organization was established to promote tourism to the United States from abroad. The USTS has six field offices—in London, Paris, Frankfurt, Tokyo, Toronto, and Mexico City.

Background Desired

Academic studies that will help get you a hearing for BEWT are international economics, Russian studies, East Central European studies, Chinese studies, and business administration. A combination of two or three of the above will be particularly helpful.

Courses in trade or maritime problems will give you an edge over many of your competitors for jobs with the Maritime Administration.

Courses in international economics, tourism, and a knowledge of French and/or Spanish will help you get the Civil Service rating required for a job with the USTS.

How to Apply

Write to: Department of Commerce
14th St. and Constitution Ave. NW
Washington, DC 20230

Department of Defense (DOD)

You should pay particular attention to the **International Security Affairs Division**. ISA develops defense positions in political-military and foreign economic affairs including arms control and disarmament. Among its functions are negotiating and monitoring agreements with foreign governments concerning military facilities and the status of armed forces. Policy guidance is provided to *defense attachés* in US embassies and to US representatives at international organizations and conferences.

Background Desired
Academic studies of optimum use are national security, military technology, international economics, US foreign policy, Russian studies, Chinese studies, and East Central European studies and languages. Either a PACE or Mid-Level rating is usually required for positions in ISA.

How to Apply
Write to: International Security Affairs Division
Department of Defense, Pentagon
Washington, DC   20301

Executive Office of the President

The major function of the **Office of Management and Budget (OMB)** is to make government service more efficient and economical. OMB has two divisions of potential interest to you, **National Security** and **International Affairs**. In these divisions are concentrated the international aspects of the following OMB functions: assisting the President in evaluating budgets for the foreign-oriented agencies (e.g., Department of State, ICA, NSA, and CIA), and keeping the President informed of the work proposed, initiated, and completed by these agencies.

Background Desired
A Mid-Level rating with a background in economics, international economics, business administration, foreign affairs, and international relations will be helpful.

How to Apply
Write to: Office of Management and Budget
Executive Office of the President
Washington, DC   20503

Department of Health, Education, and Welfare (HEW)

HEW's **Office of Education (OE)** has a **Division of International Education** that funds language and area studies. In cooperation with the Department of State, it also carries out teacher exchange activities.

Background Desired

If you are interested in this type of work, fortify yourself with courses and experience in education and area studies.

How to Apply

Write to: Division of International Education
Office of Education
Department of Health, Education, and Welfare
400 Maryland Ave. SW
Washington, DC   20202

In addition, HEW has an **Office of International Health,** an **International Staff** in the **Social Security Administration,** and an **Associate Commissioner for Institutional Development and International Education.**

International Health activities include research on global health problems. International Social Security activities include research on various social security systems throughout the world, as well as the administration of programs for those in the system who are living abroad.

Background Desired

Health, nutrition, and medicine for HEW's international health activities; social sciences and statistics for those interested in international social security matters.

How to Apply

Write to: Office of International Health
Room 18-67 Parklawn Building
Rockville, MD   20852

or

International Staff
Social Security Administration
1875 Connecticut Ave. NW
Washington, DC   20009

Federal Reserve System

The system is comprised of twelve Federal Reserve Banks located throughout the country and a Board of Governors in Washington, DC. The Board's primary function is to formulate monetary policy. To assist the Board, there is a staff of about 1,400 employees assigned to various divisions, among which is the **Division of International Finance**. This division analyzes international policies and operations of the Federal Reserve, major financial and economic developments abroad that affect the US economy, and problems related to the international monetary system. Staff members of the division serve on US delegations to international financial conferences and maintain liaison with central banks of foreign countries.

Background Desired

As you might surmise, the most pertinent curriculum for jobs in the International Finance Division is one of international economics, international finance, money and banking, accounting, and statistics. This is one of those rare government agencies for which a Civil Service rating is not required. A PhD in these fields is usually preferred, but exceptionally talented people with an MA are given consideration.

How to Apply

Write to: International Finance Division
Board of Governors of the Federal Reserve System
20th St. and Constitution Ave. NW
Washington, DC   20551

Department of Housing and Urban Development (HUD)

HUD tries to improve the quality of life in US cities and towns as well as ensure that future community growth is more orderly than it has been. This department gives financial and technical assistance to help states and cities solve urban problems.

In HUD there is an office concerned with international affairs, headed by an **Assistant to the Secretary for International Affairs**. This office coordinates the exchange of research and experience between HUD's programs and those of foreign governments. Housing and urban programs throughout the United States presumably benefit from the information exchanged under these cooperative arrangements. Some foreign programs that are said to have proved applicable to HUD's operations include: (a) industrialized building in Japan; (b) consolidation of local governments in Sweden, France, and Great Britain; (c) regional planning in France and Poland; (d) housing management in Great Britain; (e) housing allowances in several European countries; and (f) national and urban growth policy throughout the advanced countries.

Background Desired

In its researching of urban and housing programs of other countries, HUD uses *economists, program analysts, financial analysts, realty specialists,* and *loan specialists*. Civil Service is, of course, a requirement.

How to Apply
Make out a Standard Form 171 and send it, along with a Notice of Civil Service Eligibility, to:

> Assistant to the Secretary for International Affairs
> US Department of Housing and Urban Development
> 451 7th St. SW
> Washington, DC   20410

Department of Justice

The **Immigration and Naturalization Service (INS)** within this department administers the immigration laws relating to the admission, deportation, and naturalization of citizens. The INS has offices throughout the United States that provide information to those seeking US citizenship. INS also works to eliminate the flow of illegal drugs into the country. **The Board of Immigration Appeals** is the highest tribunal in immigration matters.

Another part of the Department of Justice of interest to those with international backgrounds is the **Drug Enforcement Administration**, which conducts domestic and international investigations of major drug traffickers, exchanging information with certain foreign countries.

Background Desired
In these immigration and drug enforcement functions, economists, investigators, lawyers, and statisticians are needed.

How to Apply
Write to: Department of Justice
Constitution Ave. and 10th St. NW
Washington, DC   20530

Department of Labor

The **Bureau of International Labor Affairs** (ILA) carries out the international responsibilities of the Department of Labor. The bureau helps to formulate international economic and trade policies affecting American workers. Further, it administers the trade adjustment assistance program under the Trade Act of 1974, which provides special benefits for workers economically hurt by import competition. ILA also represents the United States in trade negotiations and in such international bodies as the General Agreement on Tariffs and Trade (GATT), the International Labor Organization (ILO), and the Organization for Economic Cooperation and Development (OECD). The bureau also provides direction to the US *labor attachés* at embassies abroad.

Background Desired

Some temporary jobs in this bureau, dealing with trade adjustment assistance matters, are exempt from Civil Service; but even in these cases your qualifications will be more impressive if you have a Mid-Level economist rating. Courses in trade and labor relations are other subjects that will be helpful in getting a job in the bureau.

How to Apply

Write to: Bureau of International Labor Affairs
Department of Labor
200 Constitution Ave. NW
Washington, DC 20210

Environmental Protection Agency (EPA)

The purpose of EPA is to protect and improve our environment. It aims to check and/or eliminate pollution of all types, from excess garbage to noise to radiation. An Associate Administrator is in charge of the international aspects of these functions. Some research is undertaken on environmental standards and problems faced by other countries. The office is also involved in providing guidance to US representatives at international conferences dealing with environmental matters.

Background Desired

In-depth academic studies in economics, environment, energy, population, and related courses are of major importance in getting the Mid-Level rating of interest to this organization.

How to Apply

Write to: Associate Administrator for International Activities
Environmental Protection Agency
401 M St. SW
Washington, DC 20460

Department of Energy (DOE)

DOE was established in 1977 to bring together the many fragmented energy programs and offices created over the years in the federal government. Its purpose is to ensure that the supply of energy available to the United States is sufficient to meet our needs.

This department has an **Assistant Secretary for International Affairs**, whose office develops and implements US international energy policies. It provides the energy perspective on all international negotiations between the United States and other nations. The office also develops policy options on energy relationships between producer and consumer nations, analyzing the options' impact on these relationships and on US energy objectives. Another function is to recommend US policy toward the international oil industry. Of particular importance is the office's role in evaluating the future adequacy of world energy resources.

Background Desired
All these analytical and technical functions are met by personnel qualified in engineering, economics, and energy matters. Here, as elsewhere, a heavy dose of economics at school may get you the appropriate Mid-Level ratings.

How to Apply
Write to: Assistant Administrator for International Energy Affairs
Department of Energy
12 St. and Pennsylvania Ave. NW
Washington, DC   20461

Federal Maritime Commission (FMC)

The FMC regulates the waterborne foreign and domestic commerce of the United States, assures that US international trade is open to all nations on equitable terms, and guards against monopoly situations in US waterborne commerce.

Background Desired
To obtain the necessary Civil Service ratings for FMC jobs, take courses in trade, economics, finance, and maritime shipping.

How to Apply
Write to: Federal Maritime Commission
1100 L St. NW
Washington, DC   20573

Foreign Claims Settlement Commission of the US

This organization determines claims of US citizens against foreign governments for loss or injury. Special claims programs have been undertaken against the governments of Yugoslavia, Panama, Poland, Bulgaria, Hungary, Rumania, Italy, the Soviet Union, Cuba, Czechoslovakia, and the People's Republic of China. The commission further administers claims of ex-prisoners of war from Vietnam and civilians who were interned during the Vietnam conflict.

Background Desired

This agency has only a small staff and vacancies do not often arise. Still, if you have special interest in claims work and if you have an academic background in finance, law, or specialized knowledge of the countries listed above, you should give it a try.

How to Apply

Write to: Foreign Claims Settlement Commission of the US
1111 20th St. NW
Washington, DC   20579

General Services Administration (GSA)

The GSA is concerned with the management of US property and records, including the construction and operation of buildings, procurement and distribution of supplies, use and disposal of property, and stockpiling of strategic materials.

Since much US property is located abroad, there is an international aspect to GSA work. The government-wide supply system means that purchases ranging from automobiles to paper clips are made for federal agencies, both those in the United States and abroad. GSA also determines the amounts of travel and relocation allowances for personnel of the non-foreign affairs agencies of the government.

Background Desired

Courses in business administration, finance, and economics comprise an optimum academic background to get a Civil Service rating for these jobs.

How to Apply

Write to: General Services Administration
General Services Building
18th and F Sts. NW
Washington, DC   20405

National Science Foundation (NSF)

The Foundation supports many programs for scientific research. Its **Division of International Programs** encourages American participation in international science programs and activities. The Division also fosters the exchange of information between scientists in the United States and in foreign countries.

Background Desired

Few jobs are available, but if you are interested in a career with this orga-nization, a scientific background in addition to economics or area studies will be helpful.

How to Apply

Write to: Division of International Programs
National Science Foundation
Washington, DC   20550

Department of Transportation (DOT)

This department aims to enroll the cooperation of federal, state, and local governments, carriers, labor, and other interested parties in achieving a more effective transportation network throughout the United States.

DOT has an **Assistant Secretary for Policy and International Affairs** who is responsible for carrying out the department's international pro-grams. Among these are conducting research on transportation problems in other countries and providing policy and guidance to US representatives attending international conferences involving transportation matters.

Background Desired

For this specialized work economics will be a help. Even more pertinent for the necessary Civil Service rating, however, are courses in transportation, trade, and technology.

How to Apply

Write to: Assistant Secretary for Policy and International Affairs
Department of Transportation
400 7th St. SW
Washington, DC   20590

Civil Aeronautics Board (CAB)

The CAB promotes and regulates the civil air transport industry, both within the United States and between the United States and foreign coun-tries. It grants licenses to provide air transportation services and approves or disapproves fares. The CAB's **Bureau of International Affairs** focuses on the air transport policy of foreign governments. It also helps the Depart-ment of State negotiate bilateral air agreements with other countries. Four geographical units administer the board's international responsibilities: Western Hemisphere, Northern Europe, Mediterranean and Africa, and Pacific and Far East.

Background Desired

Of interest to the board for the occasional jobs that open up is a background in area studies, trade, economics, and, if possible, some aviation experience.

How to Apply

Write to: Bureau of International Affairs
Civil Aeronautics Board
1825 Connecticut Ave. NW
Washington, DC   20428

Legislative Branch

The search for government jobs does not end with the obvious executive agencies. The legislative branch offers a variety of positions with international content, few of which depend on Civil Service exams and ratings.

Senate and House

The Senate Foreign Relations Committee and the House International Relations Committee both have small staffs, which research international issues of interest to Congress and participate in drafting those sections of Bills with international content.

Depending on its strength and the prestige of its Chairman, the Senate Foreign Relations Committee in particular can have an important influence on the formulation of foreign policy by the State Department. Sometimes the influence is in an adversary role, sometimes in a cooperative one; but if you are interested in the formulation of foreign policy you would do well to include both Congressional Committees in your job hunting.

Background Desired

An academic background in area studies, national security, international economics, economic development, and foreign policy is helpful in getting consideration for the few job openings on the House and Senate Committees.

How to Apply

Since Civil Service ratings are usually not needed for the legislative branches, how do you go about your job hunt? If you know a friend of your Congressman—or better yet, a contributor to his or her campaign—you will be welcomed and may perhaps receive an introduction to one or both committees. You have no Congressional contacts? Don't let that fact discourage you from making a direct approach. Go to the office of your Representative or Senator. You may not get to see either of them, but you will be able to see a staff assistant who may give you suggestions and perhaps help on the job hunt.

Another tip: If you aren't able to get a paying job and can support yourself for a while, by all means offer your services on a voluntary basis. Once you are in the office, you will be on the inside track the next time there is a job vacancy. Besides your own Congressman and Senator, write to:

> House International Relations Committee
> Rayburn House Office Building
> Independence Ave. and South Capitol St.
> Washington, DC   20515

> or

> Senate Foreign Relations Committee
> Dirksen Office Building
> 1st St. and Constitution Ave.
> Washington, DC   20510

General Accounting Office (GAO)

The GAO is in the legislative branch of government and reports directly to Congress. It analyzes the efficiency and effectiveness of the operations of federal government agencies in the executive branch. Its recommendations ostensibly lead to improved management practices in these agencies. Even though the GAO is in the legislative branch, it uses Civil Service ratings for entry positions. Overseas offices of this agency are located in Frankfurt, Honolulu, and Bangkok.

GAO's **International Division** administers these offices and supervises GAO reports to Congress on various foreign policy problems. Typical of these reports are: *Progress Report on US–Soviet Cooperative Programs; Actions Recommended to Alleviate Serious Financial Problems Facing the UN;* and *Bolivia—An Assessment of US Policies and Programs.* These titles give some indication of the diversity of GAO work.

Background Desired

Far from being an accountant's paradise, the GAO is more often in search of the international relations expert, the student specializing in area studies or international economics, and the business administration graduate.

How to Apply

Write to: International Division
             General Accounting Office
             441 G St. NW
             Washington, DC   20548

Library of Congress

Here again the title of this organization is deceptive and does not hint at the scope of its functions. True, the library has an extensive collection of books on every subject and in a multitude of languages. It also administers the copyright laws. But two of its offices engage in a variety of research tasks of an international nature.

The **Research Department** has a **Federal Research Division** that is broken down into a Latin America, Asia, and Western Europe Section and a Soviet and Eastern Europe Section, both of which perform research for the Department of Defense.

The **Congressional Research Service** (CRS) is also an important source of jobs for the international relations scholar. The CRS works exclusively as the research arm of members of Congress and their staffs. Two CRS units will be of particular interest to you: (1) the **Foreign Affairs and National Defense Division**, which has three sections—**Global Issues** (international organizations, international economics, and global strategy), **Regional Issues** (Latin America, Europe, and Africa/Asia), and **Policy Management** (budget and management); and (2) the **Environment and Natural Resources Division**.

In addition, the CRS has an internship program lasting for three-month periods in which successful applicants receive a stipend and work on short-term analytical projects.

Typical CRS projects might be American cults abroad and relations with their host governments, educational system in Russia, the influence of Castro in the Caribbean.

Background Desired
Area studies, international economics, national security, foreign policy, environmental studies, and/or world resources would be valuable.

How to Apply
Send a résumé or Personal Qualifications Statement (Standard Form 171) to:

> Federal Research Division, Research Department
>
> or
>
> Congressional Research Service
> Library of Congress
> 10 1st St. SE
> Washington, DC   20540

Office of Technology Assessment (OTA)

This office is an advisory arm of Congress. Its aim is to help policy makers plan for the consequences of technological change.

Background Desired

Although a scientific background is most pertinent for OTA work, this organization has an occasional need for an international generalist or one trained in world trade and international economics.

How to Apply

Write to: Personnel Office
Office of Technology Assessment
119 D St. NE
Washington, DC 20510

☆

Congressional Budget Office (CBO)

The CBO was established in 1974 to provide Congress an overview of the federal budget and to enable it to make decisions on spending and taxing levels. CBO is the mechanism through which Congress weighs priorities for the allocation of national resources. There is a **National Security and International Affairs Division** that prepares budget studies relating to US defense and international economic programs. The division examines the impact on the economy and the federal budget of foreign programs, such as commodity agreements, aid, tariff and subsidy programs, and international monetary agreements.

Background Desired

Courses in economics, finance, national security, accounting, trade, and tariffs would certainly be a plus if you are eyeing positions in CBO.

How to Apply

Write to: National Security and International Affairs Division
Congressional Budget Office
2nd and D Sts. SW
Washington, DC 20515

Publications

The following publications will give you additional information on each government agency, its functions, organization, and top personnel:

1. *US Government Manual* An annual published by the Office of the Federal Register, the National Archives and Records Service. It costs $6.50 and may be ordered from:

> US Government Printing Office
> Washington, DC   20402

2. *Washington Information Directory* This is also an annual directory, and it may be obtained by writing:

> Congressional Quarterly, Inc.
> 1414 22nd St. NW
> Washington, DC   20037

CHAPTER SIX

The United Nations and Related International Organizations

Many of you with backgrounds in international affairs naturally think of the United Nations and its specialized agencies as the best sources of jobs after graduation. Some years ago that was true. Today, however, there are few UN positions open, even for the most talented.

In addition to the dearth of jobs, a personnel quota system adds to the difficulty in getting work in some UN organizations. These quotas, whether rigidly enforced or used only as informal guidelines, are tied to the funds contributed by each member country. If you are an American and the organization at which you are applying receives 25 percent of its funds from the United States, the target figure for all American employees would presumably be one quarter of the total personnel. In many organizations, however, you will find Americans overrepresented.

Even without definite quotas, the United Nations—with some justification—tries to unearth qualified talent from developing nations that are presently underrepresented. For these reasons, if you are a qualified national of Upper Volta or Chad, for example, you probably have a better chance at a UN job than if you are a qualified American. However, at higher levels—and in specialized fields such as law and economics—Americans with the appropriate graduate degrees and a few years of experience have a somewhat better chance.

Staffing, as you can see, is not entirely dependent on the skills and background you offer. Because there is no exam system for professional jobs similar to that used by the Civil Service, contacts, energy, and initiative in locating job opportunities are all-important.

Should I Take Courses on the United Nations to Get a UN Job?

Courses on the United Nations may be interesting and informative, but don't expect them to lead to a UN job. The United Nations in particular values MAs and PhDs in economics, economic development, and area studies, with fluency in French and/or Spanish in addition to English. An academic specialization in the UN system is nice to have, but it's not what you get hired for.

Can Pressure Help?

The higher the position for which you are applying, the more you will have to cope with political considerations. In addition to the quota or guideline system mentioned above, your application is liable to languish unless you get support from your government. Russia, America, and several other countries as well vie for the top jobs, and indeed often stake out a claim to positions considered politically sensitive and therefore especially desirable. The decision on whether you or someone of a different nationality gets a position is often made far from the Personnel Office.

Strong and consistent pressure on your behalf, if obtainable from your government, is of utmost importance. The United Nations has been known to resist light pressures from member governments but often buckles under more determined efforts. In other words, get all the political support you can—from your Mission to the United Nations, from your Foreign Ministry or Department of State, from influential friends and relatives. All such support will be crucial in your effort to join the UN household.

The UN Secretariat: New York

The Secretariat services the Secretary General of the United Nations, who is the chief administrative officer of the whole system: the General Assembly, the Security Council, the Economic and Social Council, and the Trusteeship Council. Much of the research, public relations, and administrative work in the Secretariat is generated by resolutions of the General Assembly.

The greatest need is for specialists with a concentration in economics, economic development, area studies, administration, agriculture, communications, and social sciences (among others). Languages, of course, particularly French and Spanish in addition to English, are usually required.

Professional positions are graded from P-1 to P-5 levels. Most holders of graduate degrees will qualify for a P-1 (approximately $15,000 to $20,000) or P-2 (about $20,000 to $26,000) rating depending on the degree (MA or PhD) and on the amount of experience, if any. BAs and BSs have little chance at these positions. All salaries have a habit of rising, so check to see current levels.

In filling professional vacancies, the Secretariat pays more attention to maintaining a fair balance of employees among member countries, several of which have few nationals on the Secretariat staff, than do the specialized agencies.

Types of Jobs

Lower-level research jobs are the ones for which many of you may be best qualified, but for which only a few of you will be given serious consideration. Administrative vacancies are also few and usually filled by the reassignment of existing staff.

The following positions, some of which are equally difficult to get, should still be looked at by those who have appropriate qualifications and strong motivation for UN work.

Public information officer
This type of position is found primarily in the UN **Office of Public Information** (UNOPI).

One unit of UNOPI, called the **Center for Economic and Social Information** (CESI), coordinates, plans, and where necessary helps finance information programs to stimulate international development. CESI tries to involve developed and developing countries in cooperative programs aimed at accelerating economic and social progress in the developing countries.

REQUIREMENTS   Professional posts in this office call for substantial experience in journalism, publications, radio, films, and visual media. Even junior posts ordinarily require considerable experience, not merely a degree in journalism or international communications.

Legal officers
The **Office of Legal Affairs** has a very small staff.

REQUIREMENTS   Only those with a specialization in public international law are considered.

Translators
Recruitment for this position is by competitive exam and interview, usually held annually.

REQUIREMENTS   A candidate will have to translate from at least two official languages into his or her mother tongue, which must be one of the six official UN languages (Arabic, Chinese, English, French, Russian, and Spanish).

Interpreters
Here, too, recruitment is by individual examination.

REQUIREMENTS   Applicants must be able to interpret into their mother tongue (again, one of the six official languages) and must have full auditory comprehension of at least two other official languages.

Demographers and population personnel
A need for trained staff in this field sometimes exists.

REQUIREMENTS   A doctorate in the social sciences with a major in demography is usually required. A world resources specialization in academic work is helpful.

Clerical and secretarial posts
Most vacancies in this category are for secretaries and typists. Occasionally there is a need for high-speed conference typists to serve on a shift basis in large typing pools.

REQUIREMENTS   The minimum requirement for secretarial jobs is a typing speed of 50 to 55 words per minute. Preferably, applicants should be bilingual (English plus French or Spanish).

UN guides
Guides are recruited locally, usually once a year, and begin their training in March. Personal interviews at headquarters may be arranged, usually for the fall, by writing to:

UN Central Employment Section
Room DC–200
United Nations
New York, NY   10017

REQUIREMENTS   Candidates should be from 20 to 30 years old and have a college degree. Fluency in English and one other official UN language is a requirement.

Internship Programs

Occasionally, ad hoc internships for graduate students can be arranged. These are for the academic semester and should not be confused with the summer UNOPI internships in New York and Geneva (see below). The United Nations pays no stipend.

If interested, write to:

> Recruitment Programmes Section
> Office of Personnel Services
> United Nations
> New York, NY   10017

enclosing a UN Personal History Form P-11, together with a transcript of your undergraduate and graduate grades, a sample of your research work, and a description of the type of project desired. The UN P-11 Form can usually be obtained from college placement offices. Otherwise, write to:

> Office of Personnel Services
> United Nations
> New York, NY   10017

All of this documentation should be accompanied by at least one letter of recommendation—from your employer, your university, or your Permanent Mission to the United Nations. On receipt of this material, the Office of Personnel Services will try to arrange a suitable assignment in one of the departments.

A summer internship program is conducted annually by UNOPI for college students and those doing graduate work in economics, law, international relations, sociology, communications, and related subjects. Each year about fifty candidates are selected for the New York program and about eighty for a like program in Geneva. Again, no stipend is paid to interns on either assignment. Obtain special application forms from:

> UNOPI
> UN Secretariat
> United Nations
> New York, NY   10017

The United Nations seldom recruits paid staff for the summer months only. The main exception is the addition of a few extra guides to the Visitors' Service, to handle the seasonal influx of vacationers.

Although each UN organization makes the final decision on hiring personnel, various parts of the US government are sometimes drawn into the recruitment process. The Department of State is officially charged with recommending and sometimes even recruiting US citizens for UN positions; for technical positions, the department generally delegates this responsibility to other federal agencies.

International Organization	*Responsible US Agency*
UNESCO (Teachers)	US Office of Education (HEW)
World Health Organization (Medical personnel)	International Division, Public Health Service
FAO (Nutrition/Agriculture)	Office of International Organization Affairs, Department of Agriculture
International Atomic Energy (Nuclear physics)	Office of International Affairs, US Atomic Energy Commission
ICAO (Aviation engineering)	Office of International Aviation Affairs, Federal Aviation Agency
ILO (Labor, Vocational education)	International Division, Department of Labor

If interested in any of these UN technical jobs, send the responsible federal agency an appropriate résumé. If you feel qualified for a professional post of a more general nature that is not covered by the technical posts mentioned above, send a résumé to:

> UN Recruitment Staff
> Bureau of International Organizations
> Department of State
> Washington, DC   20520

In both cases, also send a UN P-11 (Personal History) Form to:

> Recruitment Programmes Section
> Office of Personnel Services
> United Nations
> New York, NY   10017

The UN Secretariat: Outside New York

Geneva Office and Regional Economic Commissions

The UN office at Geneva is the only regional office of the UN Secretariat. In addition, there are five regional commissions aimed at economic and social development of the area in which they are located:

1. **Economic Commission for Europe** (ECE), in Geneva;
2. **Economic and Social Commission for Asia and the Pacific** (ESCAP), in Bangkok;
3. **Economic Commission for Latin America** (ECLA), in Santiago, with a branch in Mexico City;

4. **Economic Commission for Africa** (ECA), in Addis Ababa;
5. **Economic Commission for Western Asia** (ECWA), in Amman.

Aside from administrative personnel, who are usually provided through the reassignment of existing staff from headquarters or from one of the other offices, UN regional offices are staffed primarily with specialists experienced in economics, statistics, sociology, and various phases of industry.

For employment with the UN Geneva Office or any of the Regional Economic Commissions, write to:

> Recruitment Programmes Section
> Office of Personnel Services
> United Nations
> New York, NY   10017

UN Office of Public Information (UNOPI)

UNOPI also has about fifty centers overseas, which service over 130 member countries. These offices are involved in all areas of press, publications, radio, television, films, graphics, exhibitions, and public liaison. They cover the whole spectrum of UN activities in political, economic, social, and humanitarian matters. Information Center directors contact government officials, educational authorities, and media personnel in order to increase awareness in that country of UN aims and activities.

Following is a list of all UN Information Centers (UNIC) with their addresses. Send all employment applications to:

> United Nations Office of Public Information
> United Nations
> New York, NY   10017

UN Information Centers

Afghanistan

PO Box 5,
Kabul

Algeria

B.P. 823,
Alger

Argentina

Marcelo T. de Alvear 684
3rd Floor, Buenos Aires

Australia

PO Box R 226
Royal Exchange
Sydney 2000

Austria

UNIDO
PO Box 707
A-1011 Vienna

Belgium

108, rue d'Arlon
1040 Bruxelles

Bolivia

Apartado Postal 686
La Paz

Brazil

Rua Cruz Lima 19,
group 201
Flamengo, Rio de Janeiro

Burma

132 University Avenue
Rangoon

Burundi

B.P. 1490
Bujumbura

Chile

ECLA, Information Service
Edificio Naciones Unidas
Avenida Dag Hammarskjold
Santiago

Colombia

Apartado Postal 6567
Bogota

Czechoslovakia

Panska 5, 110 00 Prague 1

Denmark

37 H.C. Andersen Blvd.
1553 Copenhagen V

Egypt

B.P. 262
Cairo

El Salvador

Apartado Postal 2157
San Salvador

Ethiopia

Economic Commission for
Africa, Information Service
PO Box 3001
Addis Ababa

France

1, rue Miollis
75732 Paris

Ghana

PO Box 2339, Accra

Greece

36 Amalia Avenue
Athens 119

India

55 Lodi Estate
New Delhi 110003

Iran

PO Box 1555
Teheran

Iraq

PO Box 2398 Alwiyah
Baghdad

Italy

Palazzetto Venezia, Piazza
San Marco 50
Rome

Japan

Shin Ohtemachi Building
Room 450, 2-1 Ohtemachi
2-Chome, Chiyoda-ku
Tokyo

Jordan

UN Economic Commission
for Western Asia
PO Box 35099
Amman

Kenya

PO Box 30218

Liberia

PO Box 274
Monrovia

Malagasy Republic

B.P. 1348
Tananarive

Mexico

Presidente Mazaryk No. 29
7th Floor
(Colonia Polanco)
Mexico 5, D.F.

Morocco

"Casier ONU," Rabat

Nepal

PO Box 107, Lainchaur
Lazimpat, Katmandu

Nigeria

PO Box 1068
Lagos

Pakistan

PO Box 1107
Islamabad

**Papua
New Guinea**

PO Box 472
Port Moresby

Paraguay

Casilla de Correo 1107
Asuncion

Peru

Avenida Arenales 815
Apartado Postal 4480
Lima

Philippines

PO Box 2149
Manila

Romania

16 rue Aurel Vlaicu
Bucharest

Senegal

B.P. 154
Dakar

Sri Lanka

PO Box 1505
Colombo

Sudan

PO Box 1992
Khartoum

Switzerland

Public Relations &
Documentation Service
Information Service
United Nations
1211 Geneva 10

Thailand

UN Economic and Social
Commission for Asia
and the Pacific
Sale Sanititham
Bangkok

Togo

B.P. 911
Lomé

**Trinidad and
Tobago**

PO Box 130
Port of Spain

Tunisia

B.P. 863
Tunis

Turkey

P.K 407
Ankara

United Kingdom

14/15 Stratford Place
London, WIN 9AF

**United Republic
of Cameroon**

B.P. 836
Yaounde

**United Republic
of Tanzania**

Box 9224
Dar-es-Salaam

United States

Special Projects Unit
OPI
United Nations
New York, 10017

USSR

No. 4/16 Ulitsa
Lunacharskogo 1
Moscow

Yugoslavia

PO Box 157
Belgrade, YU-11001

Zaire

B.P. 7248
Kinshasa

Zambia

c/o UNDP
PO Box 1966
Lusaka

The UN also sponsors programs of technical cooperation, administered by the **UN Conference of Trade and Development (UNCTAD)**, the **UN Industrial Development Organization (UNIDO)**, and nine of the specialized agencies supervised by the UN Development Programme. Requests from countries for technical assistance are distributed to participating organizations on the basis of field of specialization. The requests are usually for senior expert advisers. Candidates who are relatively junior, without much experience in their fields, are seldom nominated. More on this shortly.

UN Specialized and Related Agencies

Food and Agriculture Organization (FAO)

The purpose of the FAO is to raise levels of nutrition as well as improve the efficiency of production and distribution of food and agricultural products. It has regional offices in Ghana, Ethiopia, Thailand, Chile, Egypt, and Washington, DC.

The **World Food Programme** is an agency set up by the FAO to provide food aid to all developing countries. The Programme lives by voluntary pledges from participating countries in the form of commodities, cash, or services such as shipping. Food aid has been given by the Programme for a diversity of projects, recipients, and reasons: resettlement of Bedouin tribes, dairy and livestock improvement, community development, land improvement schemes, victims of natural disasters, and refugees and displaced persons.

Background Desired
Economics (particularly agricultural economics), economic development, world resources, and nutritional subjects.

How to Apply
For information on both the FAO and the World Food Programme, write to:

> Via delle Terme di Caracalla
> 00100 Rome, Italy

International Fund for Agricultural Development (IFAD)

IFAD is a relatively new and important specialized agency within the UN system. With initial resources of a billion dollars, its primary purpose is to help increase agricultural production in developing countries. To this effect, it disburses loans on easy terms to these countries.

Background Desired
Economics (primarily agricultural economics), economic development, finance, sociology, world resources with an emphasis on food, and Third World area studies.

How to Apply

Write to: International Fund for Agricultural Development
Via del Serafico 107
EUR 00142 Rome, Italy

or

United Nations
Room 2920
New York, NY 10017

International Civil Aviation Organization (ICAO)

ICAO was established as a specialized agency of the UN to achieve international cooperation in the air. One of ICAO's chief activities has been the establishment of international standards in all aspects of aviation: licensing of personnel, rules of the air, aeronautical charts, operation of aircraft, registration marks, airworthiness of planes, accident inquiries, and aircraft noise. This organization has six regional offices, located throughout the world, for planning navigation facilities and ground services for aircraft. A particular aim of ICAO is to promote civil aviation in developing countries. To this effect, a program of technical assistance is carried out through the UN Development Programme.

Background Desired

Aeronautics, meteorology, economics, and business administration.

How to Apply

Write to: International Civil Aviation Organization
PO Box 400
1000 Sherbrooke Street West
Montreal PQ
Canada H3A 2R2

International Atomic Energy Agency (IAEA)

This agency seeks to enlarge the contribution of atomic energy to national welfare. Through an international safeguards system, it also tries to ensure that its assistance to any country is not used for military purposes. Technical assistance to developing countries is provided by the IAEA in the form of fellowships, training courses, and study tours.

Background Desired

Although a scientific background is of major interest to the IAEA, there is some place for those trained in economics, administration, public relations, and general international relations.

How to Apply

Write to: International Atomic Energy Agency
Kaertnerring 11
A-1010 Vienna, Austria

International Bank for Reconstruction and Development (IBRD)

The IBRD assists in the reconstruction and development of member countries by making loans out of its own funds when private capital is not available on reasonable terms. It also promotes private foreign investment by guarantees on loans and investments made by private investors.

The World Bank system encompasses four institutions:

1. The **World Bank** (the unofficial name for the IBRD) is the oldest and largest international organization providing development finance. In addition to loans, the Bank helps developing countries evaluate projects and draw up national programs.

2. The **International Development Association** (IDA) lends on exceptionally easy terms to very poor countries that cannot afford conventional borrowing to meet their needs for development capital.

3. The **International Finance Corporation** (IFC) invests in private or "mixed" (i.e., joint ventures between private enterprise and government) ventures. Unlike the Bank and the IDA, the IFC neither seeks nor accepts government guarantees. It is one of the few international development organizations that makes both equity investments and loans.

4. The **International Center for Settlement of Investment Disputes** (ICSID) provides a mechanism for solving disputes between governments and investors.

Entry into the World Bank structure is formalized through a **Young Professionals Program,** a mechanism for hiring talented individuals for junior professional posts. Upon entry, you are given two or three rotational assignments of from four to eight months. In each assignment, you are treated as full-fledged members of the Department to which you are assigned and are expected, through on-the-job training, to make a significant contribution. For example, one assignment might be as *loan officer* in one of the Bank's Country Program Departments; another assignment might be to work as a *project economist* or *financial analyst* in a Regional Projects Department, or as an *economist* or *investment officer* in IFC. Upon satisfactory completion of the rotational assignments, you join one of the departments of the Bank on a regular basis.

Participants in the program are selected twice yearly on a highly competitive basis. Applications are sought in all member countries. Qualifications are screened and interviews arranged for the most promising applicants. Final selection is made by a panel of senior staff members "on the basis of professional merit."

Background Desired

As many of the following as possible: banking and finance, economics, economic development, business administration, and Third World studies. In addition, professional experience in one of the above areas is highly desirable. The average age of the entering Young Professional is about 28. If you have an MA or PhD degree without practical experience, you will probably be encouraged by the Bank to first get a job elsewhere in the banking or economic development field and then apply to the Young Professionals Program. A PhD does have an edge over an MA, however.

How to Apply

Write to: Young Professionals Program
World Bank
1818 H St. NW
Washington, DC   20433

Candidates should submit:

1. Typewritten application forms (provided by the Bank if not available in your placement office);
2. References (at least three);
3. Transcripts of academic records.

Send all documentation to the Bank at least ten weeks prior to the selection date, normally set for March and October of each year.

International Monetary Fund (IMF)

The IMF is the foremost international organization involved in global monetary issues. It keeps informed of member countries' economic problems, and often provides financial assistance to help them overcome balance-of-payments difficulties. The IMF has also established a system of special drawing rights to supplement existing reserve assets of its member countries.

There are fourteen departments in the IMF. Five are area departments concerned with analyzing economic developments and financial policies in specific countries. Other departments are concerned with exchange rates, restrictions on international payments, and international liquidity.

The IMF has a **Young Professionals Program** similar to that of the World Bank. Work assignments are interspersed with courses and seminars. Over a two-year period, successful applicants will normally have assignments in one area department and one functional department in Washington headquarters, and will also take part in a mission overseas. The assignment given a candidate after this two-year stint depends on his or her background and interests.

Background Desired

Because of the specialized technical nature of IMF work, PhDs in economics, finance, and statistics are normally needed. Occasionally MAs in these fields may be considered if they also have impressive practical experience in the economic and financial fields. Area studies, business administration, and languages are additional useful qualifications.

How to Apply

The Fund's program for Young Professionals starts twice a year, in early October and early March. For application forms, the deadline date for submittal, and other information about the program, write to:

> Young Professionals Program
> International Monetary Fund
> 19th and H Sts. NW
> Washington, DC   20431

International Labor Office (ILO)

The ILO's main purpose is to improve labor conditions, raise living standards, and promote economic stability throughout the world. It is distinct from all other international organizations in that a tripartite body representing government, workers, and employers from each member country shapes ILO policies. The standards developed by the annual conference, while not obligatory, are guides for countries to follow and form an international labor code covering employment, hours of work, protection of women and young workers, workmen's compensation, trade unionism, and related matters.

Background Desired

The type of work undertaken by this organization points to the following optimum background for employment: economics, particularly labor economics; industrial relations; statistics; area studies; languages; and some experience in trade unions or the Department of Labor.

How to Apply

US relations with the ILO have wavered from whole-hearted support to resignation because of political differences with ILO policies. Accordingly, the prospects for employment will depend, among other factors, on whether the US is a full dues-paying member at the time you apply. If still interested, write to:

> International Labor Office
> 4 Route des Morillons
> 1211 Geneva, Switzerland
> or

International Labor Office
1750 New York Ave. NW
Washington, DC   20006

United Nations Educational, Scientific, and Cultural Organization (UNESCO)

UNESCO, a specialized agency of the United Nations, functions in the fields of education, science, mass communications, and cultural matters.

Education   One of UNESCO's priorities is the problem of illiteracy. In addition, UNESCO recognizes the need for educational innovation and works with countries individually and in regional groupings to improve the quality of education offered. Much of this organization's educational business is done through large-scale conferences.

Science   UNESCO seeks to advance the cause of science globally and also helps countries build up their scientific capabilities. It has set up special funds for research, has established an international exchange of information on the application of science and technology to development, and has organized regional conferences of ministers of science and technology.

Communications   UNESCO is charged by its constitution to promote "the free flow of ideas by word and image." To this end, it aims to increase each country's access to information. It has worked to help launch national and regional news agencies to promote rural newspapers and help create training centers for journalists. It pays increasing attention to television and helps train personnel to bring TV to villages throughout the developing world.

Culture   UNESCO's best-known effort in this field has been its international campaigns to save the great monuments of the world. Artistic, engineering, and archeological skills have been mobilized globally to launch cultural rescue operations, such as for the Egyptian temples that were almost submerged by the waters of the Aswan Dam. Long-term study projects are also under way to preserve and diffuse traditional and contemporary cultures of all regions of the world.

Background Desired
Because of the variety of UNESCO activities, you should determine in advance which parts or functions interest you, since qualifications will differ according to section and division. If you are educationally inclined, teaching experience and a background in academe are desirable. If you are interested in UNESCO's cultural activities, you should have some background in the arts, cultural studies, archaeology, or engineering. If commu-

nications is your field, you should be qualified in journalism, broadcasting, publishing, and communications skills.

How to Apply

Write to: United Nations Educational, Scientific,
and Cultural Organization
7 Place de Fontenoy
75700 Paris, France

or

UNESCO
UN Secretariat Building
New York, NY   10017

United Nations Children's Emergency Fund (UNICEF)

As its title indicates, UNICEF is involved with the needs of children on a global scale. About 70 percent of UNICEF's long-term aid goes to equipping health centers, schools, and day-care and community centers throughout the world. About 30 percent goes to training needed staff: nurses, health and nutrition workers, teachers, and child welfare workers. UNICEF's resources are also used for relief and rehabilitation of children suffering from natural disasters and civil disturbances.

Background Desired

Social work, welfare, health, nutrition, teaching, education, economics, area studies, and languages.

How to Apply

Write to: United Nations Children's Emergency Fund
United Nations
New York, NY   10017

United Nations Development Programme (UNDP)

UNDP activities are directed toward helping developing countries throughout Asia, Africa, Latin America, the Middle East, and part of Europe in their efforts to make effective use of available natural resources and manpower. UNDP operations have two thrusts: the most important is to help developing countries provide their people with adequate nutrition, housing, employment, education, health care, and public services; the second is to help these countries increase their output of commodities and raw materials.

Toward these ends, UNDP evaluates requests from developing countries for technical assistance. It supports thousands of projects in agriculture, industry, education, power production, transportation, communications, health, public administration, housing, trade, and related fields. These projects are closely linked with overall national development plans.

The importance attributed to UNDP work can be seen by the fact that it administers four-fifths of all the funds contributed to the UN system for development purposes. It has over 100 field offices, far more than other UN organizations. Because of UNDP's global representation, other UN organizations doing business in foreign countries are sometimes housed in UNDP offices. A list of UNDP overseas offices is found on the next page.

Each year UNDP recruits a small group of outstanding young graduates for its professional staff, placing these people at the entry level of P-1 or P-2. Successful candidates serve at any of the UNDP field offices throughout the world and usually spend the greater part of their careers overseas. A four-year tour of duty in each assignment is normal.

UNDP also has a **Junior Professional Officer Program** (JPOP), which trains young officers sponsored by their governments. These young professionals join for one- or two-year assignments, generally at a field office, after which they are expected to return to their countries. From the sponsoring country's point of view, the program provides a fine opportunity to build up a core of personnel trained in developmental work. Some industrialized countries have signed agreements with UNDP to sponsor JPOs from developing countries that are not able to afford the expense of subsidizing their own nationals.

Over 100 JPOs are in the field at any one time. Graduates of this program sometimes become full-fledged UNDP employees, although candidates are warned from the beginning that the "JPOP is emphatically not a backdoor to a UNDP career."

Background Desired

The emphasis on development work immediately points to the major qualification demanded of most applicants: a thorough grounding in economic development and economics. Graduate academic work in these fields is expected. Courses in sociology and public administration are helpful, and experience in developing countries is desirable. As with most UN organizations, fluency in French and Spanish is usually required.

How to Apply

For ordinary employment as well as for the JPOP, send a P-11 Form and a one-page statement of your motivation for UNDP work to:

Recruitment Section
Division of Personnel
United Nations Development Programme
1 UN Plaza
New York, NY   10017

UN Development Programme Offices

Afghanistan

UNDP Field Office
PO Box 5
Kabul, Republic of Afghanistan

UN agencies having offices in the country:
FAO, WHO, IBRD, IMF, UNICEF, UNFPA, WFP, UNIC

Algeria

UNDP Field Office
Boite Postale 823
Algiers, People's Democratic Republic of Algeria

UN agencies having offices in the country:
UNHCR,ILO, FAO, WHO, UNICEF, UNIC

Angola

UNDP Field Office
Catxa Postal 910
Luanda, Angola

UN agencies having offices in the country:
UNHCR

Argentina

UNDP Field Office
Apartado Postal 2257
Buenos Aires, Argentina

UN agencies having offices in the country:
UNHCR, FAO, WHO, UNIDO, UNIC

Australia

Governmental Coordinating Unit Re-UN System Development Assistance
The Secretary, Department of Foreign Affairs
Canberra A.C.T. 2600, Australia

UN agencies having offices in the country:
UNIC

Bahrain

UNDP Field Office
PO Box 814
Manama, State of Bahrain

Bangladesh

UNDP Field Office
PO Box 224
Dacca, People's Republic of Bangladesh

UN agencies having offices in the country:
ILO, FAO, WHO, IBRD, IMF, UNFPA, UNICEF, WFP, UNIDO

Benin

UNDP Field Office
Boite Postale 506
Cotonou, People's Republic of Benin

UN agencies having offices in the country:
FAO, WHO, WFP

Bolivia

UNDP Field Office
Casilla 686
La Paz, Bolivia

UN agencies having offices in the country:
FAO, WHO, UNICEF, WFP, UNIC

Botswana

UNDP Field Office
PO Box 54
Gaberones, Republic of Botswana

UN agencies having offices in the country:
UNHCR, WFP

Brazil

UNDP Field Office
CP 07/285
Brazilia, Brazil

UNDP Field Office
Caixa Postal 743
ZCOO, Rio de Janeiro, Brazil

UN agencies having offices in the country:
UNIDO, ILO, FAO, UNESCO, WHO, UNICEF, WFP, UNIC

Burma

UNDP Field Office
PO Box 650
Rangoon, Socialist Republic of the Union of Burma

UN agencies having offices in the country:
WHO, UNICEF, UNIC

Burundi

UNDP Field Office
Boite Postale 1490
Bujumbura, Republic of Burundi

UN agencies having offices in the country:
UNHCR, FAO, WHO, UNICEF, WFP, UNIC

Cameroon

UNDP Field Office
Boite Postale 836
Yaounde, United Republic of Cameroon

UN agencies having offices in the country:
ILO, FAO, UNESCO, WHO, IBRD, WFP, UNIC, UNIDO

Cape Verde

UNDP Field Office
Caixa Postal 62
Praia, Republic of Cape Verde

UN agencies having offices in the country:
WFP

Central African Republic

UNDP Field Office
PO Box 872
Bangui, Central African Republic

UN agencies having offices in the country:
WHO, WFP

Chad

UNDP Field Office
Boite Postale 906
N'Djamena, Republic of Chad

UN agencies having offices in the country:
FAO, UNICEF, WFP

Chile

UNDP Field Office
Casilla 197-D
Santiago, Chile

UN agencies having offices in the country:
UNHCR, ILO, FAO, UNESCO, WHO, UNFPA, WFP, UNIC

Colombia

UNDP Field Office
Apartado Aereo No. 3868
Bogota, Colombia

UN agencies having offices in the country:
UNHCR, FAO, WHO, UNFPA, UNICEF, IBRD, WFP, UNIC

Comoro Islands

UNDP Field Office
PO Box 1348
Tananarive, Malagasy Republic

Congo

UNDP Field Office
Boite Postale 465
Brazzaville, People's Republic of the Congo

UN agencies having offices in the country:
WHO, UNICEF, WFP

Costa Rica

UNDP Field Office
Apartado Postal 4540
San Jose, Costa Rica
UN agencies having offices in the
country:
ILO, FAO, WHO, UNFPA, WFP

Cuba

UNDP Field Office
Apartado Postal No. 4138
Havana 4, Cuba
UN agencies having offices in the
country:
FAO, WHO, UNESCO

Cyprus

UNDP Field Offices
PO Box 3521
Nicosia, Cyprus
UN agencies having offices in the
country:
WFP

Democratic Yemen

UNDP Field Office
PO Box 1188
Tawahi, Aden, People's Democratic
Republic of Yemen
UN agencies having offices in the
country:
WHO, WFP

Dominican Republic

UNDP Field Office
Apartado 1424
Santo Domingo, Dominican Republic
UN agencies having offices in the
country:
WHO

East African Community

UNDP Field Office
PO Box 228
Arusha, United Republic of Tanzania

Ecuador

UNDP Field Office
PO Box 4731
Quito, Ecuador
UN agencies having offices in the
country:
WHO

Egypt

UNDP Field Office
PO Box 982
Cairo, United Arab Republic of Egypt
UN agencies having offices in the
country:
UNHCR, UNRWA, UNIDO, UNEP,
FAO, UNFPA, ILO, UNESCO, WHO,
ICAO, UNICEF, WFP, UNIC

El Salvador

UNDP Field Office
PO Box 1114
San Salvador, El Salvador
UN agencies having offices in the
country:
WHO, UNFPA, WFP, UNIC

Equatorial Guinea

UNDP Office in Equatorial Guinea
Calie de Kenia
Malabo, Equatorial Guinea

Ethiopia

UNDP Field Office
PO Box 5580
Addis Ababa, Ethiopia
UN agencies having offices in the
country:
UNHCR, ILO, FAO, UNESCO, WHO,
UNICEF, WFP, IBRD, UNIC

French Territory of the Afars and The Issas

Governmental Coordinating Unit
Re-UN System Development
Assistance
Ministere des Affairs Etrangenes
37 Quai d'Orax
Paris 7 eme, France

Gabon

UNDP Field Office
Boite Postale 2183
Libreville, Gabon
UN agencies having offices in the country:
ITU, WFP

Gambia

UNDP Field Office
PO Box 553
Banjul, Republic of Gambia
UN agencies having offices in the country:
WFP

Ghana

UNDP Field Office
PO Box 1423
Accra, Ghana
UN agencies having offices in the country:
FAO, WHO, IBRD, WFP, UNIC

Greece

UNDP Field Office
36 Amalia Avenue
Athens 119, Greece
UN agencies having offices in the country:
UNHCR, UNIC

Guatemala

UNDP Field Office
Apartado Postale 23-A
Ciudad de Guatemala, Guatemala
UN agencies having offices in the country:
FAO, UNIDO, UNICEF

Guinea

UNDP Field Office
Boite Postale 222
Conakry, Republic of Guinea
UN agencies having offices in the country:
FAO, WHO, WFP

Guinea-Bissau

UNDP Field Office
CP 179
Bissau, Republic of Guinea-Bissau
UN agencies having offices in the country:
UNHCR, WFP

Guyana

UNDP Field Office
PO Box 726
Georgetown, Guyana
UN agencies having offices in the country:
WHO

Haiti

UNDP Field Office
PO Box 557
Port-au-Prince, Haiti
UN agencies having offices in the .country:
UNFPA, WHO, IMF, WFP, UNICEF

Honduras

UNDP Field Office
Apartado Postal 976
Tegucigalpa, Honduras
UN agencies having offices in the
country:
FAO, WHO

Iceland

UNDP Regional Office for Europe,
Mediterranean, Middle East
UNDP Headquarters
New York, NY 10017 USA

India

UNDP Field Office
PO Box 136
New Delhi, 110001, India
UN agencies having offices in the
country:
ILO, FAO, UNESCO, WHO, IBRD,
UNFPA, UNIDO, UNICEF, WFP,
UNIC

Indonesia

UNDP Field Office
PO Box 2338
Jakarta, Indonesia
UN agencies having offices in the
country:
ILO, UNESCO, WHO, IBRD, IMF,
WFP, UNICEF, UNIDO

Iran

UNDP Field Office
PO Box 1555
Teheran, Iran
UN agencies having offices in the
country:
ILO, FAO, IBRD, UNICEF, WFP,
UNIC, UNIDO

Iraq

UNDP Field Office
PO Box 2048 Alwiyah
Baghdad, Iraq
UN agencies having offices in the
country:
FAO, WHO, UNICEF, WFP, UNIC

Israel

UNDP Field Office
39 Jabotinsky Street
Jerusalem, Israel

Ivory Coast

UNDP Field Office
Boite Postale 1747
Abidjan, Ivory Coast
UN agencies having offices in the
country:
WHO, UNICEF, WFP, IBRD

Jamaica

UNDP Field Office
PO Box 280
Kingston, Jamaica
UN agencies having offices in the
country:
ILO, FAO, WHO, IMF, UNFPA

Jordan

UNDP Field Office
PO Box 565
Amman, Jordan
UN agencies having offices in the
country:
FAO, UNICEF, WFP

Kenya

UNDP Field Office
PO Box 30218
Nairobi, Kenya

UN agencies having offices in the country:
UNHCR, UNEP, FAO, UNESCO, WHO, IBRD, UNICEF, UNFPA, UNIC, UNIDO

Korea

UNDP Field Office
Central PO Box 143
Seoul, Republic of Korea

UN agencies having offices in the country:
FAO, WHO, IMF, UNICEF, WFP

Kuwait

UNDP Field Office
PO Box 2993
State of Kuwait

UN agencies having offices in the country:
ILO, UNIDO

Lao People's Democratic Republic

UNDP Field Office
Boite Postale 345
Vientiane, Lao People's Democratic Republic

UN agencies having offices in the country:
UNHCR, WHO, IMF, UNICEF

Lebanon

UNDP Field Office
PO Box 3216
Beirut, Lebanon

UN agencies having offices in the country:
UNHCR, UNIDO, UNRWA, UNFPA, ILO, UNESCO, WHO, UNICEF, WFP, UNIC

Lesotho, Kingdom of

UNDP Field Office
PO Box 301
Mascro, Lesotho

UN agencies having offices in the country:
WHO, WFP

Liberia

UNDP Field Office
PO Box 274
Monrovia, Liberia

UN agencies having offices in the country:
WHO, IMF, UNIC, UNIDO

Libyan Arab Republic

UNDP Field Office
PO Box 358
Tripoli, Libyan Arab Republic

UN agencies having offices in the country:
WHO

Malagasy Republic

UNDP Field Office
PO Box 1348
Tananarive, Malagasy Republic

UN agencies having offices in the country:
WHO, WFP, UNIC

Malawi

UNDP Field Office
PO Box 30135
Lilongwe 3, Republic of Malawi

UN agencies having offices in the country:
WFP

Malaysia

UNDP Field Office
PO Box 2544
Kuala Lumpur, Malaysia

UN agencies having offices in the country:
FAO, UNIDO, UNFPA

Mali

UNDP Field Office
Boite Postale 120
Bamako, Republic of Mali

UN agencies having offices in the country:
FAO, WFP

Mauritania

UNDP Field Office
Boite Postale, 620
Nouakchott, Mauritania

UN agencies having offices in the country:
WFP, UNICEF

Mauritius

UNDP Field Office
PO Box 253
Port Louis, Mauritius

UN agencies having offices in the country:
WFP, UNICEF

Mexico

UNDP Field Office
Apartado Postal 6719
Mexico 6, D.F. Mexico

UN agencies having offices in the country:
FAO, WHO, ICAO, UNFPA, WFP, UNICEF, UNIC, UNIDO

Mongolia

UNDP Field Office
PO Branch No. 49
Box 207
Ulan Bator, People's Republic of Mongolia

UN agencies having offices in the country:
WHO

Morocco

UNDP Field Office
Casier Onu, Rabat-Chellah
Rabat, Kingdom of Morocco

UN agencies having offices in the country:
WHO, FAO, UNIC, UNIDO

Mozambique

UNDP Field Office
PO Box 4595
Maputo, People's Republic of Mozambique

UN agencies having offices in the country:
UNHCR, UNICEF, WFP

Nepal

UNDP Field Office
PO Box 107
Katmandu, Kingdom of Nepal

UN agencies having offices in the country:
FAO, WHO, IBRD, UNICEF, UNFPA, UNIC, WFP

Nicaragua

UNDP Field Office
Apartado Postal 3260
Managua, Nicaragua

UN agencies having offices in the country:
FAO, WHO, WFP

Niger

UNDP Field Office
PO Box 256
Niamcy, Niger
UN agencies having offices in the country:
FAO, WHO, UNICEF, WFP

Nigeria

UNDP Field Office
PO Box 2075
Lagos, Nigeria
UN agencies having offices in the country:
FAO, WHO, IBRD, UNFPA, UNIDO, UNICEF, WFP, UNIC

Oman

UNDP Field Office
PO Box 87
Muscat, Sultanate of Oman

Pakistan

UNDP Field Office
PO Box 1051
Islamabad, Pakistan
UN agencies having offices in the country:
ILO, FAO, WHO, IBRD, UNFPA, WFP, UNICEF, UNIC, UNIDO

Panama

UNDP Field Office
Apartado 6314
Panama 5, Panama
UN agencies having offices in the country:
WHO, IMF

Papua New Guinea

UNDP Field Office
Private Mail Bag
Port Moresby, Papua New Guinea
UN agencies having offices in the country:
WHO, UNIC

Paraguay

UNDP Field Office
Casilla de Correo 1107
Asuncion, Paraguay
UN agencies having offices in the country:
FAO, WHO, IMF, UNICEF, UNIC, UNIDO

Philippines

UNDP Field Office
PO Box 1864
Manila, Philippines
UN agencies having offices in the country:
ILO, FAO, UNICEF, UNFPA, WFP, UNIC, UNIDO

Qatar

UNDP Field Office
Box 3233
Doha, State of Qatar

Romania

UNDP Field Office
PO Box 701
Bucharest, Romania
UN agencies having offices in the country:
UNIC

Rwanda

UNDP Field Office
Boite Postale 445
Kigali, Rwanda
UN agencies having offices in the country:
UNHCR, WHO, WFP

Saudi Arabia

UNDP Field Office
PO Box 558
Riyadh, Saudi Arabia
UN agencies having offices in the country:
WHO, ICAO

Senegal

UNDP Field Office
Boite, Postale 154
Dakar, Republic of Senegal
UN agencies having offices in the
country:
UNHCR, FAO, WHO, ILO, UNESCO,
ICAO, UNICEF, UNFPA, WFP,
UNIC, UNIDO

Sierra Leone

UNDP Field Office
PO Box 1011
Freetown, Republic of Sierra Leone

Somalia Democratic Republic

UNDP Field Office
PO Box 24
Mogadiscio, Somalia Democratic
Republic
UN agencies having offices in the
country:
FAO, WHO, UNICEF, WFP, UNIDO

South Pacific

UNDP Office
PO Box 1864
Manila, Philippines
UN agencies having offices in the
country:
FAO, UNFPA, WFP

Sri Lanka

UNDP Field Office
PO Box 1505
Colombo, Sri Lanka
UN agencies having offices in the
country:
FAO, WHO, UNICEF, UNFPA, WFP,
UNIC

Sudan

UNDP Field Office
PO Box 913
Khartoum, Democratic Republic of the
Sudan
UN agencies having offices in the
country:
UNHCR, FAO, UNESCO, WHO,
IBRD, IMF, UNICEF, WFP

Swaziland

UNDP Field Office
PO Box 261
Mbabane, Swaziland
UN agencies having offices in the
country:
FAO, WFP

Switzerland

UNDP Field Office
or
United Nations Volunteer Programme
Place des Nations
CH-1211 Geneva 20, Switzerland
Headquarters: UNHCR, WHO, UPU,
ITU, WMO, UNCTAD
Offices: UNRWA, UNITAR, UNEP,
FAO, UNESCO, IMF, IAEA,
UNICEF,WFP, UNIC

Syrian Arab Republic

UNDP Field Office
PO Box 2317
Lamascus, Syrian Arab Republic
UN agencies having offices in the
country:
UNIDO, UNRWA, FAO, UNICEF,
WFP

Tanzania

UNDP Field Office
PO Box 9182
Dar-es-Salaam, United Republic of
Tanzania
UN agencies having offices in the
country:
UNHCR, ILO, UNESCO, WHO,
IBRD, WFP, UNIC

Thailand

UNDP Field Office
PO Box 618
Bangkok, Thailand
UN agencies having offices in the country:
UNHCR, UNEP, ILO, FAO, WHO, IBRD, IMF, ICAO, UNFPA, UNIDO, UNICEF, UNIC

Togo

UNDP Field Office
Boite Postale 911
Lome, Togo
UN agencies having offices in the country:
WHO, WFP, UNIC

Trinidad and Tobago

UNDP Field Office
PO Box 812
Port-of-Spain, Trinidad and Tobago
UN agencies having offices in the country:
UNFPA, ILO, WHO, WFP, UNIC

Tunisia

UNDP Field Office
Boite Postale 863
Tunis, Tunisia
UN agencies having offices in the country:
UNHCR, FAO, WHO, UNFPA, WFP, UNIC

Turkey

UNDP Field Office
PK 407
Ankara, Turkey
UN agencies having offices in the country:
UNHCR, ILO, WHO, UNFPA, WFP, UNIC

Uganda

UNDP Field Office
PO Box 7184
Kampala, Uganda
UN agencies having offices in the country:
UNHCR, FAO, WHO, WFP

United Arab Emirates

UNDP Field Office
PO Box 3490
Abu Dhabi, United Arab Emirates
UN agencies having offices in the country:
WHO, UNICEF

Upper Volta

UNDP Field Office
Boite Postale 575
Ouagadougou, Upper Volta
UN agencies having offices in the country:
FAO, WHO, WFP, UNIDO

Uruguay

UNDP Field Office
Casilla de Correo 1207
Montevideo, Uruguay
UN agencies having offices in the country:
FAO, ILO, UNESCO, WHO, IMF

Venezuela

UNDP Field Office
Apartado 1969
Caracas, Venezuela
UN agencies having offices in the country:
FAO, WHO

Yemen Arab Republic

UNDP Field Office
PO Box 551
San'a, Yemen Arab Republic

UN agencies having offices in the country:
WHO, UNICEF, WFP

Yugoslavia

UNDP Field Office
PO Box 644
Belgrade, Yugoslavia

UN agencies having offices in the country:
UNIC

Zaire

UNDP Field Office
Boite Postale 7248
Kinshasa, Republic of Zaire

UN agencies having offices in the country:
UNHCR, ILO, WHO, UNICEF, UNIC, UNIDO, IBRD

Zambia

UNDP Field Office
PO Box 1966
Lusaka, Republic of Zambia

UN agencies having offices in the country:
UNHCR, ILO, FAO, WHO, WFP, UNICEF, IBRD

United Nations Fund for Population Activities (UNFPA)

The Population Fund, as it is popularly called, was set up in 1967 to help developing countries with high population rates and low national incomes solve their population problems. This UN organization is recognized as the focal point for the promotion and coordination of international population programs. The fund assists national efforts by: (a) promoting government awareness of the consequences of a high population growth rate; (b) providing assistance to countries seeking relief from their population problems; (c) helping organizations within the UN system to be more effective in planning and implementing population projects; and (d) assuming the leading international role in developing global population strategies.

Background Desired

A similar background to that required for UNDP applies to the fund: economics, economic development, and developing area studies. Emphasis is also placed on population, demography, and statistics. Fluency in languages is a great plus.

How to Apply

Write to: UN Fund for Population Activities
485 Lexington Ave.
New York, NY   10017

World Health Organization (WHO)

WHO plans and coordinates health action on a global basis. It assists member countries to carry out health programs, to strengthen their health services, and to train their health workers. It also promotes medical research and exchange of scientific information, makes health regulations for international travel, keeps communicable diseases under surveillance, collects and distributes data on health matters, and sets standards for the control of drugs and vaccines.

WHO has six regional offices: African region (headquarters, Brazzaville); the Americas (Washington, DC); Eastern Mediterranean (Alexandria); Europe (Copenhagen); Southeast Asia (New Delhi); and Western Pacific (Manila).

Background Desired
The type of work performed by WHO defines the type of personnel needed: medical officers, nurses, sanitary engineers, entomologists, bacteriologists, health educators, and occasionally economists and statisticians. Third World experience is desirable, as is fluency in the languages of the area applied for, of course.

How to Apply
Write to: World Health Organization
20 Ave. APPIA
CH-1211 Geneva 27, Switzerland

United Nations Volunteers (UNV)

UNV is somewhat similar to the Peace Corps (now part of ACTION) in that it enrolls the youth of many countries in a collective effort to help developing nations. The help offered ranges from community development to road construction, well digging, health services, education—in other words, much the same territory covered by the UNDP in its technical assistance work. For this reason, volunteers are associated with UNDP-assisted projects and form another wing of that organization. The primary aim of UNV is to make a contribution to the development of the recipient country. Volunteers are paid transportation expenses and a small living stipend.

Background Desired
Economics, business administration, teaching, health services, community development, engineering, and almost any other skills needed by impoverished countries.

How to Apply
Applicants must be over 21 and are recruited from both developed and developing countries. UNV does not recruit volunteers directly; applica-

tions are channeled through existing volunteer organizations. To this effect, UNV cooperates with the **International Secretariat for Volunteer Service** and the **Coordinating Committee for International Voluntary Service**, two international volunteer organizations with a membership of over 500 affiliated organizations. Applicants should seek sponsorship from recognized volunteer organizations in their own country. For a list of these organizations, write to:

> International Secretariat for Voluntary Service
> 12 Chemin de Surville
> Geneva, Petit Lancy 1213, Switzerland
> or
> Coordinating Committee for International Voluntary Service
> 1 Rue Miollis
> Paris 15, France

For other information on the UNV, write to:

> UN Volunteers
> Palais des Nations
> 1211 Geneva 20
> Switzerland

United Nations Industrial Development Organization (UNIDO)

UNIDO was established in 1967 to "promote and accelerate the industrialization of the developing countries." There is a policy-making **Industrial Development Board** on which forty-five countries are represented. The technical assistance activities of UNIDO are financed mainly by UNDP. One of UNIDO's aims is to increase the developing nations' share of world industrial production from 7 percent to 25 percent by the year 2000. UNIDO also administers an Industrial Development Fund of voluntary contributions for special operational tasks.

To summarize, UNIDO helps developing countries expand and modernize their industries; acts as liaison between developing and industrialized countries in their joint efforts toward industrialization of the former; assists developing nations to obtain financing for industrial projects; and undertakes the transfer of needed technology and the training of personnel.

Background Desired

Business administration, industrial relations, and, as elsewhere, a liberal supply of economics courses, economic development, and Third World area studies. Languages are also desirable.

How to Apply

Write to: United Nations Industrial Development Organization
PO Box 707
A-1011 Vienna, Austria

United Nations Institute for Training and Research (UNITAR)

UNITAR was established in 1963 as an autonomous institute within the UN framework for specialized training and research. The training function involves individuals primarily from the developing nations who need to improve their qualifications for UN work or for work in their own countries. Research performed is "related to the functions and objectives of the UN," thus allowing wide latitude for the studies undertaken.

Background Desired

A research and/or training ability is clearly indicated for all applicants. Specific courses in support of your application are: economics, economic development, area studies, world resources, international relations, and foreign policy.

How to Apply

Send your P-11 Form to:
United Nations Institute for Training and Research
UN Headquarters
New York, NY   10017

United Nations University

The UN University was established to "improve the conditions of human existence throughout the world." It is not organized on the basis of traditional academic departments; instead, the University's institutes employ multidisciplinary approaches to specific world problems. It is strongly oriented toward the needs of the developing countries. The University Council has chosen world hunger as the first priority. Long-range analysis of food policy, water resources, human rights, international trade, and the uses of the sea are other matters of concern.

Background Desired

Teaching credentials and experience, agriculture, world resources, Third World area studies, and of course, languages, especially Japanese.

How to Apply

Write to: United Nations University
Toho Sheimei Building
15-1 Shibuya 2-Chome, Shibuya-ku
Tokyo, 150, Japan

or

United Nations
New York, NY 10017

United Nations International School

The UN International School is not part of the UN structure, but is included here because of its close relationship to the United Nations. The School is for students whose parents are associated with the United Nations and have come to New York from abroad. It is a day school, beginning with the 5-year-old level and continuing through preparation for college and university. It has two locations: on the East River south of UN headquarters, and an elementary branch in Queens.

Background Desired
Teaching experience, area studies, languages.

How to Apply

Write to: United Nations International School
24-50 East River Drive
New York, NY 10010

General Agreements on Tariffs and Trade (GATT)

GATT, an autonomous organization within the UN system, is the focus for intergovernmental efforts to remove trade barriers. It also aims to expand international trade and economic development.

Background Desired
Economics, economic development, and trade and tariff studies.

How to Apply

Write to: General Agreements on Tariffs and Trade
Palais des Nations
CH-1211 Geneva 20
Switzerland

United Nations Environment Programme (UNEP)

The UN General Assembly, in establishing UNEP, recognized that environmental problems on the international level required a special approach. Since environment is the logical concern of many UN organizations, it was considered unwise to make environmental problems the province of one agency. Thus, in contrast to the concept that shaped other UN organizations, UNEP was created as a small coordinating body to give leadership and direction to international initiatives—not to do the work itself, but to see that it gets done.

Background Desired

Economics, economic development, world resources, population studies, energy studies, and environmental studies.

How to Apply

Write to: United Nations Environment Programme
PO Box 30552
Nairobi, Kenya

or

866 UN Plaza, 3rd Floor
New York, NY   10017

United Nations High Commissioner for Refugees (UNHCR)

This organization is concerned with any individual who lives outside his or her home country and who does not receive its protection for reasons of race, nationality, membership in a particular social group, or political opinion. UNHCR has two main functions: (1) encouraging the practice of asylum and then safeguarding the rights of refugees concerning employment, education, residence, freedom of movement, and security against being returned to a country where their lives may be in danger; and (2) helping governments and private organizations in countries of asylum in their task of enabling refugees to become self-supporting.

In recent years the UN Secretary General has designated UNHCR to coordinate several major UN programs. One concerned emergency relief for some ten million East Benghali refugees in India; another, the return of thousands of refugees to the South Sudan and their resettlement in that region. More recently, UNHCR has provided aid to hundreds of thousands of uprooted people in and from Indochina.

Background Desired

Social work, work with displaced persons or refugees, economics, economic development, and international relations.

How to Apply

Write to: United Nations High Commissioner for Refugees
Palais des Nations
CH-1211 Geneva 10
Switzerland

Consultative Group on International Agricultural Research (CGIAR)

This group was organized by the FAO, the World Bank, and the UNDP. Its purpose is to stimulate agricultural progress in the tropics and subtropics, where most of the less-developed countries lie. It tries to achieve this aim through research programs and the training of scientists and specialists in the developing world.

CGIAR supports eleven centers engaged in the investigation of the problems of tropical agriculture: **International Rice Institute** (Philippines); **International Maize and Wheat Improvement Center** (Mexico); **International Center for Tropical Agriculture** (Colombia); **International Institute of Tropical Agriculture** (Nigeria); **International Potato Center** (Peru); **International Crops Research Institute for the Semi-Arid Tropics** (India); **International Laboratory for Research on Animal Diseases** (Kenya); **International Livestock Center for Africa** (Ethiopia); **West Africa Rice Development Association** (Liberia); **International Board for Plant Genetic Resources** (Italy); and **International Center for Agricultural Research in the Dry Areas** (Lebanon).

Background Desired

Agricultural sciences, economics, and Third World area studies.

How to Apply

Write to: Consultative Group on International Agricultural Research
C/O IBRD
1818 H St. NW
Washington, DC 20433

World Intellectual Property Organization (WIPO)

WIPO is responsible for the protection of intellectual property throughout the world, and for the administration of various "Unions," each founded on a multilateral treaty and dealing with the legal and administrative aspects of intellectual property. Intellectual property consists of: (1) industrial property (chiefly inventions, trademarks, and designs); and (2) copyrights (chiefly literary, musical, artistic, photographic, and cinematographic work). Part of the activities of WIPO is devoted to assisting developing countries. Particular emphasis is placed on the transfer of technology and know-how related to industrial property.

Background Desired
Law, business administration, cultural work, library sciences, and transfer of technology.

How to Apply
Write to: World Intellectual Property Organization
              32, Chemin des Colombettes
              1211 Geneva 20
              Switzerland

              or

              WIPO Liaison Office at the United Nations
              821 UN Plaza
              New York, NY   10017

Four other specialized UN agencies whose names are self-descriptive are:

> Inter-Governmental Maritime Consultative Organization (IMCO)
> 101-104 Piccadilly
> London WIV OAE
> England
>
> International Telecommunication Union (ITU)
> Place des Nations
> 1211 Geneva 20
> Switzerland
>
> Universal Postal Union (UPU)
> Case postal
> 3000 Berne 15
> Switzerland
>
> World Meteorological Organization (WMO)
> 41, avenue Giuseppe Motta
> CH-1211 Geneva 20
> Switzerland

Publications

Additional information on UN agencies and their functions, organization, and personnel can be found in:

1. *Yearbook of the United Nations* (New York: United Nations, 1976).

2. *Europa Year Book, 1977, A World Survey, Vol. I, Part I International Organizations* (London: Europa Publications, Ltd.).

3. *World Mark Encyclopedia of the Nations* (New York and Toronto: World Mark Press, Ltd., John Wiley, 1976).

Regional UN Organizations

The following organizations, also related to the UN system, are listed separately because they have a particular regional emphasis.

Organization of American States (OAS)

The OAS is one of the world's oldest international organizations. It unites the countries of the Western Hemisphere "in a community of nations dedicated to the achievement of peace, security, and prosperity for all Americans." The OAS is thought of as a regional agency of the United Nations. In fact, its relation is limited to the maintenance of peace and the peaceful settlement of disputes. In other fields—economic, social, legal—the OAS operates independently. The **Council** of the OAS is the executive body of the organization and it functions with eight permanent committees: (1) **General;** (2) **Program and Budget;** (3) **Inter-American Conferences;** (4) **Inter-American Organizations;** (5) **Economic and Social Affairs;** (6) **Juridical–Political Affairs;** (7) **Cultural Affairs;** and (8) **Public Information, Regulations, and Procedures.** The titles of the committees represent the general scope of overall OAS functions.

The **Pan American Union** is the Secretariat of the OAS. In addition, there are five inter-American specialized organizations with which the OAS Council maintains working agreements: (1) **Pan American Health Organization** (headquarters in Washington, DC); (2) **Inter-American Children's Institute** (headquarters in Montevideo); (3) **Inter-American Commission of Women** (headquarters in the Pan American Union in Washington, DC); (4) **Pan American Institute of Geography and History** (headquarters in Mexico City); and (5) **Inter-American Institute of Agricultural Sciences** (headquarters in the Pan American Union in Washington, DC). This prolific network of agencies and organizations, all dedicated to the improvement of the quality of life for North and South Americans, has personnel working in a wide variety of jobs: economic, political, social, health.

Background Desired

Latin American studies, Spanish and Portuguese economics, economic development, communications, and public relations.

How to Apply

Write to: General Secretariat
Organization of American States
Constitution Ave. & 17th St. NW
Washington, DC   20006

Inter-American Development Bank

The purpose of the bank is to promote economic development of its member countries from Latin America. The United States and several countries from Europe and Asia have also been admitted as members. The bank finances high priority economic and social development projects in the private and public sectors; it provides technical cooperation, research, and training in the development field; and it acts as a clearing house for the exchange of information on economic and social questions in Latin American countries. Bank offices are located in most Latin American countries.

Background Desired

Finance and banking, economics, economic development, Latin American studies, and Spanish and Portuguese.

How to Apply

Write to: Inter-American Development Bank
808 17th St. NW
Washington, DC   20577

Organization for Economic Cooperation and Development (OECD)

The OECD is the successor to the Organization for European Economic Cooperation, which administered the Marshall Plan for European recovery after World War II. The organization is composed primarily of European countries, although the United States, Canada, Japan, and several other countries are also members. The OECD tries to achieve the highest sustainable economic growth, employment, and standard of living in member countries while maintaining financial stability. Another purpose of the organization is to expand world trade.

Background Desired

The specialized economic nature of this organization puts a premium on PhDs in economics, industrial relations, manpower studies, economic development, statistics, and finance. Business administration, European studies, and languages are also helpful.

How to Apply

Write to: Organization for Economic Cooperation and Development
2 Rue Andre-Pascal
75775 Paris 16, France

Intergovernmental Committee for European Migration (ICEM)

One purpose of the ICEM is to arrange for transporting immigrants from certain overpopulated European countries to other countries willing to absorb them. Unemployed workers in industrialized European countries and refugees are other groups helped by ICEM. The reunification of families and the provision of needed language training are among tasks performed by this organization.

ICEM also cooperates with the UN High Commissioner for Refugees (UNHCR) on occasion: the resettlement of refugees from Vietnam, Laos, and Cambodia was jointly undertaken by both organizations. The ICEM has also worked on the resettlement of Chileans "detained under the provisions of the state of siege." Its efforts have been directed towards obtaining entry visas to allow migration of these people to other countries.

Background Desired

Economics, law, sociology, and international relations.

How to Apply

Write to: Intergovernmental Committee for European Migration
16 Avenue Jean Trembley Petit Saconnex
Geneva, Switzerland

Asian Development Bank

The bank's function is to promote economic growth in member countries, most of which are from Asia. The United States became a member in 1966 and provides significant funding for the organization.

Background Desired

Banking and finance, economics, economic development, and Asian studies.

How to Apply

Write to: Asian Development Bank
2330 Roxas Boulevard
Pasay City
Philippines

UN Relief and Works Agency for
Palestine Refugees in the Near East (UNRWA)

UNRWA has existed as a temporary UN agency since 1950, with its mandate being renewed periodically by the General Assembly. It provides services to Palestinian refugees, specifically those persons (or their descendants) who were residents of Palestine for the last two years before the 1948 Arab-Israel conflict and who then lost their homes and means of livelihood.

UNRWA operates almost 600 schools for refugee children and employs over 8,000 teachers, mostly Palestinians, to staff these schools. This educational program is run jointly with UNESCO. UNRWA's health program for refugees is also run jointly—in this case with the WHO. Its other major program is a relief program consisting of food distribution, staffed mostly with local personnel. The agency's areas of operation are Lebanon, Syria, East Jordan, the West Bank, and the Gaza Strip.

Background Desired
UNRWA's international staff is limited in number, and the organization requires the following specializations as well as experience: law, accounting, information and public relations, administration, personnel, education, health, nutrition and feeding, and languages. Since UNRWA is a temporary organization, new hiring is at a minimum.

How to Apply
If you are qualified and sufficiently motivated, write to:

> UN Relief and Works Agency
> for Palestine Refugees in the Near East
> United Nations Secretariat
> New York, NY   10017

CHAPTER SEVEN

Nonprofit Organizations

From a world of standardized application forms (US government and United Nations) and competitive exams (US government), we move to more individualized world with a diversity of application forms (or no forms at all) and no entrance exams.

What Is a Nonprofit Organization?

The US government and the United Nations are not run for profit, but they are public enterprises and their size and importance warrant separate consideration. What we are now considering is the myriad of organizations in the private sector to which profit making is irrelevant and indeed impossible considering their functions, such as helping refugees, making the public aware of foreign policy issues, helping American students traveling abroad, family planning, placing foreign students in American homes and schools, arranging study trips to Russia, analyzing issues before the General Assembly, researching and promoting human rights, supporting community development in African nations, exhibiting art from South East Asia.

All of these organizations service people in various ways and are intended to enhance the public good. Some have consultative status with the United Nations and are known as NGOs (nongovernment organizations); a few cooperate with the US government on some of its minor functions, such as hosting foreign officials in the United States. Others operate without relationship to either the government or the United Nations.

A few of these organizations are large (the Ford Foundation); many are so small that their offices are cubbyholes, open only part-time and staffed by volunteers.

If you are out for personal profit, you will hardly be attracted to organizations that make none. Except for the largest of these organizations, the entry salaries are about the lowest you will find on the international totem pole (fortunately, mid- and top-level positions offer respectable salaries). In close competition for the dubious award of poor initial reimbursement are the publishing and journalism jobs. (More about this in Chapter Nine.)

However, if you are service-oriented and wish to work on behalf of people and worthwhile ideas—or if you are turned off by the competitive rat race around you, disturbed by the bureaucracy of the United Nations and the government, and willing to accept a lower salary in return for job satisfaction—the nonprofit world may be right for you.

Don't be thrown off by the opprobrious appellation "do gooder," which you may hear about employees of nonprofit organizations. The term conjures up an image of idealistic but disorganized, woolly minded, and inefficient individuals. Not necessarily so. Many employees of these organizations are hardheaded administrators, economists, scientists, and sociologists who "do good" in the best sense of the term.

The funding of these organizations is often precarious. Many of them depend on private donors who, in a down stock market, close their purse strings. Corporate donors may also be less generous in a recession. Lack of financial support in trying times often results in budget cuts and curtailed projects for which you may be admirably qualified. Job possibilities, then, may depend not only on the size of the organization, but also on the state of the economy and particularly the state of business, an ironic dependence if the business world has turned you off from the beginning.

You may notice that quite a few nonprofit organizations seem to have overlapping functions. Some of them seek "to increase understanding between peoples," and this phrase appears again and again in the description of functions publicized by their public relations officials. You will also notice that several organizations are involved with "global interdependence," others with "hemispheric solidarity," and many seem concerned with economic development in Latin America, population problems, and environmental issues. There is undoubtedly duplication. Still, the enormity of the job to be done in increasing both understanding and development may justify the number of organizations in these fields. The question of efficiency of operations (couldn't the job be better done by combining all these smaller organizations into one master conglomerate?) can reasonably be posed. That the question arises at all highlights the state of the nonprofit organization today: its independence and goodwill plus a certain amount of inefficiency and lack of discipline.

Since very few of these organizations have branches overseas, work will almost always be at US headquarters. Business trips abroad for short-term conferences or consultation take place only with the largest nonprofit organizations and even then only occasionally.

Because travel is rare, language fluency is seldom needed. An exception exists in the case of some headquarters jobs involving research from original sources, where translation ability may be required. A background in area studies, however, may be at a premium in nonprofit organizations geared to a particular region, such as the Asia Society, the Citizen Exchange Corps, or the Center for Inter-American Relations.

Internships

If you cannot find a paying job in a nonprofit organization, you may wish to consider an internship in this field. Voluntary work is a valuable way of gaining experience and may subsequently lead to a job. If you decide to go the internship route, consult the *International Directory for Youth Internships with the United Nations, Its Specialized Agencies, and Non-Government Organizations*. This booklet is published through the cooperative effort of the UN Headquarters NGO Youth Caucus and the Foreign Area Materials Center of the University of the State of New York. It is available from either organization at $2.00 a copy.

The nonprofit organizations in the listing that follows are the most important with international interests. They are grouped under the following headings: Foreign Affairs; Area Interests; Educational, Cultural, and Exchange; Economics and Economic Development; Energy, Environment, and Population; Business and Labor; Relief, Rehabilitation, and Human Rights; and Others. Organizations and centers attached to universities, such as the Economic Growth Center at Yale and the Research Institute on International Change at Columbia, are not included here because any jobs that may open up will probably be filled from within.

For each organization we will list some of the qualifications usually desired of an applicant should a job opening occur. (Some organizations may depend on volunteers with few, if any, jobs ever available. Still, if motivated and qualified, do not hesitate to apply.) Any necessary academic degree will be noted. Organizations marked with an asterisk (*) are relatively large and more likely to have a job opening from time to time. Check addresses before you write or visit, since there is much movement, especially among the smaller of these agencies. Some of them also pass out of existence with alarming frequency. For a complete listing of nongovernment organizations that have consultative status with the Economic and Social Council of the UN, consult *Non-Government Organization Profiles and Statistical Data*, 1977, by William Heery. This book is available in the UN library in New York. A list of directories of various types of nonprofit organizations is found in the bibliographies.

Foreign Affairs

American Political Science Association

This is an organization for students and professors interested in the study of government and politics. It publishes the *American Political Science Review*, a quarterly journal of scholarly articles and book reviews in political science, including international affairs.

Background Desired
International relations, editing skills, and administrative experience. An MA or PhD is preferred.

How to Apply
Write to: American Political Science Association
1527 New Hampshire Ave. NW
Washington, DC 20036

Council on Foreign Relations, Chicago*

The council engages in a program of foreign policy seminars, briefings, study groups, conferences, and publications designed to serve its large constituency in the Chicago area. It generally gives priority to issues of international economic policy.

Among the council's programs are: an annual conference on a specialized international topic; a noon lecture series; a lecture forum subscription series; a womens' luncheon forum supplemented by evening meetings; and a secondary school program composed of seminars and workshops for teachers. In summary, the council aims to increase the Chicago public's awareness of international issues.

Background Desired
International relations, foreign policy, economics, economic development, conference and seminar organization. An MA or PhD is preferred.

How to Apply
Write to: Chicago Council on Foreign Relations
116 South Michigan Ave.
Chicago, IL   60603

Council on Foreign Relations, New York*

The origins of the council lay in the disappointment of its founders in what they considered lack of understanding of international affairs in the United States. Its membership of about 1,700 persons throughout the country is made up of individuals with special interest and experience in international problems.

In order to increase the awareness of Americans to the importance of international issues, the council conducts meetings to give its members an opportunity to talk with knowledgeable US and foreign officials. It does not take any position on questions of foreign policy.

The studies program of the council explores questions of international importance through individual scholarly research by its professional staff and through study groups and conferences involving members and non-members. Since 1922 the council has published the quarterly journal *Foreign Affairs.*

The **Committees on Foreign Relations** are another important facet of the council. Thirty-seven of these committees, located in as many US cities, schedule meetings from time to time on problems of international relations. The purpose of this program is to help develop in important US communities a nucleus of informed opinion on current issues of international affairs. The committees are almost always run by volunteers, but even if involvement in a local committee may not bring a job, it does provide contact with individuals who have similar interests.

Background Desired
International affairs, foreign policy, economics, and area studies. A PhD is preferred for scholarly research. For some administrative jobs, a BA suffices. For *Foreign Affairs:* editing.

How to Apply

Write to: Council on Foreign Relations
              58 East 68th St.
              New York, NY   10021

Council on International and Public Affairs

This organization, formerly called Conference on World Affairs, seeks to "promote the study of the problems and affairs of the peoples of the United States and other nations of the world through conferences, research, publications, and other means."

The council operates in four main areas: (1) improvement of college and university instruction so that the policy analysis skills of students can be strengthened and applied to important public issues; (2) increase of citizen participation in world affairs; (3) an international literature and arts program to strengthen "world cultural literacy of Americans and other peoples"; and (4) a program in international science and technology.

Background Desired

International relations, publishing, communications, and conference and seminar organization. An MA or PhD is preferred.

How to Apply

Write to: Council on International and Public Affairs
              60 East 42nd St.
              New York, NY   10017

Council on Religion and International Affairs (CRIA)

This council, founded in 1914 by Andrew Carnegie, seeks to apply "the insights of ethics and religion to international affairs, including the formulation of foreign policy."

CRIA's programs include: biweekly dialogues in which policy makers discuss current topics with influential people from government, business, and religious and educational organizations; an annual lectureship on ethics and international affairs; study groups; task forces; and publications.

Background Desired

International affairs, foreign policy, experience in organizing conferences and seminars. A BA is sometimes accepted.

How to Apply

Write to: Council on Religion and International Affairs
              170 East 64th St.
              New York, NY   10021

Foreign Policy Association*

FPA has as its purpose the development of an "informed, thoughtful, and articulate public opinion on international affairs." FPA provides informational and educational materials and sponsors meetings designed to increase American interest in foreign policy issues. Its **Great Decisions Program** involves thousands of people in discussion groups on world affairs throughout the country. Through Great Decisions ballots and meetings in Washington, FPA's national participants make their views known to governmental policy makers. FPA also publishes a *Headline* series and *Foreign Policy Briefs,* kits with briefing cards on current world problems that are used by voter groups and political candidates.

Background Desired
International relations, foreign policy, economics, area studies, communications studies and experience, and public relations. An MA or PhD is preferred for most jobs.

How to Apply
Write to: Foreign Policy Association
345 East 46th St.
New York, NY 10017

or

1800 K St. NW
Washington, DC 20006

Hudson Institute*

This is one of the better "think tanks," with an impressive scope of research ranging from "social policy to the Prospects of Mankind, from national security issues to corporate environment." Its goal is to meet the need for research and analysis to supplement the decision maker's sources of ideas. It analyzes major issues, projects long-range problems, and suggests alternative means of coping with them.

Background Desired
Economics, economic development, area studies, and research ability. A PhD is preferred.

How to Apply
Write to: Hudson Institute
Quaker Ridge Road
Croton-on-Hudson, NY 10520

Institute of Current World Affairs

The institute (the Crane-Rogers Foundation) provides financial assistance to a few persons of unusual promise for the firsthand study of particular foreign areas or problems of contemporary significance. With this end in view, the institute normally gives one or two fellowships a year for study and research ordinarily not connected with work toward an academic degree.

Background Desired
Administration, area studies, international relations. A BA is sometimes accepted, especially if the job is administrative in nature.

How to Apply
Write to: Institute of Current World Affairs
535 Fifth Ave.
New York, NY   10017

Institute of Defense Analysis *

IDA aims to promote national security by conducting studies and analyses on matters of interest to the US government. Originally, IDA's research was done almost exclusively for the Department of Defense; in this role it came under attack from students in the 1960s because of its assistance to the military during the Vietnam War. Now there has been some broadening of its role and it assists other government agencies in problems of significant national and international interest. IDA's program includes science and technology, systems evaluation, communications research, foreign affairs, and social studies.

Background Desired
Science, military technology, foreign policy, national security, computer science, international relations, and economics. A PhD is preferred.

How to Apply
Write to: Institute of Defense Analysis
400 Army-Navy Drive
Arlington, Virginia   22202

International Study and Research Institute

The institute offers non-degree programs on vital national and international topics. In addition to a regular curriculum, the institute organizes seminars and conferences on critical issues and develops programs of interest to business groups and educational institutions. It also arranges orientation sessions for executives of private business and voluntary agencies engaged in international operations.

Background Desired
Research ability, teaching, foreign policy, international relations, business administration, and seminar and conference organization. An MA or PhD is preferred.

How to Apply
Write to: International Study and Research Institute
55 West 44th St.
New York, NY   10036

Charles Kettering Foundation*

Originally started to support scientific research, the foundation has broadened its interests to include research programs in education, urban affairs, and internationalism. Among the grants given under the latter category are: East-West communication; North-South communication on food and development; communication with hemispheric neighbors; international education in public schools; and community education on critical world issues.

Background Desired
International relations, economics, economic development, Third World country studies, communications, teaching, and educational studies. An MA or PhD is preferred.

How to Apply
Write to: Charles Kettering Foundation
5335 Far Hills Ave.
Dayton, OH   45429

National Strategy Information Center

The objective of the NSIC is to conduct educational programs in international security affairs. It tries to encourage "civil-military partnership" in the belief that an informed public opinion is necessary to the establishment of a defense system in the United States capable of protecting the country.

NSIC carries out its program by holding seminars and conferences on national security matters, conducting workshops on geopolitics and defense budgets, and publishing books and papers to inform the public on strategy and military security.

Background Desired
National security, military studies, and research ability.

How to Apply
Write to: National Strategy Information Center
111 East 58th St.
New York, NY 10022

Social Science Research Council

Fellowships are offered for doctoral dissertation research in the social sciences to be carried out in Africa, Asia, Latin America, the Near and Middle East, or Western Europe. Programs are designed to support scholars who intend to become specialists in the area where the research is conducted.

Background Desired
Full-time enrollment at a US or Canadian university and completion of all PhD requirements except the dissertation.

How to Apply
Write to: Social Science Research Council
605 Third Ave.
New York, NY 10016

Twentieth Century Fund

The purpose of the fund is to inform and stimulate national public debate on critical issues. It sponsors individual scholars pursuing independent research efforts and also uses task forces composed of distinguished authorities to report on policy issues in the fund's research program.

The fund's research concentrates on four broad areas: (1) business, economics, and public administration; (2) urban problems; (3) politics and communications; and (4) international affairs. Among some of the international subjects researched are Soviet–American economic relations, nationalization of US enterprises in Latin America, arms races and arms control, and nuclear proliferation.

Background Desired
Economics, international affairs, economic development, nuclear technology, arms control, area studies, and research ability. A PhD is preferred.

How to Apply

Write to: Twentieth Century Fund
41 East 70th Street
New York, NY 10021

United Nations Association of the USA *

The philosophy of this organization is expressed in the following quote: "The United Nations is the only institution in the history of man that has become indispensable before it has become possible." Putting its faith in the United Nations, the UNA is not unwilling to admit its weaknesses but emphasizes its strengths and potential.

UNA seeks to stimulate American public opinion in support of constructive US policies in the United Nations. It tries to develop new ideas on how to make the United Nations more effective, and provides American citizens with factual information on current UN issues through its information, research, education, and community action programs.

UNA conducts a variety of programs. Its **Policy Studies Program** brings together independent panels of experts in specific fields to apply their knowledge to controversial international programs. Its **Economic Policy Council** examines international economic issues and their impact on US relations with industrialized and developing countries. Its **Public Information Service** works with the media and Congress, trying to get objective information on the United Nations and its activities across to the American public.

UNA is the official coordinating body for the annual observation of National United Nations Day on October 24. Although headquartered in New York, UNA has a Washington office that feeds information on the United Nations to Congress and the Executive Branch.

Background Desired

International organizations, international relations, economics, disarmament and military technology, public relations, research ability, and publications experience. An MA or PhD is preferred.

How to Apply

Write to: United Nations Association of the USA
300 East 42nd St.
New York, NY 10017

World Affairs Councils

These councils exist in most major US cities. In general, their function is to help Americans gain a better understanding of significant issues in US foreign policy and to stimulate informed citizen participation in world affairs. At one time directly connected with the Foreign Policy Association, these councils are now independent and provide their own funding and programming. Most of the councils depend to a large extent on volunteers, although there are a few paid positions in the largest councils.

Background Desired
International affairs, economics, foreign policy, and occasionally area studies. A BA may be acceptable.

How to Apply
A list of councils and related community organizations follows. If you are interested in working for a specific council, contact it at the address indicated.

World Affairs Councils and Related Community Organizations

Although local world affairs councils are often volunteer agencies without a paid staff (or with only one or two professionals), they are a good source of information about international activities, programs, internships, and the like. If you find yourself situated in a place other than New York or Washington and still have the desire to be involved internationally (or if you have spare time and can afford to do volunteer work), contact the appropriate group listed below and see how your needs and theirs might mesh.

Alaska

Executive Director
Alaska World Affairs Council
Egan Library, University of Alaska
3211 Providence Drive
Anchorage, AK 99504
(907) 278-3938 or 274-9217

Arizona

President
Phoenix World Affairs Council
401 North 1st St.
Phoenix, AZ 85004

California

Executive Director
Los Angeles World Affairs Council
900 Wilshire Blvd., Suite 230
Los Angeles, CA 91105
(213) 628-2333

President
World Affairs Council of the Desert
471 East Tahquitz-McCallum, Rm. 24
Palm Springs, CA 92262
(714) 325-9317

Executive Director
World Affairs Council of Inland
Southern California
Riverside, CA 92521
(714) 787-5744

President
World Affairs Council of San Diego,
Inc.
House of Hospitality, Studio One
San Diego, CA 92101
(714) 231-0111

Executive Director
World Affairs Council of Northern
California
312 Sutter St., Suite 200
San Francisco, CA 94108
(415) 982-2541

World Affairs Council of San Joaquin
County
7400 Pacific Ave.
Stockton, CA   95207

Colorado

Director
Rocky Mountain Forum on Inter-
national Issues
University of Denver
University Park
Denver, CO   80208

Executive Director
Adult Education Council of Metropolitan Denver
1100 Acoma St.
Denver, CO   80204

Connecticut

Director
Service Bureau for Connecticut
Organization
956 Main St.
Hartford, CT   06105
(203) 249-9711

Executive Secretary
World Affairs Center, Inc.
1380 Asylum Ave.
Hartford, CT   06105
(203) 236-5277

Executive Director
Institute of World Affairs
Twin Lakes Campus
Salisbury, CT   06068

Chairman
Stamford Forum for World Affairs
19 Crestview Ave.
Stamford, CT   06907
(203) 323-6178

Florida

Director
Miami Council on World Affairs
Center for Advanced International
Studies
University of Miami
PO Box 8123
Coral Gables, FL   33124
(305) 284-4303

World Affairs Council
441 Neadiw Karj Drive
Sarasota, FL   33577

PO Box 1056
Seffner, FL   33584
(813) 681-3105

International Cultural and
Economic Center
PO Box 24626
Tampa, FL   33623
(813) 961-6823

Georgia

Southern Center for International
Studies
Suite 1239, Lenox Towers North
3400 Peachtree Road NW
Atlanta, GA   30326
(404) 261-5763

Hawaii

Executive Director
Pacific and Asian Affairs Council
2004 University Ave.
Honolulu, HI   96822
(808) 941-6066 or 941-5355

Illinois

President
Chicago Council on Foreign Relations
116 South Michigan Ave.
Chicago, IL   60603
(312) 726-3860

Director
The Chicago Great Decisions Council
c/o Union League Club
65 West Jackson Blvd.
Chicago, IL   60604
(312) 427-7800

Chairman
World Affairs Conference of
Northwestern Illinois
Rock Valley College
3301 North Mulford Road
Rockford, IL   61601
(815) 226-2688

Director
The Quad-Cities World Affairs Council,
Inc.
Quad-Cities Graduate Study Center
639 38th St.
Rock Island, IL   61201
(309) 794-7376

Indiana

Indianapolis Council on World Affairs
School of Business, Indiana University
830 East 38th St.
Indianapolis, IN   46205
(317) 926-0696

President
Indianapolis World Affairs Council
Chase & Partners, Inc.
300 Circle Tower Building
Indianapolis, IN   46204
(317) 634-8010

Iowa

Quad-Cities World Affairs Council, Inc.
Marycrest College
1607 W. 12th St.
Davenport, IA   52804
(319) 326-9512

Louisiana

Director of Operations
Foreign Relations Association of
New Orleans
611 Gravier St., Room 408
New Orleans, LA   70130
(504) 524-2168 or 837-8151

Maryland

Project Director
Baltimore Council on Foreign Relations
(In process of organization)
Department of Political Science
University of Maryland–Baltimore
County
5401 Wilkins Ave.
Baltimore, MD   21228
(301) 455-2568

Massachusetts

Executive Director
The World Affairs Council of Boston
70 Hereford St.
Boston, MA   02110
(617) 267-6674

Program Coordinator
World Affairs Council of Connecticut
Valley
1476 Parker St.
Springfield, MA   01129
(413) 782-2054

Executive Secretary
World Affairs Council of the
Connecticut Valley, Inc.
Box 264
Wilbraham, MA   01095

Michigan

Executive Secretary
Detroit Council for World Affairs
Center for Peace and Conflict Studies
5229 Cass Ave., Room 101
Detroit, MI   48202
(313) 577-3453 or 577-3468

Executive Director
World Affairs Council of Western
Michigan
210 Federal Square Building
Grand Rapids, MI   49503
(616) 458-9535

Minnesota

Director
World Affairs Center
University of Minnesota
306 Wesbrook Hall
Minneapolis, MN   55455
(612) 373-3799

Missouri

Executive Director
International Relations Council
210 Westport Road
Kansas City, MO   64111
(816) 531-0090 or 333-5546 (home)

Director
St. Louis Council on World Affairs
Chase-Park Plaza Hotel
212 North Kingshighway Blvd.
St. Louis, MO   63108
(314) 361-7333

New Hampshire

Consultant
New Hampshire Council on World
Affairs
11 Rosemary Lane
Durham, NH   02824
(603) 862-1683

New Mexico

President
Santa Fe Council on International
Relations
PO Box 1223
Santa Fe, NM   87501
(505) 982-4931

New York

President
World Affairs Council of Broome
County
Roberson Center
30 Front St.
Binghamton, NY   13905

Executive Director
Buffalo Council on World Affairs, Inc.
237 Main St., Room 346
Buffalo, NY   14203
(716) 854-1240

President
Council on Foreign Relations
58 East 68th St.
New York, NY   10021

Executive Director
Lake Placid Council on Foreign Policy
PO Box 845
Lake Placid, NY   12946

Chairman
Foreign Policy Association
345 East 46th St.
New York, NY   10017
(212) 557-8736

President
Syracuse World Affairs Council
1147 Westmoreland Ave.
Syracuse, NY   13210
(315) 637-8577

North Carolina

President
North Carolina Council on World
Affairs
University of North Carolina
Charlotte, NC   28213
(704) 597-2254

Ohio

Director
Institute for Civic Education
The University of Akron
Akron, OH   44325
(216) 375-7575

President
Cincinnati Council on World Affairs
Dixie Terminal Building, Suite 1028
Cincinnati, OH   45202
(513) 621-2320

President
Cleveland Council on World Affairs
601 Rockwell Ave.
Cleveland, OH   44114
(216) 781-3730

Administrative Assistant
International Council of Mid-Ohio
1375 Perry St.
Columbus, OH   43201
(614) 421-2155

World Affairs Council
CARE
Eight East Chestnut St.
Columbus, OH   43215

Executive Director
Dayton Council on World Affairs
40 South Main St., Suite 520
Dayton, OH   45402
(513) 233-6203

President
Toledo Council on World Affairs
248 East Front St.
Perrysburgh, OH   43551
(419) 874-6274

President
Toledo Council on World Affairs, Inc.
2373 Robinwood Ave.
Toledo, OH   43620

Oregon

Oregon Great Decisions Council
Room 330, Extension Hall
Oregon State University
Corvallis, OR   97331

Executive Director
World Affairs Council of Oregon
1912 SW Sixth Ave., #252
Portland, OR   97201
(503) 229-3049

Pennsylvania

Chairman
Foreign Policy Association of the
Lehigh Valley
722 Beverly Ave.
Bethlehem, PA   18018
(215) 697-6515

President
Foreign Policy Association of Harris-
burg
PO Box 1221
Harrisburg, PA   17108

Executive Director
World Affairs Council of Philadelphia
John Wanamaker Store
Third Floor Gallery
1300 Market St.
Philadelphia, PA   19107
(215) 563-5363

Executive Director
World Affairs Council of Pittsburgh
Kaufmann's Department Store
400 Fifth Ave.
Pittsburgh, PA   15219
(412) 281-7970

Foreign Affairs Council of Reading and
Berks County, YMCA Building
Reed and Washington Sts.
Reading, PA   19601
(215) 375-4291

Rhode Island

Executive Director
World Affairs Council of Rhode Island
15 Opechee Drive
Barrington, RI   02806
(401) 245-5449 or 421-8622 (ans. serv.)

South Carolina

Director
Institute for International Studies
Columbia Forum on World Affairs
University of South Carolina
Columbia, SC   29208
(803) 777-8180

Tennessee

Executive Director
Adult Education Council
526 Vine St.
Chattanooga, TN   37403
(615) 267-1218

Texas

Executive Director
Dallas Council on World Affairs
3409 Oak Lawn, Suite 115
Dallas, TX   75219
(214) 521-2171

President
Houston Council on World Affairs
The Crispin Company
World Trade Center
1520 Texas Ave.
Houston, TX   77002
(713) 223-6311

Chairman
Gulf Coast Council on Foreign Affairs
8001 Palmer Highway
Texas City, TX   77590
(713) 938-0360

Vermont

Executive Director
Vermont Council of World Affairs
Trinity College
Burlington, VT   05401
(802) 863-3539 or 862-3251 (home)

Chairman
Windham World Affairs Council
Windham County, Vermont
PO Box 1105
Brattleboro, VT   05301
(802) 464-5495

Virginia

Chairman
World Affairs Council of Greater
Hampton Roads
PO Box 3304, Customhouse Station
Norfolk, VA   23514
(703) 627-6848

Washington

President
World Affairs Council of Seattle
405 Olive Way
Seattle, WA   98101
(206) 682-6986

Wisconsin

Director
Institute of World Affairs
The University of Wisconsin-
Milwaukee
PO Box 413
Milwaukee, WI   53201
(414) 963-4251

Chairman
World Affairs Council of Milwaukee
W63 N650 Washington Ave.
Cedarburg, WI   53012
(414) 375-0625

Canada

President
The Niagara Institute for
International Studies
Niagara-on-the-Lake, Ontario
Canada
(416) 468-2151

Worldwatch Institute

Worldwatch seeks to anticipate global problems and social trends. Through
its publications and research, Worldwatch focuses public attention on
emerging international issues. Its concerns cover a broad area: global
energy alternatives; environmentally induced illnesses; the changing status
of women and its impact on society; current global trends in population
growth; and economic and political discontinuities facing the world in the
last years of this century. The small staff of the institute is said to be
"future oriented."

Background Desired
Energy and environmental studies, population studies, economics, foreign
policy, and research ability. An MA or PhD is preferred.

How to Apply
Write to: Worldwatch Institute
1776 Massachusetts Ave. NW
Washington, DC   20036

Area Interests

Accion International

This organization specializes in research, evaluation, and implementation of development programs in Latin America. Accion focuses on the problems of low-income populations and stresses the need for self-help in local, regional, and national development plans.

Background Desired
Economic development, economics, Latin American studies, knowledge of Spanish and Portuguese, agricultural studies, and sociology.

How to Apply
Write to: Accion International
               10-C Mount Auburn St.
               Cambridge, MA   02138

African-American Institute *

The AAI program has three main thrusts:

1. *To promote African development* To this end, the AAI has arranged graduate study in the United States for over 1,000 Africans and undergraduate study in America for an even larger number of Africans. These studies benefit Africans in the development field, university administration, and actuarial sciences, among others.
2. *To strengthen African–American understanding* To this effect, the AAI grants travel award to Africans for visits to the United States.
3. *To inform Americans about Africa* The AAI provides low-cost study and travel opportunities in Africa for thousands of Americans. It also tries to expand and improve teaching in the United States about Africa.

The AAI has field offices in all large African countries.

This organization also publishes a free booklet, *Opportunities in Africa,* listing job opportunities, technical assistance positions, teaching jobs, volunteer work experience, research opportunities, study opportunities in African universities, and information on grants, fellowships, and scholarships for travel and research in Africa.

Background Desired
African studies, African languages, economics, economic development, cultural studies, educational administration, teaching, and actuarial sciences. A BA is occasionally accepted.

How to Apply

Write to: African–American Institute
833 United Nations Plaza
New York, NY   10017

African–American Labor Center

The AALC was established by the AFL–CIO in 1964 to assist and strengthen free democratic trade unions in Africa. Major activites of the center include worker education, leadership and vocational training, cooperatives and credit unions, social services, and study and exchange programs for Africans engaged in trade unionism.

Background Desired

Trade unionism, African studies and/or experience, African languages, industrial relations, vocational training, and teaching. A BA is often accepted.

How to Apply

Write to: African–American Labor Center
345 East 46th St.
New York, NY   10017

African Fund for Endangered Wildlife

This organization works with various African governments to protect wildlife. In Kenya, for example, the fund, with money raised in the United States and with the help of the Phelps Stokes Fund, is assisting the government in capturing and relocating a special breed of giraffes that is threatened with extinction.

Background Desired

African studies, conservation, world resources, economics, public relations, and fund raising. A BA may be accepted.

How to Apply

Write to: African Fund for Endangered Wildlife
c/o Phelps Stokes Fund
Washington, DC   20005

American Committee on Africa

The committee is devoted to supporting African people in their struggle for freedom and independence. ACOA also informs Americans about significant African issues and mobilizes public support on behalf of African freedom.

To carry out its objectives, the committee has established the **Africa Defense and Aid Fund** to support African liberation movements. It also arranges meetings, conferences, and speaking tours in America for African representatives.

Background Desired
Public relations, fund raising, African studies and experience, and administration. A BA is accepted.

How to Apply
Write to: American Committee on Africa
305 East 46th St.
New York, NY   10017

☆

American Council on Germany

This organization, as might be surmised from the name, seeks to promote better understanding between the United States and West Germany. Drawing on resources from both countries, the council sponsors group discussions, personal exchanges, and joint working projects. In addition, it supports efforts by government, academe, and business that can yield benefits to both peoples.

The **John J. McCloy Fund**, which was a gift to the council from the German government, provides fellowships to young Germans and Americans, giving each the opportunity to work in the other country. Fellowships have been in the fields of trade unionism, journalism, state and municipal government, law, and creative writing.

Other council projects include biennial meetings of American and German leaders to examine urgent global issues biennial meetings of American and German young adults, workshops, seminars, lectures, and programs for freshman legislators of both countries.

Background Desired
German studies and language, economics, administration, exchange program experience, seminar and conference organization, and public relations. An MA or PhD is preferred.

How to Apply
Write to: American Council on Germany
680 Fifth Ave.
New York, NY   10019

American Fund for Czechoslovak Refugees

The fund exists to help Czech refugees adjust to American life and customs. Specifically, it aids them in getting housing and employment, attempts to reunify separated families, and obtains organizational sponsorship for each refugee so that the immigration status can be regularized. This organization also aids refugees from Indochina in much the same way as it aids Czech refugees.

Background Desired
Czech studies and languages, East Central Europe studies, knowledge of employment market, social work, and experience with refugees. A BA may be accepted.

How to Apply
Write to: American Fund for Czechoslovak Refugees
1790 Broadway
New York, NY   10019

American Jewish Committee *

In addition to local and domestic goals, the AJC is very much involved internationally. It helps Israel's efforts to safeguard her existence; it supports the United Nations in its human rights work; it protects the rights of Jews in countries where they may be oppressed; and it assists Jews in all lands to enjoy equal status with other inhabitants in those countries.

Background Desired
International relations, Middle East studies, and human rights work. A BA may be accepted.

How to Apply
Write to: American Jewish Committee
165 East 56th St.
New York, NY   10022

American-Korean Foundation

The foundation supports many South Korean orphanages with food, clothing, and medical supplies and carries on the work of the "Burma Surgeon" in South Korea through its support of the Gordon Seagrave Memorial Hospital. It aids Korean 4-H Clubs and teaches rural Korean youth modern agricultural techniques. It provides technical instruction and tools to enable Korean refugees to build their own homes. It offers scholarships for needy Korean students, and it carries out demonstrations and training programs in land reclamation in South Korea.

Background Desired

Economics, economic development, Korean studies and language, agricultural economics, social work, sociology, and medical and nutrition subjects. A BA may be accepted.

How to Apply

Write to: American–Korean Foundation
             345 East 46th St.
             New York, NY   10017

American–Mideast Educational and Training Services *

Amideast is the new name for the American Friends of the Middle East. Formerly a small organization that encouraged cultural exchange between Americans and the people of the Mideast, it is now involved in all aspects of the development of human resources in the Middle East and Africa.

Amideast's newest programs concern technical training in areas where rapid economic growth places a premium on management and technological skills. Under contracts with corporations and governments, Amideast services help increase the reserve of trained manpower—teachers and administrators, personnel managers, pilots, accountants, computer programmers, electronics experts, and many other kinds of technicians.

Background Desired

Middle East studies and languages, business administration, vocational training, personnel work, computer studies, electronics, and accounting. A BA may be accepted.

How to Apply

Write to: American–Mideast Educational and Training Services
             1717 Massachusetts Ave. NW, Suite 100
             Washington, DC   20036

American–Scandinavian Foundation

This foundation advances cultural relations between the United States and Scandinavian countries. Among the programs carried out are: exchange of persons; publication of books and periodicals; and cultural projects such as concerts, lecture tours, and exhibitions of arts and crafts.

Background Desired

Scandinavian studies and/or languages, cultural activities, exchange programs, and publishing skills. A BA may be accepted.

How to Apply

Write to: American–Scandinavian Foundation
127 East 73rd St.
New York, NY 10021

American Zionist Youth Foundation

The foundation offers both summer and long-term programs to bring American youth into contact with Israel. Summer programs, for college and high school students, range from kibbutz living to archaeology seminars to art and dance workshops. Long-term programs involve a spring semester at Tel Aviv University and other work-study programs in Israel.

Background Desired

Middle East studies, and a strong commitment to Israel. A BA is accepted.

How to Apply

Write to: American Zionist Youth Foundation
515 Park Ave.
New York, NY 10022

Asia Society *

The Asia Society is dedicated to increasing American understanding of Asia. It is concerned with both the traditional arts and humanities and with contemporary social, political, economic, and cultural issues.

Asia House Gallery, one of the best known of the society's programs, introduces many Americans to Asian art treasures. The **Performing Arts Program** brings to America the finest Asian theatre, music, and dance. The society's **Education Program** seeks to strengthen the study of Asia throughout the curriculum of American schools at all levels.

The society also has a **Meetings and Studies Program,** which brings outstanding Asian and Western scholars, politicians, and economists before American audiences, at Asia House and elsewhere in the country. This program depends on the advice and participation of the society's **Country Councils,** each of which is composed of Asia Society members with special interest in and knowledge of an Asian country. There are councils for Afghanistan, Bangladesh, Burma, Cambodia/Laos, China, the Himalayas, India, Indonesia, Iran, Korea, Malaysia/Singapore, Pakistan, the Philippines, Sri Lanka, and Thailand.

Of special interest to those of you with an Asian studies background is *Organizations Interested in Asian Studies Education,* a list issued by the society and available for the asking from its Education Department.

Background Desired
Asian studies, cultural interests and experience, conference organization, business administration, education studies, and museum work. A BA is sometimes accepted.

How to Apply
Write to: Asia Society
112 East 64th St.
New York, NY 10021

Asia Foundation *

The foundation aims to strengthen Asian educational, cultural, and civic activities with American assistance. It makes private American support available to Asian individuals and institutions that are helping to modernize and develop their own societies. It also encourages cooperation among Asian, American, and international organizations working toward these goals.

Background Desired
Cultural studies and experience, Asian studies, exchange of individuals, and fund raising. A BA is occasionally accepted.

How to Apply
Write to: Asia Foundation
550 Kearny St.
San Francisco, CA 94108

Asian–American Free Labor Institute

Under policy guidance from the AFL/CIO, AAFLI encourages the development of strong free trade unions throughout Asia. It helps provide a framework within which Asian trade unionists can build programs and institutions suited to their needs. Help consists of funds in some cases as well as training programs for Asian officials of trade unions.

Background Desired
Trade union experience, Asian studies and languages, vocational training, and business administration. A BA may be accepted.

How to Apply

Write to: Asian–American Free Labor Institute
815 16th St. NW
Washington, DC   20006

Atlantic Council of the United States *

The council seeks to promote ties between Western Europe, North America, Japan, Australia, and New Zealand. The objective is to increase the security of all and to harmonize economic, monetary, energy, and resource policies in member countries. The council fosters debates on issues of international security and political and economic problems, and makes policy recommendations to both the executive and legislative branches of the US government as well as to appropriate international organizations. A typical council publication is its paper, "Improving NATO Force Capabilities."

Background Desired
National security studies, military technology, Western Europe studies, foreign policy, international relations, and Russian and communist studies. An MA or PhD is preferred.

How to Apply
Write to: Atlantic Council of the United States
1616 H St. NW
Washington, DC   20006

Center for Inter-American Relations *

In a very general way, the center works toward strengthening understanding between the United States and other nations in the Western Hemisphere. The center has a **Public Affairs Program** that provides for seminars and conferences on current political and economic problems of the hemisphere; a **Literature Program** that promotes the publication in the United States of Latin American and Caribbean fiction, poetry, and drama; a **Visual Arts Program** that holds exhibits in the center's art gallery; and a **Music Program** that brings Latin American music and performers to audiences in the United States.

Background Desired
Latin American studies and languages, cultural studies, conference organization, and museum experience. A BA is sometimes accepted.

How to Apply

Write to: Center for Inter-American Relations
680 Park Ave.
New York, NY   10021

China Institute in America*

The institute has a dual purpose: (1) to educate Americans in various aspects of Chinese culture; and (2) to help Chinese-Americans adjust to the life and customs of their new country. The institute operates a **School of General Studies** that offers courses on Chinese history and culture especially for school teachers. The school also offers courses in computer programming for Chinese immigrants wishing to make a career in this field. Lectures, seminars, and conferences are held on a wide range of political, economic, and cultural subjects relating to China. Small art exhibitions are presented from time to time at the institute's gallery.

Background Desired
Chinese studies and language, teaching, administration, international relations, economics, museum work, and cultural studies. A BA may be accepted.

How to Apply
Write to: China Institute in America
125 East 65th St.
New York, NY   10021

Citizen Exchange Corps*

The CEC offers opportunities to Americans to participate in intercultural programs with citizens of nations having different political and/or economic systems. Education, mutual understanding, and cooperation are the goals of CEC programs. The corps emphasizes the exchange of cultures, ideas, vocations, and values on a one-to-one basis. There are three facets to CEC work: **Intercultural Travel, Hospitality,** and **Special Activities** (including Soviet-American exchange conferences, seminars for American citizens, and Soviet-American art exchanges). The emphasis of each of the three programs is on the Soviet Union.

Background Desired
Soviet studies and language, cultural studies, exchange programs. A BA may be accepted.

How to Apply

Write to: Citizen Exchange Corps
18 East 41st St.
New York, NY 10017

Council on Hemispheric Affairs (COHA)

The council brings together US leaders from the academic, business, professional, and public sectors to analyze policies and problems in inter-American relations. Typical of the issues studied are: the region's economic interrelationships; military assistance programs in Latin America; advancing respect for human rights; opportunities for women and minorities in Latin America; and the right of Latin American trade unions to organize and function freely.

Background Desired

Latin American studies and languages, economics, international affairs, industrial relations, and military technology. An MA or PhD is preferred.

How to Apply

Write to: Council on Hemispheric Affairs
30 Fifth Ave.
New York, NY 10011

or

1125 15th St. NW
Washington, DC 20005

Council of the Americas*

Though nonprofit, the council is a business organization, directed and operated by its corporate members, that acts as an interpreter of the interests and operations of US businesses investing in Latin America. It seeks to increase cooperation and understanding between Latin American countries and foreign investors. Toward these ends, the council: (a) provides for a direct dialogue between Latin American government officials and US corporate executives; (b) coordinates the work of its member companies in sponsoring managerial education and grass roots self-help in Latin America; (c) encourages direct dialogue between US corporate executives and officials of the US government concerned with Latin America; and (d) exchanges information on Latin American social, economic, and political development among its members.

Background Desired

Latin American studies and languages, economics, business, administration, finance, and marketing. A BA may be accepted.

How to Apply

Write to: Council of the Americas
680 Park Ave.
New York, NY   10021

English-Speaking Union of the United States

The function of the E-SU is to "further peace, mutual understanding, trust, and friendship with the English-speaking people of the world." Its activities include administering exchange scholarships and travel grants, scheduling speakers, and printing pamphlets and newsletters.

Background Desired

English and Commonwealth studies, experience in exchange programs, and experience in organizing lectures and seminars. A BA may be accepted.

How to Apply

Write to: English-Speaking Union of the United States
16 East 69th St.
New York, NY   10021

European Community Information Service *

As its name indicates, the ECIS provides information through its New York and Washington offices about the European community. It publishes a monthly magazine and periodic brochures and provides groups with speakers. It creates exhibits about the European community for conferences and seminars. It issues press releases to the media and provides films for conferences and classrooms.

Background Desired

Communications, Western Europe studies, and economics. A BA is sometimes accepted.

How to Apply

Write to: European Community Information Service
2100 M St. NW
Washington, DC   20037
                or

277 Park Ave.
New York, NY   10017

German Marshall Fund of the United States

The purpose of the fund is to assist individuals and organizations in the United States, Europe, and elsewhere to understand and resolve contemporary and emerging problems common to industrial societies. It operates both domestically and internationally.

The fund was started as a gesture of gratitude from the German government for the help given Europe by the Marshall Plan. It has a wide variety of programs, including grants for: documentary films on new approaches to work in the United States and Europe; the establishment of a **Council for International Urban Liaison** to coordinate the international urban activities of US local government associations; the establishment of an **International Urban Technology Exchange Program** to serve municipal governments in the United States and Europe by disseminating information about user needs and available technologies; meetings on international trade issues; exchanges of US and Common Market experts; and European–American studies programs.

Background Desired
European studies, tariffs and trade, industrial relations, business administration, and economics. An MA or PhD is preferred.

How to Apply
Write to: German Marshall Fund of the United States
            11 Dupont Circle NW
            Washington, DC   20036

Institute for Policy Studies

The **Latin American Program** of the institute examines hemispheric relations with the goal of establishing an improved relationship between the two regions of the continent.

A prime part of the program is the **Latin American Round Table**, which is a forum for hemispheric debate. LART meets monthly to follow current developments in Latin America and to aid in the formulation of alternative US policies toward that area. In addition to LART, the Latin American Program of the institute includes conferences, research, publications, and a student program.

Background Desired
Latin American studies and languages, international relations, economics, and conference and seminar organizing. An MA or PhD is preferred.

How to Apply

Write to: Institute for Policy Studies
            1901 Q St. NW
            Washington, DC   20009

International Research and Exchanges Board (IREX)*

IREX administers academic exchange programs between the United States and countries of Eastern Europe and the Soviet Union. The several IREX exchange programs operate under reciprocal agreements with the countries concerned. Scholars from Bulgaria, Czechoslovakia, Hungary, Poland, Romania, Yugoslavia, and the USSR are placed on the campuses of American universities for periods of two months to an academic year. Both graduate students and professors are included in the program. The sending country provides international transportation for its participants, and the host country grants allowances for housing, food, tuition, and research expenses.

Background Desired

Russia and East Central Europe studies and languages and exchange program experience. An MA or PhD is preferred.

How to Apply

Write to: International Research and Exchanges Board
            110 East 59th St.
            New York, NY   10022

Japan Productivity Center

The JPC sends teams of businessmen and government officials to the United States for observation and study tours. The professional program is arranged by the JPC with the help of community organizations. The latter arrange for home hospitality and for team participation in community activities. The JPC is also active in various training and research activities in Japan, including receiving study teams from abroad.

Background Desired

Japanese studies and language, exchange program experience, and business administration. A BA may be accepted.

How to Apply

Write to: Japan Productivity Center
            1-1, 3-chome, Shibuya, Shibuyaku
            Tokyo, Japan
            or

1001 Connecticut Ave. NW
Washington, DC   20036

John D. Rockefeller III Fund

The fund supports cultural exchange in the visual and performing arts between Asia and the United States. Fellowship awards are given in the following fields: archaeology, architecture, art history, crafts, dance, film, music, painting, sculpture, and theatre.

Background Desired
Cultural studies and experience, Asian studies and languages, and exchange program experience. An MA or PhD is preferred.

How to Apply
Write to: John D. Rockefeller III Fund
50 Rockefeller Plaza
New York, NY   10020

Middle East Institute *

The institute was founded in 1946 to increase understanding between the people of the Middle East and the United States. Obviously, there are many different ways of approaching this type of goal, and the institute focuses on the following: a rather complete library on Middle East documentation; publication of the *Middle East Journal;* conferences, seminars, and lectures; a business advisory service for businesses interested in trade expansion; and a language training program.

Background Desired
Middle Eastern studies and languages, communications and journalism, research ability, economics, business administration, library science, and seminar and conference organization. An MA or PhD is preferred.

How to Apply
Write to: Middle East Institute
1761 N St. NW
Washington, DC   20036

National Committee on US–China Relations *

The National Committee believes that increased knowledge of China and US-China relations is essential to international understanding and the effective conduct of US foreign policy. This belief is carried out through a program of educational, cultural, civic, and sports exchanges with the People's Republic of China and through educational activities enhancing such exchanges. Conferences, meetings, and information services are other adjuncts of the committee's activities. Many high-level delegations of Americans have been invited for study tours of China, and many Chinese cultural and sports attractions—dance groups, a table tennis team, an acrobatic troupe, and a gymnastics team—have toured the United States under the auspices of the committee.

Background Desired
Chinese studies and language, cultural and educational exchange experience, communications, and public relations. An MA or PhD is preferred.

How to Apply
Write to: National Committee on US-China Relations
             777 UN Plaza
             New York, NY   10017

Near East Foundation*

This is one of the oldest US organizations involved in technical assistance and rural development overseas. Although it emphasizes the Near East area, it is also involved in parts of Asia and Africa. The NEF invests its resources in trained US technicians who set up overseas projects that benefit people in that area.

Among the kinds of work performed are: training of young people for vocations; helping farmers by introducing crops suited to special weather conditions and by making available superior breeds of livestock; and helping villages by training teachers and showing people how to control diseases.

Background Required
Middle East, Asian, and African studies and languages, economics and economic development, agricultural economics, health studies, nutrition, community development, and teaching. An MA or PhD is preferred.

How to Apply
Write to: Near East Foundation
             50 East 64th St.
             New York, NY   10021

Operation Crossroads Africa*

Operation Crossroads arranges work camps, study tours, and other projects for North American college students in African countries during the summer months. Eight to ten Americans, an Operation Crossroads leader, and African volunteers will live in a rural community in Africa on a project that usually requires vigorous physical labor: digging foundations, hauling water, mixing cement. Crossroads offers an intense cross-cultural and educational experience, and, at the same time, an opportunity to make a contribution to community development in Africa.

Background Desired

If applying for leadership of one of the groups, African studies and language, community development, economic development, sociology, and leadership training or potential. A BA usually suffices.

How to Apply

Write to: Operation Crossroads Africa
150 Fifth Ave.
New York, NY   10011

Partners of the Americas

This organization fosters a closer relationship between the people of the United States and the people of Latin America by means of self-help projects. The program operates through technical assistance programs of economic, social, and cultural development. A "partnership" links a state in the United States with a country or an area in Latin America, for example Utah with Bolivia, Iowa with Yucatan (Mexico), and Maine with Rio Grande do Norte (Brazil). One example of how the partnership works: to build a school, one partner contributes the land and labor, the other provides the equipment or funds.

This organization also sponsors certain special programs, including vocational rehabilitation and services for the handicapped in thirty-two US states and seventeen Latin American countries and sports programs involving two-way educational exchanges of coaches and players in basketball, soccer, and other sports.

Background Desired

Latin American studies and languages, economic development, exchange program experience, public relations, and administration. A BA is often adequate.

How to Apply

Write to: Partners of the Americas
2001 S St. NW
Washington, DC   20009

Tinker Foundation

The foundation attempts to "create a climate of better understanding between the peoples of the US and Ibero-America, Spain, and Portugal." A sampling of subjects for which grants have been given are: a two-year grant to enable the American Field Service to establish a two-way exchange program of high school teachers from Argentina, Brazil, Colombia, and the United States; the purchase of a liberal arts library for the Bilingual Institute of Biscayne College; defraying the travel costs of Latin American participants to a meeting of the Atlantic Conference sponsored by the Chicago Council on Foreign Relations; an award to the Department of Agricultural Economics of Cornell University to work on the economic and social aspects of agricultural development in the Mexican tropics; and an award to Johns Hopkins University to support its Latin American Diplomats Program.

Background Desired
Latin American studies and languages, educational and cultural studies, knowledge of exchange programs, and administration. An MA or PhD is preferred.

How to Apply
Write to: Tinker Foundation
             645 Madison Ave.
             New York, NY   10022

Trilateral Commission *

The commission is an organization of distinguished individuals from North America, Western Europe, and Japan who aim to: (1) enhance cooperative relations among these three industrially advanced areas of the world; (2) analyze major issues affecting the three regions; (3) develop practical proposals on questions of mutual interest; and (4) obtain endorsement of these proposals from influential citizens of the three areas. The commission issues a quarterly publication called *Trialogue,* with articles such as the following: "Avenues for Trilateral-Communist Collaboration," "US–Soviet Agricultural Cooperation," and "East–West Relations."

Background Desired
Research ability, Japanese, West Europe, or Russian studies, economics, international affairs, and administration. A PhD is preferred.

How to Apply
Write to: Trilateral Commission
             345 East 46th St.
             New York, NY   10017

US–USSR Trade and Economic Council *

This organization of American and Soviet business-related enterprises is devoted to facilitating trade expansion between the two countries. It draws its authority from a government-to-government protocol and its effectiveness from the support of the governments and business people of both countries. The council has the dual responsibility of market development and individual trade facilitation for members. Through a binational Board of Directors, it works to develop new business projects to meet the special conditions of US–Soviet trade. It provides a full range of trade assistance services for members through its New York and Moscow offices, which both maintain binational staffs of trade and economic specialists. In addition, the council offers its members complete business support facilities to handle day-to-day dealings in both countries.

Background Desired
Economics, trade, Soviet studies and language, and business administration. A BA may be accepted.

How to Apply
Write to: US–USSR Trade and Economic Council
280 Park Ave.
New York, NY   10017

Youth Institute for Peace in the Middle East

This institute was established to educate young people about the history of the Arab–Israeli conflict, to impress students with the need to defend Israel's existence, and to work for an Arab–Israeli reconciliation. It sponsors conferences and seminars to achieve these aims.

Background Desired
Middle East studies, particularly of Israel, public relations, and experience in seminar and conference organization. A BA may be accepted.

How to Apply
Write to: Youth Institute for Peace in the Middle East
275 Seventh Ave.
New York, NY   10001

Educational, Cultural, and Exchange

Academy for Educational Development*

The AED helps schools and colleges, governmental agencies, and other educationally oriented institutions to improve their present plans and develop future programs. The academy provides advisory and staff services to these organizations and conducts in-depth research designed to make education more effective. Its international functions include assisting the development of educational and social programs in foreign countries.

Background Desired
Teaching, educational studies, economics, and administration. An MA or PhD is preferred.

How to Apply
Write to: Academy for Educational Development
680 Fifth Ave.
New York, NY   10019

International Association of Economics and Management Students (AIESEC)*

AIESEC is a student organization whose major activity is the exchange of students between member countries on a work-traineeship basis. Traineeships—in all parts of the world—are in the field of management for such areas as hospital, public, and university administration, development corporations, city government, and businesses. The traineeship is usually taken during the summer but can last up to eighteen months. Each student receives a stipend to cover living and incidental expenses; transportation expenses are not paid.

Background Desired
For both national headquarters and international headquarters staff, campus experience with AIESEC, program coordination, finance, and management. Work toward the BA usually suffices if you are applying for a traineeship.

How to Apply
AIESEC operates on a decentralized basis, with offices on the campus of many large American universities. Find out if there is a local representative on your campus. If not, write to:

AIESEC US National Committee
622 Third Ave.
New York, NY   10017

Local campus workers are not paid; professional staff in the United States and in international headquarters are. For the latter, write to:

> AIESEC International
> 45 Avenue Legrand
> 1050 Brussels, Belgium

American Council on Education *

The ACE's function is to extend the range and enhance the quality of higher education in the United States. It acts as a coordinating council among the national educational associations, and provides a center of communication between the academic community and the federal government in matters of higher educational policy.

The ACE has some international functions as well, which are carried out by an **Overseas Liaison Committee,** the **International Education Project,** and the **Council for International Exchange of Scholars.** The committee provides a means of communication between the higher education professionals in the United States and the academic communities in Africa, Asia, Latin America, the Caribbean, and the Pacific. The **Rural Development Network,** a major committee program, promotes the exchange of information among researchers and professionals active in rural development.

The International Education Project tries to enlarge the constituency and resource base of international education and international studies. Much of the project's work is done through task forces that explore subjects such as transnational research and language and library resources. The Council for International Exchange of Scholars recommends senior scholars for university lecturing and post-doctoral research under the Fulbright-Hays program.

Background Desired
Teaching experience and courses on education, economics, and area studies. A PhD is preferred.

How to Apply
Write to: American Council on Education
One Dupont Circle
Washington, DC   20036

American Field Service *

The AFS offers an opportunity for students between the ages of 16 and 18 to live for a summer or a year with families of different cultures. American students are sent abroad, and foreign students are welcomed to the United

States. In the United States there are over 400 field representatives and 2,600 host families that receive students. Abroad, AFS works with hundreds of local committees and almost 2,000 host families on six continents.

In case you connect the American Field Service with ambulances during the first World War, you are on the right track. The AFS was started as a volunteer ambulance service for the French army in 1914. The American-French understanding that resulted from this association led to scholarships for American students at French universities. From there AFS broadened its activities to include its present concentration on the high school student.

Background Desired
International relations, area studies, languages, cultural studies, student counseling. A BA is accepted.

How to Apply
Write to: American Field Service
313 East 43rd St.
New York, NY   10017

Association for World Education

The association was organized in 1970 by a group of individuals and institutions interested in introducing a world view in education. Programs have included summer seminars in Denmark, conferences on the aims of the UN University, a world conference on "World Education and the Roles of Women," workshops in Austria at the World Citizens Assembly, and the quarterly publishing of *Journal of World Education.*

Background Desired
Education studies, teaching, international relations, conference organizing, and (for the *Journal*) editing and research. An MA or PhD is preferred.

How to Apply
Write to: Association for World Education
3 Harbor Hill Drive
Huntington, NY   11743

Boy Scouts of America

The **International Division** of the Boy Scouts participates in international activities by arranging the following international services for visiting foreign scouts: visits to the National Office of the Scouts and to its National

Training Center; consultations with leaders of the National Office; and contacts with local Boy Scout groups.

Background Desired
Boy Scouts training and some interest in international affairs. A BA is accepted.

How to Apply
Write to: Boy Scouts of America
Route 1-130
North Brunswick, NJ 08902

Carnegie Corporation*

This corporation is a philanthropic foundation created by Andrew Carnegie that is primarily interested in education and in certain aspects of governmental affairs. Grants for projects are made to colleges, universities, and professional associations. Approximately 7 percent of the income is allocated to educational endeavors in British Commonwealth areas.

Background Desired
Commonwealth studies, program and grants experience, economics, and education. A PhD is preferred.

How to Apply
Write to: Carnegie Corporation
437 Madison Ave.
New York, NY 10022

Council for Intercultural Studies and Programs

CISP is a cooperative association of some 400 colleges, universities, and higher educational associations. It conducts (a) conferences on new directions for old problems in international studies, (b) seminars here and abroad for faculty, and (c) projects to develop teaching materials. It also publishes a monthly bulletin, *Intercultural Studies Information Service,* and distributes materials through **Learning Resources on International Studies.**

Background Desired
International relations, cultural and communications studies, research ability, teaching, and seminar and workshop organization. An MA or PhD is preferred.

How to Apply

Write to: Council for Intercultural Studies and Programs
60 East 42nd St.
New York, NY   10017

Council on International Educational Exchange (CIEE)*

The council has a membership of US academic institutions and national organizations that send American students abroad or bring foreign students to the United States. It maintains permanent staffs in New York, Paris, and Tokyo offices.

Student travel services available to individuals and groups include authorization of the International Student Identity Card, group air charters, student railpasses, car plans, and publications. The council also sponsors study programs abroad for US students and hospitality programs in the United States for foreign students and teachers.

The CIEE publishes a fact sheet on working abroad and a booklet, *Employment Abroad,* that lists information on employment in foreign countries.

Background Desired

International studies, administrative ability, travel background, and experience in exchange programs. A BA may be adequate.

How to Apply

Write to: Council on International Educational Exchange
777 UN Plaza
New York, NY   10017

Council for International Exchange of Scholars

The council, which is administered by the American Council on Education, is a private agency cooperating in the administration of Fulbright-Hays grants for American University lecturers and advanced research scholars to study and work abroad.

Background Desired

International relations, exchange program experience, and administration. An MA or PhD is preferred.

How to Apply

Write to: Council for International Exchange of Scholars
Eleven Dupont Circle NW
Washington, DC   20036

Eisenhower Exchange Fellowships

This organization provides for travel and observation in the United States for foreign individuals who have demonstrated leadership potential in their own countries. Programs in the United States are developed on the basis of the professional interests of the fellows.

Background Desired
Experience in exchange programs and international studies. A BA may be accepted.

How to Apply
Write to: Eisenhower Exchange Fellowships
256 South 16th St.
Philadelphia, PA   19102

Experiment in International Living

The EIL focuses on cross-cultural communication with the belief that living with foreign people is the best way to understand their culture. Thousands of young Americans "experiment" annually by living with foreign families, and many foreigners live with American families. The EIL also has a school that offers undergraduate and graduate courses in language teaching and world issues.

Background Desired
Experience with exchange programs, teaching, and languages. A BA is sometimes adequate.

How to Apply
Write to: Experiment in International Living
Brattleboro, Vermont   05301

Foreign Student Service Council

The programs of this council are designed to give the university-level foreign student an understanding of the US government and an introduction to people in Washington. A member of COSERV, a national organization that coordinates services to students and visitors from abroad, the council offers three-day hospitality stays with American families as well as a series of seminars to acquaint foreign students with American life and customs. The council also issues a quarterly newsletter.

Background Desired

Experience in organizing hospitality programs and seminars and general international relations. A BA is adequate.

How to Apply

Write to: Foreign Student Service Council
1623 Belmont St. NW
Washington, DC   20009

Franklin Book Programs *

The purpose of this nonprofit organization is to help developing countries with their needs for educational materials and books. FBP has four broad objectives: (1) to increase local capabilities for producing books and other educational materials; (2) to increase international exchange of books; (3) to strengthen indigenous book marketing and distribution; and (4) to develop "the reading habit." The programs' board of directors consists of leading publishers, educators, and corporation executives.

Background Desired

Area studies, educational studies and experience, teaching, and publishing. A BA may be accepted.

How to Apply

Write to: Franklin Book Programs
801 Second Ave.
New York, NY   10017

Girl Scouts of the United States

This organization has an **International Department** that assists in developing programs for international visitors. Assistance includes home hospitality and opportunities to observe Girl Scout activities.

Background Desired

Exchange program experience and a background in the Scouts. A BA is usually adequate.

How to Apply

Write to: International Department
Girl Scouts of the United States
830 Third Ave.
New York, NY   10022
or

132 Ebury St.
London SWI W9QQ
England

Institute of International Education (IIE)*

The IIE is a leading organization in the field of educational and cultural exchange. It administers scholarships and fellowships for foreign students and arranges for their admission to US colleges and universities. It also services US students, screening applicants for Fulbright grants for overseas study. Among its other functions are: organizing travel, study, internships, and research programs for US and foreign leaders and specialists; providing information and advice on higher education in the United States and abroad to individuals and institutions throughout the world; planning itineraries and providing hospitality for foreign students and leaders in the United States; and conducting seminars and conferences on major issues in international education.

The IIE has regional offices in Atlanta, Chicago, Denver, Houston, Los Angeles, San Francisco, and Washington. Its overseas offices are located in South America, East Africa, Southeastern Asia, Japan, and Europe.

Background Desired
Educational studies, economics, area studies, experience in exchange programs, and administration. A BA is sometimes adequate.

How to Apply
Write to: Institute of International Education
              809 UN Plaza
              New York, NY   10017

Interfuture*

This organization selects promising students (usually undergraduates) to carry out independent studies on issues important to the world community. Three global themes have been chosen: "Individual and Society," "Habitat," and "Internationalism." Each student participant explores one of these themes through a study project of his or her choice. This research is carried out in a North Atlantic and in a Third World nation. Over an eight-month preparatory period, the IF scholar prepares the project with the help of a faculty advisor on campus; abroad for seven months, the student becomes immersed in the local culture. Scholars present their findings as research papers to their home institutions for academic credit.

Background Desired
International relations, area studies with an emphasis on Europe and Third World countries, research, and administration. An MA or PhD is preferred.

How to Apply

Write to: Interfuture
420 Lexington Ave.
New York, NY 10017

☆

International Council on the Future of the University

Formerly known as the International Council on the University Emergency, this organization examines the wide range of problems experienced by universities of Western industrialized countries. These problems involve "meeting the new demands imposed on universities by society without diminishing the institutions' ability to maintain academic standards, to train future scholars, and to conduct fruitful research." The council's purpose is to make a constructive contribution to these problems through the involvement of its members in conferences, studies, and publications.

Background Desired
Educational studies, teaching, international studies, and Western Europe studies. An MA or PhD is preferred.

How to Apply

Write to: International Council on the Future of the University
745 Fifth Ave.
New York, NY 10022

or

c/o Giorgio Cini Foundation
31024 Venice, Italy

☆

International Student Service (ISS)*

The ISS offers its services to all students and trainees from abroad. Among the services provided are: meeting students at port of entry; facilitating student–community contacts; administering the **International Camp Counselor Program**; and sponsoring programs of educational travel.

Background Desired
Exchange program experience, international relations, and languages. A BA is usually accepted.

How to Apply

Write to: International Student Service
291 Broadway
New York, NY 10007

International Youth and Student Movement for the United Nations (ISMUN)

The aims of ISMUN, as stated in its 1975 constitution, are "to work with young people and students for the aims and ideals of the United Nations.... to strive for national liberation ... for peace and disarmament ... against imperialism, colonialism, neocolonialism. ...." In addition, ISMUN desires to work with students and young people in order to promote through research greater knowledge of the United Nations.

Background Desired
International relations, international organizations studies, economics, and experience in youth movements. A BA may be accepted.

How to Apply
Write to: International Youth and Student Movement
for the United Nations
PO Box 3021
Grand Central Station
New York, NY   10017

or

ISMUN Secretary General
5 Chemin des IRIS
1216 Cointrin, Geneva
Switzerland

Management Institute for National Development

The institute's main concern is to help increase administrative efficiency in the management of educational institutions and nonprofit organizations. The institute has focused on voluntary agencies engaged in international work, particularly those involved in overseas development. Administrative studies have been made of many of these agencies and recommendations offered for increased organizational effectiveness. The institute has also explored ways of strengthening the teaching of world development in US schools and colleges. Research reports have been written on this subject and given wide distribution in the academic community.

Background Desired
Administration, business administration, educational studies, and economic development. An MA or PhD is preferred.

How to Apply
Write to: Management Institute for National Development
PO Box 522
Madison, NJ   07940

National Association for Foreign Student Affairs

NAFSA serves as a source of professional training and as a spokesman for international educational exchange programs in government and academic circles. It supports research and developmental projects, issues numerous publications on international educational interchange, and conducts conferences and workshops in this field.

Background Desired
Educational exchange, student personnel work, international relations, conference and seminar organizing, communications, and public relations. A BA may be accepted.

How to Apply
Write to: National Association for Foreign Student Affairs
1860 19th St. NW
Washington, DC   20009

National Council for Community Services
to International Visitors (COSERV)

COSERV serves as a bridge between organizations receiving visitors from abroad, such as the Department of State, and organizations that host these visitors in local communities. In linking these "sending" and "receiving" groups, COSERV provides opportunities for the exchange of ideas and for consultation on the varying experiences of these visitors. COSERV has a nationwide network of affiliated organizations that receive these guests and plan their schedules for local observation. A list of COSERV community groups follows.

Background Desired
International relations, languages, and exchange program experience. A BA may be accepted.

How to Apply
Write to: National Council for Community Services
to International Visitors
1630 Crescent Place NW
Washington, DC   20009

National Council for Community Services to International Visitors (COSERV)

Member Community Organizations

ALBANY—The International Center

ALBUQUERQUE—Albuquerque Committee for International Visitors

ANN ARBOR—International Center, University of Michigan (UC)*

ATLANTA—Atlanta Council for International Visitors

AUSTIN, TX—International Hospitality Committee of Austin

BALTIMORE—Baltimore Council for International Visitors

BOSTON—Center for International Visitors of Greater Boston

BOULDER, CO—Boulder Council for International Visitors

BOZEMAN, MT—Montana State University

BUFFALO—Buffalo World Hospitality Association

BURLINGTON, VT—Vermont Council on World Affairs

CAMBRIDGE, MA—Harvard University Marshal's Office (UC)*

CAMBRIDGE, MA—Massachusetts Institute of Technology, Registry of Guests (UC)*

CHICAGO—International Visitors Center of Chicago

CINCINNATI—Cincinnati International Visitors Center

CLEVELAND—Cleveland Council on World Affairs

COLUMBIA, SC—Columbia Council for Internationals

COLUMBUS—Central Ohio Council for International Visitors

DALLAS—Dallas Committee for Foreign Visitors

DAYTON—Dayton Council on World Affairs

DENVER—Institute of International Education, Rocky Mtn. Office

DENVER—International Hospitality Center of the Colorado Division, UNA, USA-UNESCO

DES MOINES—Des Moines Area Council for International Understanding

DETROIT—International Visitors Council of Metropolitan Detroit

DURHAM, NH—New Hampshire Council on World Affairs

EAST LANSING, MI—Community Volunteers for International Programs

EL PASO—El Paso Council for International Visitors

EPHRATA, WA—Ephrata's International Friends

FLINT, MI—Flint Committee to Welcome International Visitors

FREEPORT, IL—International Fellowship Committee

GAINESVILLE, FL—Gainesville Council for International Friendship

GRAND ISLAND, NB—Grand Island Council for International Visitors

GRAND RAPIDS—World Affairs Council of Western Michigan

HARTFORD—World Affairs Center

HOUSTON—Houston International Service Committee, Institute of International Education, Southern Office

*(UC) University Center offers limited on-campus services.

HUNTSVILLE, AL—Huntsville-Madison County Council for International Visitors

INDIANAPOLIS—International Visitors Service of the Indianapolis Council on World Affairs

KANSAS CITY, MO—Committee for International Visitors and Students

KNOXVILLE—Knoxville Area International Council, University of Tennessee

LINCOLN, NB—Mayor's Committee for International Friendship

LITTLE ROCK—Little Rock Council for International Visitors

LOS ANGELES—International Student Service of Southern California

LOS ANGELES—Los Angeles World Affairs Council

LOUISVILLE—International Center, University of Louisville

MEMPHIS—Memphis Council for International Friendship

MIAMI—Council for International Visitors of Greater Miami

MILWAUKEE—Hospitality Council, International Institute of Milwaukee County

MINNEAPOLIS—ST. PAUL—Minnesota International Center

NEW ORLEANS—Council for International Visitors of Greater New Orleans

NEWPORT—Newport Council for International Visitors

NEW YORK CITY—International Center in New York

NEW YORK CITY—National Council of Women of the United States

NORFOLK—VIRGINIA BEACH —Committee for International Visitors

OKLAHOMA CITY—International Visitors Council, Oklahoma City Chamber of Commerce

OMAHA—Kiwanis Club of Omaha

ORLANDO-WINTER PARK, FL—Mid-Florida Council for International Visitors

PARIS, IL—International Thanksgiving Fellowship

PHILADELPHIA—Philadelphia Council for International Visitors

PHOENIX—World Affairs Council of Phoenix

PITTSBURGH—Pittsburgh Council for International Visitors

PORTLAND, OR—World Affairs Council of Oregon

PROVIDENCE, RI—World Affairs Council of Rhode Island

RIVERSIDE, CA—International Relations Council of Riverside

ROCHESTER, NY—International Hospitality Service, Rochester Association for the United Nations

ROCHESTER, NY—Rochester International Friendship Council

SACRAMENTO—People-to-People Council of Greater Sacramento

ST. LOUIS—St. Louis Council on World Affairs

SALT LAKE CITY—International Visitors-Utah Council

SAN DIEGO—International Visitors Council of San Diego

SAN FRANCISCO—International Hospitality Center of the Bay Area

SANTA FE—Santa Fe Council on International Relations

SEATTLE—World Affairs Council of Seattle

SIOUX CITY—Mayor's Committee for International Visitors

SPOKANE—Spokane International Exchange Council

SPRINGFIELD, IL—Springfield Commission on International Visitors

SPRINGFIELD, MA—World Affairs Council of the Connecticut Valley

STANFORD, CA—Bechtel International Center, Stanford University (UC)*

STERLING/ROCK FALLS, IL—International Fellowship Committee

SYRACUSE—International Center of Syracuse

TOLEDO—International Institute of Greater Toledo

TULSA—Tulsa Council for International Visitors

WASHINGTON, DC—Foreign Student Service Council of Greater Washington

WASHINGTON, DC—International Visitors Information Service

WESTPORT, CT—International Hospitality Committee of Fairfield County

WICHITA—International Visitors Council, Wichita Area Chamber of Commerce

WILLIAMSBURG, VA—Colonial Williamsburg

WILMINGTON, DE—Delaware Council for International Visitors

WORCESTER, MA—International Center of Worcester

WORTHINGTON, MN—Worthington-Crailsheim International

YAKIMA, WA—Yakima Valley Council for International Visitors

North American Students Association

This association finds university placement in England for Canadians and Americans. Its general aim is to link North American students with their counterparts in Europe or on American campuses. The association also provides a social and cultural program to promote a greater understanding of the member countries involved.

Background Desired
English, American, or Canadian citizenship and knowledge of exchange programs. A BA is usually accepted.

How to Apply
Write to: North American Students Association
23 Bloomsbury Square
London WC 1, England

Overseas Education Fund (of the League of Women Voters)

The fund offers to women from abroad briefings and training sessions at its Washington, DC headquarters on the techniques of citizen participation. Opportunities are given these visitors to observe government and voluntary groups in action at the grass-roots level.

Special emphasis is placed on helping women in developing nations to help themselves. The fund helps these women to start and operate job training programs, day care centers, craft cooperatives, shops, and health clinics. OEF's field representatives have worked in forty-four countries, their main thrust being the training of women in those countries to organize their own voluntary organizations.

Background Desired

International relations, vital knowledge of the American scene, particularly the role played by nonprofit organizations in the life of the United States. A BA is sometimes accepted.

How to Apply

Write to: Overseas Education Fund
              League of Women Voters
              1730 M St. NW
              Washington, DC   20036

Phelps Stokes Fund (PSF)

The PSF creates educational opportunities for blacks, American Indians, and poor whites in the United States. Similarly, African education is a primary concern, and PSF programs have been broadened to include emerging colleges in the Caribbean.

The fund provides opportunities for Americans to meet with Africans: American scholars are sent to African institutions, and African professors serve as visiting faculty at American colleges and universities. In addition, interest-free emergency loans are given to African students in American colleges. Much research has also centered around the state of African education.

Background Desired

African studies and languages, educational studies, exchange program experience, and administration. An MA or PhD is preferred.

How to Apply

Write to: Phelps Stokes Fund
              10 East 87th St.
              New York, NY   10028

Putney Student Travel

PST arranges travel plans and tours for teenage students. Most of the destinations are in Europe, although travel is also arranged on other continents.

Background Desired

For a tour guide, international affairs, a good knowledge of Europe and its languages, and administration. A BA is accepted.

How to Apply

Write to: Putney Student Travel
              Putney, VT   05346

Travel Program for Foreign Diplomats

This program invites foreign diplomats assigned to the United States to travel across the country and live with Americans, participating in community life. Local businesspeople show them industry, farmers take them to round up livestock or to plow fields. The diplomats meet with Americans representing different professions and different points of view. The whole purpose of this exercise is to expose foreign diplomats, who normally see little of America outside of Washington and New York, to a broad spectrum of American life, customs, and culture.

Background Desired
Knowledge of American life, geography, and culture, administration, international relations, and languages. A BA is accepted.

How to Apply
Write to: Travel Program for Foreign Diplomats
211 East 53rd St.
New York, NY   10022

World University Service of the United States

Originated in 1920, the WUS is an international student-faculty organization that has as its objective the promotion of international university solidarity and mutual service between universities in different parts of the world. It further believes that participation in university life should be open to all regardless of race, religion, or political beliefs. The Board of WUS is 50 percent students and 50 percent faculty-administration.

Background Desired
University administration, teaching, and educational studies. An MA or PhD is preferred.

How to Apply
Write to: World University Service
20 West 40th St.
New York, NY   10018

Economics and Economic Development

Agricultural Development Council

Concern about inadequate food supplies for rapidly growing populations in Asia led John D. Rockefeller to organize the ADC in 1953. The organization is involved in research and training to provide the manpower needed to help Asian countries use their agricultural resources more effectively. Although the initial impetus was toward Asia, the ADC is also involved to a limited extent in other areas of the world. The council pursues its goals through fellowships (to Asian students to travel and study), grants (for Asian research projects), publications, and meetings.

Background Desired
Economics, economic development, Asian studies and languages, agricultural economics, and administration. A PhD is preferred.

How to Apply
Write to: Agricultural Development Council
1290 Avenue of the Americas
New York, NY   10020

American Economic Association

This association prides itself on being the "Headquarters for Simplified Economics." It has written *How We Live,* which, it indicates, is the "world's best-selling primer on economics." Another "world's best" is the "Ten Pillars of Economic Wisdom," which was promoted at a World's Fair and has since become "the world's best-known economic document."

Background Desired
These claims are difficult to substantiate, but if any of you want to give this organization a whirl, you might do well to have some economic background. Also be prepared to couch the language of economics in the simplest of terms and concepts. An MA or PhD is preferred.

How to Apply
Write to: American Economic Association
1313 Twenty-first Ave. South
Nashville, TN   37212

American Enterprise Institute for Public Policy Research *

The institute is a center for the study of problems in economics, foreign policy, law, and government. It fosters research, analyzes public policy proposals, and identifies and presents varying points of view on the issues studied. To achieve this objective, it commissions scholars to undertake original research and publishes their findings. It sponsors conferences and debates on these issues and makes the proceedings available to the public.

This procedure is designed to bring about a broader understanding of controversial issues.

Background Desired

Institute personnel function in the following capacities, each of which defines the kind of background desired: seminar programs, health policy, economic policy, legal policy, government regulation, foreign and defense policy, and research on advertising. For the internationally trained student, foreign policy analysis, economics, international relations, and area studies provide a desirable background. A PhD is preferred.

How to Apply

Write to: American Enterprise Institute
1150 17th St. NW
Washington, DC   20036

American Freedom from Hunger Foundation

The foundation has as its aim the awakening of "American consciousness . . . to global hunger problems." It focuses public attention on food and hunger-related issues and it tries to mobilize public and private action to alleviate hunger and malnutrition in the world.

It achieves its objectives through holding community conferences; through raising funds to support projects of the Food and Agriculture Organization of the United Nations; through monitoring hearings and legislation of the US Congress affecting food policy; and through responding to emergency relief needs as they arise in the developing world, as in Bangladesh and the Sahel.

Background Desired

Fund raising, agriculture, economics, economic development, Third World area studies, and nutrition. An MA or PhD is preferred.

How to Apply

Write to: American Freedom from Hunger Foundation
1625 I St. NW
Washington, DC   20006

Bread for the World

This organization is a citizens' lobby, similar to Common Cause. Its membership is church-based and is concerned with world hunger and development issues. The organization welcomes interns, who help prepare Congressional profiles, undertake lobbying in Washington, and prepare educational materials.

Background Desired
International relations, economics, economic development, nutrition, agriculture, and Third World area studies. A BA is usually adequate.

How to Apply
Write to: Bread for the World
207 East 16th St.
New York, NY   10003

Brookings Institution *

Brookings is devoted to research and education in economics, foreign policy, government, and the social sciences. Its main purpose is to bring knowledge to bear on current and emerging public policy problems facing the United States. It organizes conferences and seminars on these issues and publishes its findings for the public.

Its activities are carried out through three research programs: **Economic Studies, Governmental Studies,** and **Foreign Policy Studies.** It also has an **Advanced Study Program** and a **Publications Program.** In all these activities, Brookings acts as an independent analyst and critic.

Background Desired
A PhD is preferred, since Brookings requires proven excellence in scholarship, research ability, international relations, foreign policy analysis, area studies, and economics.

How to Apply
Write to: Brookings Institution
1775 Massachusetts Ave. NW
Washington, DC   20036

Center for Environmental Education

The center is involved in alerting the public to environmental issues on an international scale and tries to enroll support for its special projects. One of these has been the **Whale Protection Fund,** designed to inform the public of the fact that Japan and Russia have ignored the whaling moratorium recommended by the UN Conference on the Environment. To pressure these countries into observing the moratorium, the center called for a boycott of products manufactured in Russia and Japan.

Background Desired

Environmental studies, world resources, population and demography, and economic development. An MA or PhD is preferred.

How to Apply

Write to: Center for Environmental Education
2100 M St. NW
Washington, DC   20037

Committee for Economic Development (CED)

CED's purpose is "to propose policies that will help to bring about steady economic growth at high employment and reasonably stable prices, increase productivity and living standards, provide greater and more equal opportunity for every citizen and improve the quality of life for all." Most of the trustees of this organization are businesspeople and educators.

The CED develops recommendations for business and public policy. Among the international issues considered by CED have been international trade, the world monetary system, and global energy policy.

Background Desired

Research, economics, and economic development. A PhD is preferred.

How to Apply

Write to: Committee for Economic Development
477 Madison Ave.
New York, NY   10022

Conference Board *

This is a research organization concerned with economic trends and management practices. Major areas of research in the international field are: international economics, international operations management, financing overseas operations, export management, investment climate analyses, compensation of third-country nationals, and industry–government relations.

Background Desired

International economics, finance, business administration, and trade. A PhD is usually required.

How to Apply

Write to: Conference Board
845 Third Ave.
New York, NY   10022

Ford Foundation*

One of the largest foundations in the world, Ford gives funds for educational, developmental, research, and experimental efforts designed to produce significant advances in selected problems of national and international importance. Much of its overseas effort is concerned with economic development, and substantial programs of developmental assistance are in effect in many developing nations. It has eleven overseas offices in the less-developed world and one in Japan. Even though in recent years Ford has reduced its staff, vacancies still arise in the economic and economic development fields.

Background Desired
Economics or economic development combined with an area studies and language background (Latin America or Africa or Asian or Middle East). Sometimes, also, there are vacancies for those with communications experience. An MA or PhD is preferred.

How to Apply
Write to: Ford Foundation
             320 East 43rd St.
             New York, NY   10017

International Agricultural Development Service

IADS provides services to needy nations trying to increase food supplies to hungry populations. Its programs, which aim to accelerate agricultural and rural development, are "country-oriented." This organization has established an international network of expert scientists and administrators who are prepared to undertake short- or long-term assignments in developing countries.

Background Desired
Economics, agricultural economics, Third World area studies, nutrition, and administration. An MA or PhD is preferred.

How to Apply
Write to: International Agricultural Development Service
             1133 Avenue of the Americas
             New York, NY   10036

International Development Research Center

The center was set up by Canada and is dedicated to "initiate, encourage, support, and conduct research into the problems of the developing regions of the world, and into the means for applying and adapting scientific, technical, and other knowledge to the economic and social advancement of those regions." Regional offices are located in Singapore, Bogota, Dakar, Beirut, and Nairobi, indicating the areas of greatest interest to the center.

The professional staff is made up of citizens of many countries, including the United States.

Background Desired
Agriculture and nutrition sciences, information activities, population and demography studies, social sciences, international relations, Third World area studies, and economics. An MA or PhD is preferred.

How to Apply
Write to: International Development Research Center
PO Box 8500
Ottawa, Canada K1G3H9

International Economic Policy Association

The association analyzes US and foreign government policies affecting international trade, aid, investments, finance, and taxation. Courses of action are recommended as a result of these evaluations. The guiding philosophy of IEPA is that freedom in economic enterprise is necessary to ensure political liberty. Its membership consists of business organizations, to which the results of these studies are submitted.

Background Desired
International business, economics, trade, finance, and taxation. An MA or PhD is preferred.

How to Apply
Write to: International Economic Policy Association
1625 I St. NW
Washington, DC 20006

International Voluntary Services (IVS)

IVS does in a private capacity what the Peace Corps does for government: enrolling American youth for person-to-person work in developing countries. It has developed teams in education—teaching English and teaching in English. Its volunteers have also been successful in community development projects, both rural and urban. The thought behind the IVS is that nongovernmental personnel can have a greater impact in working with foreign people than can government employees, who often are suspect for their official affiliations.

Background Desired

Teaching, community development, and a service ideal. A BA is often adequate.

How to Apply

Write to: International Voluntary Services
1717 Massachusetts Ave. NW
Washington, DC   20036

National Bureau of Economic Research

The bureau is one of the largest economic research organizations in the world. It works on economic problems of a domestic as well as international importance. The results of its research are issued in the form of scientific reports entirely divorced from recommendations on policy. In this way the bureau aims to provide well-researched documentation on important problems, objectively presented as a basis for discussion by policy makers.

Among the subjects of an international nature previously undertaken have been: (a) the effect of world commodity prices on US manufacturing prices; (b) multinational firms; (c) alternative trade strategies and employment; (d) US–USSR scientific and technical programs of cooperation; and (e) the international transmission of inflation through the world monetary system.

Background Desired

Research ability, economics, world resources, energy and environmental studies, and trade. A PhD is preferred.

How to Apply

Write to:·   National Bureau of Economic Research
261 Madison Ave.
New York, NY   10016

Natural Resources Defense Council*

The NRDC attempts to protect America's endangered natural resources and to improve the quality of the human environment. It combines legal action, scientific research, and citizen education in an environmental program. NRDC's major involvements are in the areas of air and water pollution, energy policy, nuclear safety, natural resource management, and the international environment.

The international functions of the council are being developed. Together with the Sierra Club and other environmentally conscious organizations, it helps plan national positions on the environment for use by US representatives at international conferences and discussions.

Background Desired

Environmental studies, world resources, energy, and public relations. A BA may be accepted.

How to Apply

Write to: Natural Resources Defense Council
15 West 44th St.
New York, NY   10036

or

917 15th St. NW
Washington, DC   20005

or

2345 Yale St.
Palo Alto, CA   94306

New TransCentury Foundation

This foundation, under a grant from the Agency for International Development, provides technical assistance in various management areas to private organizations working toward Third World development. One form that assistance takes is the *Job Opportunities Bulletin,* a publication listing all job vacancies in developmental work in the Third World. None of these positions is with TransCentury. The foundation usually provides a preliminary screening of applicants and sends the résumés of the most qualified to the agency with the vacant position.

Background Desired

Job placement work, Third World area studies, economic development, economics, finance, and administration. (This background is applicable for work with TransCentury and also for the type of jobs listed in the *Job Opportunities Bulletin.*) A BA may be accepted.

How to Apply

Write to: New TransCentury Foundation
1789 Columbia Road NW
Washington, DC   20009

Overseas Development Council*

The ODC seeks to increase American understanding of the economic and social problems confronting the developing countries of the world. Through research, conferences, and publications, this organization seeks to make the American public, businesses, and policy makers aware of the importance of development and developing countries to the United States.

Among the subjects researched by the ODC are: the United States and Third World development; international economic systems; alternative development strategies and basic human needs; a global approach to energy; world hunger and food scarcity; and private organizations and development. Visiting fellows from business, government, and universities regularly participate in the work of the ODC.

Background Desired

Third World area studies, economic development, public relations, and conference and seminar organizing. An MA or PhD is preferred.

How to Apply

Write to: Overseas Development Council
1717 Massachusetts Ave. NW
Washington, DC   20036

Public Administration Service*

For students interested in public administration as well as in international affairs, the Service aims to improve the quality and effectiveness of governmental operations at all levels. In all cases, the central concern is with the effective accomplishment of public purposes. Frequently the focus is on central management problems, policy planning, financial management, and staff development. Outside the United States, PAS has a record of substantial activity in Canada, Central and South America, Asia, and Africa.

Background Desired

Business administration, public administration, finance, area studies, personnel, and human resources. An MA or PhD is preferred.

How to Apply

Write to: Public Administration Service
1313 East 60th St.
Chicago, IL   60637

or

1776 Massachusetts Ave. NW
Washington, DC   20036

Rockefeller Foundation*

In addition to involvement in a great number of national projects, the foundation also funds many projects of an international nature. Among its international concerns are the conquest of hunger, problems of population, the quality of environment, and university development. A random sampling of projects undertaken by the foundation show that it has funded: (a) an increase of agricultural productivity among small landowners in El Salvador; (b) an experimental program to increase the productivity of disadvantaged Asian rice farmers; (c) research on the formulation of population policy in Chile; (d) research on the motivation for delayed marriage of Hong Kong women; (e) support costs of East Asian graduate scholars at the University of Nairobi; and (f) staff development at the University of Zaire.

Background Desired
Economics, economic development, sociology, Latin American, Asian, or African studies and languages, population studies, education, and teaching. A PhD is preferred.

How to Apply
Write to: Rockefeller Foundation
111 West 50th St.
New York, NY 10020

Rockefeller Brothers Fund

This fund makes grants under three programs: **National, New York City,** and **International.** The last program has two objectives: (1) structuring interdependence among nations, and (2) helping the developing countries of Asia, Africa, and Latin America provide for their basic needs. In the first category, grants are concentrated on specific projects in international economic management, international cooperation, and science and technology. In the second category, grants concentrate on the diversification of economic opportunities, especially employment in small businesses and the management of wildland resources, such as forest lands and parks.

Background Desired
Economics, economic development, Third World area studies, business administration, world resources, environment, and population. A PhD is preferred.

How to Apply
Write to: Rockefeller Brothers Fund
30 Rockefeller Plaza
New York, NY 10020

Society for International Development

The society provides a forum for the exchange of ideas, facts, and experiences among all those professionally concerned with the problems of economic and social development in modernizing societies. To this effect, the SID publishes the *International Development Review,* which presents opinions and comments of scholars and practitioners in the field. It also holds conferences on regional and international levels. Sponsors of SID comprise many national banks in various parts of the world, and its members include such diverse organizations as Planned Parenthood, the OECD, and banks, development bodies, research organizations, and foundations in many countries.

Background Desired
Economics, economic development, Third World area studies, sociology, and conference organization. A BA may be accepted.

How to Apply
Write to: Society for International Development
1346 Connecticut Ave. NW
Washington, DC   20036

For a list of nonprofit organizations engaged in development work abroad, consult *US Non-Profit Organizations in Development Assistance Abroad,* issued by the Technical Assistance Information Clearing House in New York.

Environment, Energy, and Population

Conservation Foundation *

This foundation was organized in 1948 to prevent the destructive exploitation of natural resources. It has advanced its cause with educational campaigns, research, and studies to impress the public and government with the need for action to halt this exploitation. It has seen itself as a mediating institution that builds bridges between research and action. The foundation has also helped organize the **International Union for the Conservation of Nature and Natural Resources.**

Background Desired
Environmental studies, demography, energy studies, and world resources. An MA or PhD is preferred.

How to Apply
Write to: Conservation Foundation
1717 Massachusetts Ave. NW
Washington, DC   20036

International Institute for Environment and Development

Formerly the International Institute for Environmental Affairs, the new name of this organization indicates its increasing scope and functions. Among its concerns have been: habitat and the UN Conference on this subject in 1976; compiling the most accurate information available on the environment; publishing a newsletter on world environment matters; the law of the sea; the World Food Conference; analysis of the energy crisis; and establishment of an international environmental fellowship program.

The IED devotes much of its time to two special priorities: making environmental issues known to a wider citizen audience and attempting to ensure that commitments entered into by governments are in fact implemented.

Background Desired

Environmental studies, research ability, economics, economic development, energy studies, population and demography, and Third World area studies. A PhD is preferred.

How to Apply

Write to: International Institute for Environment and Development
27 Mortimer St.
London W1A 4QW
England

or

1525 New Hampshire Ave. NW
Washington, DC   20036

International Planned Parenthood Federation *

The IPPF encourages the formation of national centers to pioneer family planning services in each country of the world and to bring about a favorable climate of public opinion in which governments can be persuaded to take responsibility for family planning.

The IPPF has seven regions, with offices in Beirut, Colombo, Kuala Lumpur, London, Nairobi, New York, and Tokyo. All of them assist family planning associations in their areas. In addition, IPPF has several regular publications: the monthly *International Planned Parenthood News* and two specialist bimonthly publications, the *Medical Bulletin* and *Research in Reproduction.* The central and regional libraries of the IPPF are an important source of information on all aspects of human fertility and contraception.

Background Desired

World resources, population studies, research, public relations, sociology, and family planning. A BA is sometimes accepted.

How to Apply

Write to: International Planned Parenthood Federation
18–20 Lower Regent St.
London SW1Y 4PW
England

or

111 Fourth Ave.
New York, NY   10003

Population Council *

The functions of the council are to conduct research and provide professional services in the broad field of population: encompassing development issues and population policies; investigation into safe and effective means of birth planning; and design, implementation, and evaluation of programs to provide birth planning services and information.

The council is in contact with institutions overseas having similar interests. Occasionally it provides financial support for the work of institutions and trains professionals in specialized areas of population studies. The council also distributes publications and information on population matters to interested professionals.

Background Desired

Demography studies, medicine, biology, public relations, publishing, and research ability. An MA or PhD is preferred.

How to Apply

Write to: Population Council
One Dag Hammarskjold Plaza
New York, NY   10017

Population Institute *

The philosophy of the institute is that continued world population growth threatens resources, destroys the environment, and degrades human life. The institute approaches this problem by trying to bring about a change in attitudes, of individuals as well as of societies.

Its **Communication Center** helps the television industry try to create a turnabout on population issues. It is responsible for many population articles in newspapers and magazines and works with national education leaders to promote population programs in the media.

The institute also has a **Student Project** that has arranged student-faculty meetings on all levels—state, national, and international—to discuss the problems of human ecology. Finally, the institute's **Ethics Project** recognizes that the choice of population policy—individual and national—is a moral choice. This project has brought together leading Catholic, Jewish, and Protestant theologians with population experts to rethink present population doctrines.

Background Desired

Population and demographic studies, world resources, Third World area studies, economics, economic development, and public relations. An MA or PhD is preferred.

How to Apply

Write to: Population Institute
777 UN Plaza
New York, NY   10017

Population Resource Center＊

The center is a service to donors, offering professional assistance to help them identify population problems that relate to their own goals. Essentially, the center evaluates population projects and programs for funding. Before projects are recommended, the center screens them to ensure that they are valid projects capable of achieving their objectives. A portfolio of approved projects is maintained by the center. This organization also occasionally combines gifts from several donors to fund a project that none can fully fund individually.

Background Desired

Population studies, research and analytical ability, and administration. An MA or PhD is preferred.

How to Apply

Write to: Population Resource Center
622 Third Ave.
New York, NY   10017

Sierra Club*

The slogan of the club is, "Not blind opposition to progress, but opposition to blind progress." This pretty well defines the attitude and activities of this environmentally conscious organization. It helped bring the National Park Service and the Forest Service into existence; it played a leading role in the establishment of many national parks; it tries to curtail overcutting in forests and to keep the wilderness in its natural state. The International Office of this organization works closely with the UN on international activities pertaining to the environment.

Background Desired
Environmental studies, world resources, international organization studies, and international relations. A BA may be accepted.

How to Apply
Write to: Sierra Club
     530 Bush St.
     San Francisco, CA 14108

     or

     800 Second Ave.
     New York, NY 10017

Zero Population Growth

Here is yet again another population-oriented nonprofit organization. It has a new dimension, however, in its emphasis on illegal immigration as an example of the dangers of unlimited population growth. The economic motive is therefore stressed in the organization's appeals for public attention and funds. ZPG maintains that unlimited population growth is threatening the quality of life of future generations. It also mentions urban blight, poverty, and the depletion of resources as additional results of uncontrolled population increase.

Background Desired
Population studies, labor relations, economics, and labor economics. A BA may be accepted.

How to Apply
Write to: Zero Population Growth
     1346 Connecticut Ave. NW
     Washington, DC 20036

Business and Labor

Amalgamated Clothing Workers of America, AFL—CIO

This association has an international program that works toward "international labor unity." It has supported labor organizations in other countries and has sent funds to workers hit by natural disasters in various parts of the world. Amalgamated has been active in preventing unrestricted imports of textiles, and has also been instrumental in getting voluntary quotas imposed on Asian countries from which competition has been experienced.

Background Desired
Trade unionism experience and motivation, industrial relations, economics, Asian studies, trade, and textiles. A BA is adequate if you have any of the above.

How to Apply
Write to: Amalgamated Clothing Workers of America
15 Union Square
New York, NY   10003

American Federation of Labor—Congress of Industrial Organizations*

The AFL-CIO has a **Department of International Affairs** that recommends foreign policy positions to the trade union leadership and to the rank and file. Among the international issues covered by this department are: AFL-CIO policy toward the International Labor Organization, the International Confederation of Free Trade Unions, and other international labor organizations; US-USSR relations; the need for strong US defenses; the nonexistence of trade unions and the exploitation of labor in communist countries; the Arab-Israeli conflict; and the revision of the Panama Canal treaty.

     The AFL-CIO is in contact with the embassies of foreign governments in an effort to promote better understanding of the American labor movement. The Department of International Affairs also furthers AFL-CIO policies through publications, conferences, orientation of foreign visitors, trade union missions overseas, and proposals for government action.

Background Desired
Trade unionism, industrial relations, international relations, area studies (particularly of East Central Europe, Russia, and China), and economics. A BA may be accepted.

How to Apply

Write to: Department of International Affairs
AFL–CIO
815 16th St. NW
Washington, DC   20006

American Institute for Free Labor Development

The institute is engaged in technical assistance for the development of the democratic trade union movement in Latin America. The AFL–CIO sponsors the institute, which has chosen two principal means of achieving its objective: education and social projects.

In collaboration with Latin American trade unions, the institute teaches union members the rights and responsibilities of democratic trade unionism. Central to its social projects work is the training of trade union members to participate in national and regional economic planning leading to the economic development of Latin America.

Background Desired

Trade unionism, industrial relations, economic development, and Latin American studies and languages. A BA may be accepted..

How to Apply

Write to: American Institute for Free Labor Development
1925 K St. NW
Washington, DC   20036

Business Council for International Understanding *

The BCIU provides a cross fertilization between the foreign affairs community of the US government and American business, especially companies with foreign operations or affiliates. It focuses on improving the climate for international business–government relations at the policy-making level as well as in day-to-day operations.

BCIU briefs American business people and their families who are going to be stationed abroad through seminars at the American University in Washington. Another important BCIU function is to arrange consultations and briefings for American ambassadors going overseas.

Background Desired

Business administration, international relations, area studies, seminar organization, and research capability. A BA is sometimes adequate.

How to Apply

Write to: Business Council for International Understanding
420 Lexington Ave.
New York, NY   10017

International Management and Development Institute

The purpose of the institute is to "provide education which will strengthen corporate and government management teams internationally." Put another way, it hopes to increase government and public understanding of "the international corporation as a constructive force in the domestic and world community." It works to achieve its aims through government–business training programs, executive seminars, Washington briefings, and through a general education campaign pointed toward government and the public.

Background Desired

International business, business administration, economics, trade, and finance. A BA may be accepted.

How to Apply

Write to: International Management and Development Institute
Watergate Office Building, Suite 905
2600 Virginia Ave. NW
Washington, DC   20037

International Metalworkers Federation (IMF)

The IMF is an international organization of metal workers' unions. The Secretariat staff has departments for research, women, youth, vocational training, and publications. In addition to these concerns, the IMF is engaged in strengthening trade unions in developing countries. To this effect, it has regional representatives for Latin America, West Asia, East Asia, and Africa. These representatives channel aid from the IMF to local trade unions needing assistance.

Background Desired

Trade unionism, industrial relations, metal work experience, economics, research, and Third World area studies. A BA suffices.

How to Apply

Write to: International Metalworkers Federation
54 bis, route des Acacias
CH 1227, Carouge—Geneva, Switzerland

International Transport Workers Federation

The ITWF is one of the most active of international trade union movements and has worked well in furthering the economic and social interests of transport workers and their national unions. It has developed a comprehensive research arm, which has studied labor legislation, collective bargaining problems, and working conditions affecting its members.

Background Desired
Trade unionism, industrial relations, transport experience (road, air, sea, railway), and labor economics. A BA may be accepted.

How to Apply
Write to: International Transport Workers Federation
Maritime House
Old Town
London SW4 OJR, England

National Foreign Trade Council *

Sound economic growth is an objective with which it is hard to disagree, although the means of achieving such growth may be subject to a great deal of controversy. The NFTC believes that foreign trade and investment are key instruments in achieving this growth; it further believes that close coordination of US domestic and international economic policies is required to establish a favorable climate in which international business can operate to make effective use of these instruments. Specifically, the council performs research, issues documentation and policy statements, and holds conferences and seminars to make its point of view known.

Background Desired
Business administration, economics, trade, finance, and conference and seminar organization. A BA may be accepted.

How to Apply
Write to: National Foreign Trade Council
10 Rockefeller Plaza
New York, NY   10020

Young Presidents Organization

YPO is an educational association for chief executives who become president of their companies before age 40—a key membership requirement. Its main purpose is to help members become better presidents through education and an exchange of ideas.

With a membership in more than thirty countries, YPO is an international organization. In addition to the United States, chapters are located in Europe, Canada, Japan, Mexico, Korea, Australia, and the Carribean. To fulfill the educational purpose of the organization, seminars, conferences, and major meetings (called Universities for Presidents) are held each year. Both a quarterly magazine and a monthly newsletter are published, which features reports on a wide range of subjects of interest to YPOers.

Background Desired
Business administration, educational studies, teaching, and seminar and conference organizing. A BA may be accepted.

How to Apply
Write to: Young Presidents Organization
             201 East 42nd St.
             New York, NY   10017

Relief, Rehabilitation, and Human Rights

American Council for Emigrés in the Professions

This council assists refugees who are professionally and academically trained to find appropriate work in the United States. Its services, which are free to clients, include technical counseling, résumé preparation, English language training, and placement in professional jobs. In addition, the council maintains career training programs to prepare those refugees unable to enter their professions in the United States for jobs in other professions where manpower shortages exist. Each year this organization assists about 2,500 persons.

Background Desired
Languages, international relations, area studies, counseling, and job placement. A BA is adequate.

How to Apply
Write to: American Council for Emigrés in the Professions
             345 East 46th St.
             New York, NY   10017

American Council for Nationalities Service

This organization promotes understanding and cooperation between the many nationality and racial groups in the United States. It assists immigrants—including Puerto Ricans—to adjust to American life and become participating citizens. Assistance provided to immigrants covers finding jobs, learning English, reuniting their families, and generally helping them adjust to the eccentricities and ordinary customs of American life. ACNS offices are located in most important American cities.

Background Desired
International relations, area and language studies, counseling, job placement, and social work. A BA is sometimes adequate.

How to Apply
Write to: American Council for Nationalities Service
20 West 40th St.
New York, NY 10018

American Friends Service Committee (AFSC)

The AFSC was founded in 1917 by American Quakers to provide conscientious objectors to war with an alternative to military service, such as aiding civilian victims during war. Its work began with relief and medical services during World War I, then broadened to include an emphasis on nonviolent solutions to international conflicts. Conferences and seminars involving individuals of many nations are held frequently in order to increase understanding among all nations. In addition, in various countries of Africa, Asia, Latin America, and the Middle East, AFSC workers conduct programs of social and technical assistance "to enable people to discover and utilize their own power and resources." AFSC has international headquarters in Philadelphia and ten regional offices across the United States.

Background Desired
More than any particular curriculum or even experience, the service ideal is required of applicants for jobs. The AFSC expects its employees to be dedicated to the principles and work of the Friends. In addition, a background in international studies is helpful. A BA is adequate.

How to Apply
Write to: American Friends Service Committee
1501 Cherry St.
Philadelphia, PA 19102

Amnesty International*

Through writing letters, holding publicity campaigns, sending missions and observers, and publishing special reports, Amnesty works to gain the freedom of prisoners of conscience. It also seeks humane treatment for all prisoners and detainees. This organization came into special prominence as a result of President Carter's emphasis on human rights. In 1977 it won the Nobel Peace Prize.

Background Desired

International relations work and studies, and in particular a commitment to human rights activities. A BA is adequate.

How to Apply

Headquarters is in London, but there are two offices in the United States.
Write to: Amnesty International USA
2112 Broadway
New York, NY   10023

or

3618 Sacramento St.
San Francisco, CA   94118

CARE (Cooperative for American Relief Everywhere)*

CARE was established to help meet the needs of millions of people left destitute in Europe after World War II. The founders were twenty-two American organizations—cooperative, relief, religious, refugee, and labor.

CARE's initial efforts were centered around food packages. It has since moved into an additional type of aid with its self-help programs around the world. Partnership programs in nutrition, development, and health are now a key feature. CARE also helps victims of natural disasters, such as those suffering from famine in India, or the victims of floods, earthquakes, and civil strife in all parts of the world.

Background Desired

Third World area studies and languages, nutrition, economic development, and health studies. A BA is adequate.

How to Apply

Write to: CARE
660 First Ave.
New York, NY   10016

Catholic Relief Services*

CRS is the official overseas relief and development agency of the Catholic Church in the United States. It channels foodstuffs to the world's needy. To help solve the world's food problem, it places high priority on projects designed to assist the small rural farmer; it emphasizes consumer cooperatives and rural credit structures; and it stresses water resource projects and agricultural training programs.

Background Desired
Social work, Third World area studies, economic development, agricultural economics, and food and nutrition studies. A BA suffices.

How to Apply
Write to: Catholic Relief Services
1101 First Ave.
New York, NY   10022

Church World Service*

The CWS, which represents most of the Protestant denominations, has a relief and rehabilitation aim of feeding the hungry and resettling refugees, and a long-range aim of "development of people and peace in our time." Its programs operate in all areas of the world and its representatives are stationed on all continents. Its work in general is similar to that of CARE and Catholic Relief Services.

Background Desired
Area studies, international relations, social work, nutrition, economic development, agricultural economics, and above all the service ideal. A BA is adequate.

How to Apply
Write to: Church World Service
475 Riverside Drive
New York, NY   10027

Foster Parents Plan International*

FPPI seeks foster parents in developed countries as sponsors for needy children and their families in developing areas. Current programs operating in Latin America, Asia, and Africa consist of medical services, technical and vocational education, community development, and social services for needy families.

Background Desired
African, Asian, or Latin American studies with the appropriate language, plus the service ideal. Social work experience is also useful, as is some back-

ground in nutrition, medical services, agriculture, and vocational education. A BA is adequate.

How to Apply

Write to: Foster Parents Plan International
              Box 400
              Warwick, RI   02887

Freedom House

Freedom House was started to combat totalitarianism and to strengthen democratic institutions and the right of individuals to free choice. The organization gives an annual Freedom Award to those who, as Archibald MacLeish has said, "in one way or another, and sometimes at great cost to themselves, loved human liberty and acted out their passion." It issues a periodic *Survey of Freedom*, which evaluates the state and degree of freedom in every country in the world. In the headquarters lobby of Freedom House is a 20-foot map depicting the current status of individual freedom in every nation. The organization also has conferences on issues revolving around freedom and publishes a bimonthly magazine, *Freedom at Issue*, which is given wide circulation.

Background Desired

Dedication to the ideal of freedom, ability to organize conferences, and research. A BA may be accepted.

How to Apply

Write to: Freedom House
              20 West 40th St.
              New York, NY   10018

International League for Human Rights *

The league does in the international field what the American Civil Liberties Union does domestically: protect civil rights of individuals wherever they are being violated. This organization is devoted wholly to the task of advancing human rights throughout the world.

International League activities include: (a) supporting all UN efforts on behalf of human rights; (b) gathering facts on human rights violations and intervening directly with governments; (c) protesting political trials; (d) assisting political prisoners; (e) aiding refugees and exiles; (f) participating in international meetings on human rights; (g) providing counsel to governments; and (h) printing bimonthly news bulletins and other publications.

Background Desired

Interest in civil rights and international relations. A BA suffices sometimes.

How to Apply

Write to: International League for Human Rights
             236 East 46th St.
             New York, NY   10017

International Red Cross*

The International Committee of the Red Cross acts as a neutral intermediary in time of conflict to protect victims of war in accordance with the Geneva Convention. **The League of Red Cross Societies,** another part of the International Red Cross, coordinates the efforts of member societies in meeting the needs of victims of natural disasters and refugees from war situations. Through special missions, the loan of experts, seminars, and publications, the league helps national societies to expand and improve their programs of disaster relief, nursing, blood donations, and public relations.

   The American Red Cross, one of the more advanced of the league's members, helps meet emergency needs of victims of disaster, gives assistance to sister societies in extending their programs, and provides opportunities for officials of other countries to study American Red Cross programs.

Background Desired

International relations and the service ideal. A BA is usually adequate.

How to Apply

Write to: International Red Cross
             7 Ave. de la Paix
             Geneva, Switzerland

International Rescue Committee*

The IRC is in the forefront of all refugee crises. In the Vietnam holocaust, IRC teams of doctors and nurses were responsible for the medical care of half the refugees in Thai camps. IRC trained refugees to become paramedics in keeping with its emphasis on self-help. In the United States, ten IRC offices provided resettlement services for the Indochinese it sponsored. The goal is to absorb them into American life and help them obtain employment, housing, education, and language training. In Paris, the IRC office helped many of the Indochinese admitted into France.

Financial aid, counseling, and resettlement services are provided also for refugees from the Soviet Union and Eastern Europe, as well as from . Angola and Uganda.

Background Desired
Area studies and languages, work with refugees, and social work. A BA sometimes suffices.

How to Apply
Write to: International Rescue Committee
386 Park Ave. South
New York, NY   10016

Save the Children Federation

Founded in 1932 to help Appalachian victims of the Depression, Save the Children is a pioneer in community-based development programs aimed at helping children by improving life in the communities where they live. It is involved in over 200 overseas communities in eighteen countries. Projects have included cooperatives, nutrition and health programs, school, home, roadway and water system construction, and various food activities.

Background Desired
International relations, nutrition and health studies, social welfare, community development, economic development, and Third World studies and languages. A BA may be accepted.

How to Apply
Write to: Save the Children
48 Wilton Road
Westport, CT   06880

Others

American Council of Learned Societies

This council, composed of national scholarly organizations concerned with the humanities, administers programs of fellowships and grants designed to advance research in the following fields: area studies; languages, literature, and linguistics; archaeology; anthropology; economics and geography; and political science. The ACLS also offers travel grants to scholars in certain fields to participate in research conferences abroad.

Background Desired

A small executive staff administers these ACLS programs, with the help of an extensive system of Committees, such as the **Committee on Studies of Chinese Civilization** and the **Joint Committee on Swiss–American Cooperation in the Humanities and Social Sciences**. Applicants should have skills in administration, Asian studies, and grant programs. A PhD is usually required.

How to Apply

Write to: American Council of Learned Societies
              345 East 46th St.
              New York, NY   10017

American Council of Voluntary Agencies for Foreign Service *

The council provides a forum for cooperation, joint planning, and the exchange of ideas and information among American voluntary agencies engaged in overseas work in relief, rehabilitation, and development. The council is organized as a confederation of member agencies and is governed by a Board of Directors, composed of one representative from each member organization. It is supported by its membership.

Three committees form the basis of council activity for exchange of information and joint planning: the committees on refugees, material resources, and development assistance.

The council operates the **Technical Assistance Information Clearing House** under contract with the **Agency for International Development**. The Clearing House issues a directory that covers the foreign development assistance activities of American organizations engaged in agriculture, community development, education, and health.

A membership list of organizations in the American Council of Voluntary Agencies for Foreign Service follows.

Background Desired

International relations, economics, agricultural economics, economic development, community development, statistics, library sciences, and world resources. A BA may be accepted.

How to Apply

Write to: American Council of Voluntary Agencies for Foreign Service
              200 Park Ave. South
              New York, NY   10003

American Council of Voluntary Agencies for Foreign Service, Inc.

Membership List

American Council for Judaism Philanthropic Fund, Inc.

American Council for Nationalities Service

American Friends Service Committee, Inc.

American Foundation for Overseas Blind

American Fund for Czechoslovak Refugees, Inc.

American Jewish Joint Distribution Committee, Inc.

American Mizrachi Women

American National Committee to Aid Homeless Armenians

American ORT Federation, Inc.

Assemblies of God, Foreign Service Committee

Baptist World Alliance

CARE, Inc.

Catholic Relief Services, US Catholic Conference

Christian Children's Fund

Church World Service

CODEL, Inc. (Cooperation in Development)

Community Development Foundation, Inc.

Foster Parents Plan, Inc.

Foundation for the Peoples of the South Pacific, Inc.

Hadassah, The Women's Zionist Organization of America, Inc.

Heifer Project International

HIAS

Holt International Children's Service, Inc.

Interchurch Medical Assistance, Inc.

International Rescue Committee, Inc.

Lutheran Immigration and Refugee Service

Lutheran World Relief, Inc.

MAP, Inc. (Medical Assistance Programs)

Mennonite Central Committee, Inc.

Migration and Refugee Service, US Catholic Conference

Near East Foundation

PACT, Inc. (Private Agencies Collaborating Together)

Project Concern, Inc.

Save the Children Federation, Inc.

Seventh-Day Adventist World Service, Inc.

The Salvation Army

Tolstoy Foundation, Inc.

Travelers Aid–International Social Service of America

United Israel Appeal, Inc.

United Lithuanian Relief Fund of America, Inc.

World University Service

Young Men's Christian Association, International Division

Young Women's Christian Association of the USA, National Board, World Relations

American Society of International Law

This society fosters the study of international law and promotes the practice of international relations based on law and justice. It is a forum for the exchange of views on current international legal topics; a center for research on issues concerning international law. It publishes books and periodicals on international law and sponsors student activities in this field.

Background Desired

International law. A law degree is preferred.

How to Apply

Write to: American Society of International Law
2223 Massachusetts Ave. NW
Washington, DC   20008

Arms Control Association

The ACA tries to promote public understanding of policies and programs in respect to arms control and disarmament. It aims to get public acceptance for limiting armaments and to otherwise reduce international tensions. It puts out a monthly periodical, *Arms Control Today,* a product of the research conducted by the Association.

Background Desired

Russian and Chinese studies, military technology, disarmament studies, and research experience. An MA or PhD is preferred.

How to Apply

Write to: Arms Control Association
11 Dupont Circle NW
Washington, DC   20036

Ralph Bunche Institute on the United Nations *

This is the only American academic institution concentrating exclusively on the United Nations. For its faculty, it draws on the resources of the graduate school of CUNY as well as on Columbia and New York Universities. The institute emphasizes developing scholarship on the United Nations among graduate students and postdoctoral researchers. The latter are teamed up with scholars in various ways (e.g., coauthorship, panel discussions, manuscript reading). The aim is to develop not only current research and writing about the United Nations, but also a new generation of scholars dedicated to research about the world organization. The institute also carries on a program of seminars and workshops to promote understanding of the United Nations.

Background Desired
International relations, UN studies, conference organizing, and research. A PhD is preferred.

How to Apply
Write to: Ralph Bunche Institute on the United Nations
Graduate School and University Center
33 West 42nd St., Room 1640
New York, NY   10036

Carnegie Endowment for International Peace *

The Carnegie Endowment has as its objectives the following: the study of the causes of war and practical methods to prevent it; the development of international law and its acceptance by all nations; public education regarding the causes and prevention of war; and the acceptance of peaceable methods in the settlement of international disputes. It operates programs in **Diplomacy, International Law,** the **Changing Role of Military Force, International Organization,** and the **Advancement of International Relations Research.** In the field of international law, major activities are aimed at improving international law training in developing nations.

Background Desired
International relations, international law, foreign policy analysis, military technology, national security, international organizations, and UN studies. A PhD is preferred.

How to Apply
Write to: Carnegie Endowment for International Peace
345 East 46th St.
New York, NY   10017

or

Carnegie Endowment
58, rue de Moillebeau
1211 Geneva 19, Switzerland

Governmental Affairs Institute *

This organization programs international visitors in the fields of politics, government, information media, law, economics, agriculture, and youth activities.

Like the Public Administration Service, with which it is connected, it also engages in research dedicated to improving the quality and effectiveness of government operations, not only in the United States but overseas. One of the organizations for which it acts as a consultant is the Agency for International Development. One assignment for AID has been the **Agricultural Sector Implementation Project,** which aims to bridge the gap between planners and farmers by improving the capabilities of those developing countries concerned with agricultural and rural development. Other GAI studies have been directed at the solution of agricultural and rural development problems in developing countries.

Background Desired

Economics, economic development, Third World area studies, administration, and exchange program experience. An MA or PhD is preferred.

How to Apply

Write to: Governmental Affairs Institute
              1776 Massachusetts Ave. NW
              Washington, DC   20036

Institute for World Order

IWO's worldwide research and educational programs are aimed at building "a new global system that is peaceful, just, and ecologically secure." Inspired by the Abolitionist Movement, IWO is dedicated to the abolition of "obsolete institutions that perpetuate war, social injustice, poverty, and ecological decay, and to the construction of new ones that will help . . . realize a just world order."

Of special importance to the job seeker in the field of world order is *A Preliminary Directory of Organizations and Publications for Peace and World Order Educators,* published by IWO. The list of organizations is divided into three groups: Global/National (outside USA); United States (national); and United States (regional). The directory is available free of charge.

Background Desired

Interest in peace studies, international studies, ecology and environment, and economics. A BA is adequate for some types of work.

How to Apply

Write to: Institute for World Order
              1140 Avenue of the Americas
              New York, NY   10036

Institute of Public Administration*

IPA is one of the oldest centers for research and education in public administration and public policy analysis in the United States. Its current program is focused on three fields: urban planning and administration, application of interdisciplinary analysis to broad policy questions, and overseas technical assistance in public administration, policy analysis, and urbanism.

Background Desired

Economics, education, engineering, law, planning, political science, public administration, sociology, statistics, business administration, and international relations. A PhD is preferred.

How to Apply

Write to: Institute of Public Administration
55 West 44th St.
New York, NY 10036

or

1250 Connecticut Ave. NW
Washington, DC 20036

Interface

This organization, primarily of interest to those taking public administration, uses university resources to help solve priority problems of public agencies. Among the projects on which university talent (faculty and students) has been used are: a study of cultural needs in six Bronx community planning districts; a feasibility study for the creation of a city-wide plant information service; a directory of field experience programs at Metropolitan area colleges; and a survey of how the city's neighborhood houses could better solve their problems through the use of college students.

Background Desired

Public administration, urban studies, and sociology. An MA or PhD is preferred.

How to Apply

Write to: Interface
52 Vanderbilt Ave.
New York, NY 10017

International Center *

International Center provides assistance to international visitors facing the complexities of American life, particularly in New York City. The foreign clientele served by the center consists not only of the casual visitor but also of business people on assignment, UN employees, and officials of foreign diplomatic missions. Center services include social activities, tours, visits to American homes, conversational practice in English, advice and counseling, and help in locating housing.

Background Desired
International relations, languages, program organization, and knowledge of New York. A BA is adequate.

How to Apply
Write to: International Center
Abbey Victoria Hotel, 23rd Floor
151 West 51st St.
New York, NY   10019

International Documentation

IDOC is concerned with documents and analysis generated by Third World movements and organizations on the subject of "international justice and order." It is also involved with pertinent documentation arising out of the West. It publishes a monthly magazine, each issue devoted to a special theme. Typical themes have been oil politics and the energy crisis, the environment, repression of civil liberties and civil rights, and trends in Latin America, Asia, and Africa.

Background Desired
Journalism, economic development, Third World area studies, economics, environment, world resources, and energy studies. An MA or PhD is preferred.

How to Apply
Write to: International Documentation
145 East 49th St.
New York, NY   10017

International Peace Academy *

IPA concentrates on teaching basic practical skills associated with the achievement of peace: conflict analysis, mediation, negotiation, and the presence of an impartial third party to prevent or limit hostilities. It cooperated with educational institutions throughout the world to organize courses on conflict resolution; it conducts courses and seminars on its own on this theme; it publishes material on peace keeping; it performs research to strengthen education and training for peace; and it organizes new national committees. IPA national committees now exist in Finland, France, India, Italy, the United Kingdom, the United States, and other countries.

Background Desired
Peace studies, conflict resolution, international organizations, administration, and seminar organization. An MA or PhD is preferred.

How to Apply
Write to: International Peace Academy
              777 UN Plaza
              New York, NY   10017

National Endowment for the Humanities

The National Endowment is a national grant-making agency supporting projects of research, education, and public activity in the humanities. The humanities include "those aspects of the social sciences employing historical or philosophical approaches," which in turn have been defined as including cultural anthropology, political theory, and international relations. Only a small part of available funds is granted in the international sector, but its existence may be of interest to those of you with an international relations background.

Background Desired
International relations and experience in grant making. An MA or PhD is preferred.

How to Apply
Write to: National Endowment for the Humanities
              806 15th St. NW
              Washington, DC   20506

National Geographic Society

This is a scientific and educational organization for increasing geographic knowledge and promoting research and exploration in all parts of the world. The work of the society is much in evidence through its publication, *National Geographic.*

Background Desired

Geography studies, research ability, editing of articles, and environmental studies. A BA may be accepted.

How to Apply

Write to: National Geographic Society
1145 17th St. NW
Washington, DC   20036

New Directions

This is a political action organization hoping to influence people and legislators in a number of directions. Among the priority issues of this organization in the international field are: an increase in US assistance to developing countries in the areas of food production, rural development, health care, and family planning; reduction in arms sales overseas; and combatting the proliferation of nuclear weapons.

Background Desired

International relations, energy and environment, nuclear technology, economic development, economics, and public relations. A BA suffices.

How to Apply

Write to: New Directions
2021 L St. NW
Washington, DC   20036

New York City Commission for the United Nations *

This is the result of the recognition by the City of New York that it has responsibility for establishing the best possible relationship with personnel of the United Nations and foreign diplomatic missions. The commission therefore helps diplomatic personnel assigned to New York with any and all problems encountered, such as housing, schooling, and traffic tickets.

Background Required

International relations, international organization studies, and a thorough knowledge of New York and its bureaucracy. Legal background is helpful. A BA is adequate.

How to Apply

Write to: New York City Commission for the United Nations
809 UN Plaza
New York, NY   10017

New York State Government

New York and other state governments offer a variety of possible employments for those with international training. New York actually has overseas offices for its tourism and commerce departments, and in education has extensive employment in foreign languages, social studies, and bilingual education. For some fifteen years the State Education Department has maintained a network of small offices concerned directly with education about the Third World—**The Center for International Programs and Comparative Studies, The Foreign Area Materials Center,** and **The Educational Resources Center** (located in New Delhi, India).

Background Desired
While opportunities for permanent employment with these organizations are rare, they do sponsor a number of short-term projects, which may have employment possibilities for persons skilled in education as well as international studies.

How to Apply
Write to: New York State Education Department
             Albany, NY   12210

US Committee for UNICEF*

This organization aims to inform Americans about UNICEF and the problems of the world's children, as well as to raise funds for UNICEF. The committee produces educational material for primary and secondary schools. Major fund-raising programs include the Trick-or-Treat Halloween collections, greeting card sales, a bike-a-thon and a swim-a-thon, recycling for UNICEF, and film benefits.

Background Desired
Knowledge of UNICEF, work with children, public relations, fund raising, administration, teaching, and educational studies. A BA is adequate.

How to Apply
Write to: US Committee for UNICEF
             331 East 38th St.
             New York, NY   10016

United Service Organizations (USO)

USO, which came to prominence in World War II as a center of entertainment for the armed forces, has continued its work in peace time. About a hundred USO centers are operated in various parts of the US and in foreign countries where there are significant US forces. These "away from home" centers provide social, educational, recreational, religious, and welfare services for all service men and women. The famous USO shows offer entertainment to patients in veterans' hospitals and to the military on active duty abroad.

Background Desired
Show business (if applying for a performer's job); administration and organizational abilities for those in headquarters. A BA is adequate.

How to Apply
Write to: United Service Organizations
             237 East 52nd St.
             New York, NY   10022

US Youth Council

The goal of the Youth Council is to increase the participation of young people in democratic institutions, both in the United States and abroad. During the 1950s, it sponsored biracial student and youth conferences in the South. From its early days it has also brought young leaders from other countries to the United States to examine and participate in our institutions. More currently, it is active in helping young people in developing countries build their own representative institutions.

Background Desired
Work with students and youth, exchange program experience, and developing country studies. A BA suffices.

How to Apply
Write to: US Youth Council
             910 17th St. NW
             Washington, DC   20036

World Without War Council

The principal objective of World Without War is to establish the goal of ending war as a guiding force in American life. It believes that the United States should be a leader in demonstrating new ways of resolving international disputes without violence. The council implements its strategy through a variety of programs, including leadership training, publications, education, and analysis of current international issues. Regional offices of the organization are located in Seattle, Portland (Oregon), Berkeley (California), and Chicago.

The council is managing **The International Conflict and American Organizations Project,** which aims to bring together about 2,000 peace and world affairs organizations interested in the nonviolent resolution of international conflict. Part of this project, an inventory of the organizations concerned, will be of special interest to the job seeker in this field. Ask the council for details.

Background Desired
Devotion to the "world without war" ideal, international relations, international organizations, public relations, and peace studies. A BA is usually adequate.

How to Apply
Write to: World Without War Council
175 Fifth Ave.
New York, NY   10010

CHAPTER EIGHT

International Business and Banking

International Business

So far we have looked at nonprofit organizations, both public and private. Now we turn to quite a different world, sometimes called the "real world," where profit is the motivating force.

The two worlds, real and unreal if they exist at all in such raw terms, are similar in one important respect: Before you are offered a job in any profit or nonprofit organization, you will have been evaluated in terms of the help you are expected to give that organization in carrying out its task. The salient point on which you are judged by the employer really is: How much can this person help me to do my job? Whether the employer's job is to increase some company's international profit, increase world interest in family planning, or help some despairing refugee adapt to America, the criterion of potential usefulness is the same. But with a business, the results of your performance tend to be more measurable.

Unlike a nonprofit organization, where your performance is often difficult to evaluate (how does an employer measure your success in helping a refugee adapt to America or in making the public aware of a foreign policy issue?), business operations result in hard figures on profit and loss. If profits are lagging, the stockholders are unhappy and may call management to account. The accounting may well entail a good look at personnel and jobs. Reorganization of sections and head rolling are not uncommon as an aftermath.

What Is the Best Background?

Just because you have an international relations background does not mean that you will be a prime target for eager recruiters from companies that do substantial international business. True, you will have part of the desired background, but only *part*. Likewise, language fluency and a concentration of courses in some area of the world—say Russia or Western Europe—won't necessarily get you a job with companies doing business in that area, although by all apparent logic it should. Even though a business may be impressed with your knowledge of Russia and its language or Western Europe and your fluency in French, Spanish, German, Italian, and Portuguese, you will rarely be offered a job unless you have something more to offer.

For example, some years ago an automotive manufacturer planned to expand in Russia. Students with a Russian studies background thought they would be needed for the new undertaking. Not so. When asked why not, an official of the organization said that the best marketing experts would be negotiating with the Russians. "But how," one student asked, "can you understand the Russians without having on the negotiating team people steeped in Russian politics, economics, and history?" "No problem at all," came the reply, "We will use interpreters."

Although this provides the brightest illumination of the gap between corporate operations and the international political expert, other examples are not hard to find. Some time ago a large multinational hired a retired high ranking officer of the Department of State to analyze the implications of increasing nationalism on the company's overseas expansion plans. After two years the officer retired a second time and the organization, as far as can be determined, did not repeat the experiment.

How, you may well ask, can business not be aware of the importance to their operations of international know-how? Don't casually dismiss this attitude as idiocy. After all, if business believed that an international background in itself could increase profits, they would be foolish not to hire internationally oriented people such as yourselves. The probability is that many of these organizations have analyzed the effect on company profits of hiring one or more political experts and have concluded that the benefits do not justify the costs.

The record is not all negative, however, In a third example, a giant communications conglomerate, bruised from public disclosure of its political dealings abroad, has tried to improve its public image and prevent similar errors by starting a small unit of political thinkers headed up by a retired American ambassador.

Another repair job was undertaken by an oil company as a result of adverse publicity received during the oil crisis of the early 1970s. A great deal of research was undertaken, much of it by PhDs in political science and international relations, which has been used to improve the public image of the oil industry.

In the case of the last two organizations, creative use of internationally knowledgeable personnel came into play only as a result of crises. In the case of the multinational, a well-intentioned attempt to use international training for political forecasting apparently was not successful enough to inspire emulation. Certainly, none of the four cases provided any incentive for other large organizations to get on the international bandwagon.

The Key to Hiring

The key may well be in the amount of international business being done by a company. If the international operations of an organization become increasingly important—not only in absolute figures but also as an increasing percentage of total business—that company is likely to recognize the need for personnel with international training. In this section, we will see that this is what has been happening to most large commercial banks. As profits from international operations have increased, these banks have been hiring more and more graduates of schools of international affairs.

A related factor is the existence of an expanding pool of foreign-born personnel who are getting their training in the business schools of America. These people are bilingual, have a built-in international content, are technically trained, and understandably eager to assume responsible positions in their own countries. This explains why so few Americans are now being sent abroad for long-term assignments and why an international background for an American is less valued in the business world than you think it should be.

If you get hired for international work, then you will probably do it at US headquarters of the company, with occasional travel abroad for conferences, negotiations, or consultation. Sometimes, however, assignments to company offices and factories overseas can be arranged for shifts of several years at a time, despite the adverse trend mentioned above.

There are some signs of a policy change in favor of hiring American students with special types of international training. Occasionally, a Chinese language specialist is employed by a business trading with China, or a Japanese language expert is hired by a Japanese firm in the United States. But these are exceptions. The rule for area specialists still is: You usually don't get hired by business for your international relations and area studies alone. You need something more.

What Is This "Something More?"

Simply stated, it is the conglomerate of technical business courses: the accounting, marketing, and finance courses that the MBA brings to the job hunt. You don't have to have an MBA to receive serious consideration from some internationally oriented businesses, but you do have to have these technical courses. How many? Perhaps five or six, divided into two basic tracks: accounting-marketing and accounting-finance.

Those of you who hate numbers may be dismayed to see accounting figure prominently in both tracks. Even though no one wants to turn you into an accountant (unless you want to be one), you do have to know what the work of the accountant is. In the course of a long career in business you will find an understanding of accounting vital for the insight it will give you into overall company policy and prospects.

Marketing is the heart and guts of most businesses. It is often the main highway for fast progress up the promotional ladder. Most companies manufacture a product that has to be sold to other companies or to the consumer. This is what marketing is: sales, advertising, market research, and product management.

In this *accounting-marketing* track, the following courses, or their equivalent, are recommended: basic accounting; basic marketing; two in advanced marketing, such as international and foreign marketing, marketing research, and product management; international business; and one or two in finance, especially business finance, money and financial markets, or international investments.

The *accounting-finance* track is a bit more specialized but it has one great advantage: Not only can it be used on the financial side of business, but it will also qualify you for international banking jobs.

Recommended courses for this track are basic accounting; four or five different classes in finance, such as international finance, business finance, money and financial markets, monetary policy, corporate financial reporting, financing international transactions, money markets, or international banking. International business or intermediate accounting is also good.

Don't be sidetracked into other business courses unless you have special reasons for taking them. Courses in statistics, industrial relations, managerial behavior, economics of the firm, and the like, while interesting and beneficial, will not ordinarily help you get a job in international business. Businesses will usually judge you by how many courses you have in accounting, finance, and marketing, and then look at your international courses.

Can I Substitute International Economics for Some of These Courses?

You may think that because business and the economy are dependent on each other, economics is essential to getting a business job. Not really.

Economics is the science—often theoretical—that investigates the laws affecting production, distribution, and consumption. Understanding how the economy works is always useful, employers admit, especially as you rise in the corporate ladder. For a beginning job, however, they usually consider business courses—as listed above—more valuable than an economics background.

However, international economics courses have enormous value in many other fields and will help you get an entry-level job in government, nonprofit organizations, foundations, some banks, and almost every other line of work—except many businesses.

MBA or MA?

If you know you want a career in business and you don't much care if it's international or domestic, an MBA is better. This degree commands immediate respect from most businesses and may get you farther in the long run.

However, if the international aspect is important to you, take your chances on the MA track since your international know-how will be a solid asset when you apply for jobs. But you can maximize your chances by taking the business courses indicated above and by including in your job strategy the following:

1. *Approach with employers* When interviewing with employers, stress that you offer the best of both worlds: the basic technical business courses that MBAs offer, plus something that most MBAs do not—international know-how.

2. *Define your targets* It makes no sense to apply to companies that do very little international business. Your target rightly will be those heavily involved in the international. Better yet, consult the annual reports of the major companies and identify those organizations whose profits from international operations are growing faster than domestic profits. Zero in on these companies, since your international training will be offered just when the need for your background may be greatest.

3. *Special target: Export–import companies* Another way to capitalize on your background is to try export–import companies. There is nothing more international than the work performed by these organizations. In addition, they are usually not the target for MBAs, nor do these companies usually recruit on campus since they are small and have relatively few openings. MBAs, moreover, do not usually seek them out.

Beginning salaries are often less than those offered by the conglomerates, and the initial work may be in the stock room acquainting yourself with shipping forms, bills of lading, and other documentation you should know about. But promotion comes rapidly for the talented, and long-term career opportunities are great.

For lists of exporters and importers, consult the *American Register of Exporters and Importers,* a directory of some 30,000 manufacturers and export–import buying agencies, broken down by product class.

4. *Special target: Foreign companies in the United States* Whether these companies are businesses or banks, you will be better able to compete with the MBA if you have international training plus business–banking courses. For lists of companies, contact the Washington embassies or New York consulates of the following countries: Japan, Germany, England, Israel, Brazil, and France. One disadvantage: Your chances for advancement may be limited if the company gives priority for top assignments to its own nationals.

Training Programs

Training programs in business can vary considerably. Sometimes there is no specialized training for a new employee. He or she is ushered into an office, shown the rudiments of a job, and expected to produce.

Where training programs exist they may be small and individually tailored to the successful applicant. Others are elaborate, with each stage of training defined and organized so that a new recruit feels like a product in the process of being packaged. Generally, it can be said that the largest companies have training programs and that recruits entering them are considered to have executive potential.

The length of training may vary from several weeks to several years. In some companies, course work at school is mixed with on-the-job training. Because of the diversity of the training provided, the only typical program is the atypical one.

A rather sophisticated program we have come upon involves one year of on-the-job training in marketing or finance, depending on your specialty. During that year you will be shuttled from one section to another. In each section you may have a specific job or you may act as general assistant to the officers of the section. Occasionally, you may even be made temporary supervisor of a section so that your supervisory talents may be evaluated. At the end of the year you will be assigned a full-time job in the marketing or finance section of the company.

You will notice that no specific assignment to the international is mentioned. It will probably be included in the training program, but there is no certainty that it will be. Sometimes, even with an international academic background, you may be hired for the domestic operations of the company, with the understanding that when vacancies occur in the international you will be given special consideration.

The rest of this section deals with a few specific companies that do substantial international business. The list is obviously incomplete.

Amerada Hess

This is an integrated petroleum company engaged in every phase of the petroleum business, from finding new deposits of crude oil and natural gas to refining and marketing petroleum products.

The corporationa's exploration and production activities abroad are conducted in Canada, Abu Dhabi, Libya, and the Norwegian and United Kingdom sectors of the North Sea. Its refineries produce residual fuel oil, heating oil, gasoline, and other petroleum products.

Background Desired

Petroleum engineering, marketing, accounting, finance, business administration, and Middle East studies.

How to Apply

Write to: Amerada Hess Corporation
1185 Avenue of the Americas
New York, NY   10036

American Home Products

American Products is an important world supplier of prescription drugs, packaged medicines, household products, housewares, and food and candy products. About 40 percent of its gross sales are made in Europe, Latin America, Australia and New Zealand, Asia, and Africa. It has the following international divisions: **Ayerst International** (prescription drugs); **Boyle Midway International** (household products); **Whitehall International** (packaged medicines); **Wyeth International Ltd.** (prescription drugs); and **Prestige Group Ltd.** (housewares).

Background Desired

Marketing, finance, accounting, chemistry, physics, biology, and business administration.

How to Apply

Write to: American Home Products
685 Third Ave.
New York, NY   10017

Armco International

A wholly owned subsidiary of Armco Steel, Armco International handles the marketing of steel and metallurgical products overseas. Although involved in many parts of the world, in recent years Armco has focused on business with Russia and Eastern Europe. In fact, in these areas it offers exceptional opportunities to those with a background in international affairs, primarily because a specialization in Russian and Eastern European studies and languages—without marketing, finance, or accounting—is often enough to lead to a job offer.

Background Desired
Area studies and languages, business administration, economics, marketing, finance, and accounting.

How to Apply
Write to: Armco International
345 Park Ave.
New York, NY   10022

Bordens International

Bordens has had an uninterrupted growth record since it was established in 1967 as a separate operating division of the company. At present, international sales amount to about 20 percent of the total, and international earnings are about 25 percent of total earnings. International operations are found primarily in Europe, Canada, Asia, and Latin America.

Background Desired
Business administration, finance, marketing, and accounting.

How to Apply
Write to: Bordens International
420 Lexington Ave.
New York, NY   10017

Chesebrough–Pond's

This company is a diversified manufacturer and marketer of consumer products, including foods, children's apparel, cosmetics, fragrances, and health-care products. Some of the company's best-known brand names are Vaseline, Pond's, Cutex, Prince Matchabelli, Pertussin, and Q-tips. Overseas sales amount to about 30 percent of total sales.

Background Desired
Business administration, marketing, and accounting.

How to Apply
Write to: Chesebrough–Pond's International
33 Benedict Place
Greenwich, CT   06830

Corning Glass Works

In its worldwide operations, Corning operates seventy-eight plants, has operations or affiliates in more than twenty-five countries, and exports products to more than ninety nations. Corning produces about 60,000 different products. A large proportion of the business is in glass for electrical and electronic applications. Another substantial market area is in products used for food preparation, including Pyrex and Corning Ware.

In the mid-1960s Corning decided to increase its international operations substantially. To this end, it put increasing emphasis on exports and gained majority ownership in manufacturing facilities in many countries. It is now a multinational organization with sales outside the United States accounting for almost 40 percent of the corporate total.

Background Desired
Business administration, marketing, finance, accounting, and science.

How to Apply
Write to: Corning Glass Works
Corning, NY   14830

CPC International

CPC is a worldwide family of consumers and industrial food businesses. It has manufacturing plants in over forty-five countries. Sales and earnings from the international market are about 60 percent of total company sales and earnings. Its best-known consumer names are Hellmann's, Mazola, and

Best Foods. For industrial customers, CPC manufactures cornstarch and glucose syrups.

International operations are organized into three divisions: **CPC Europe, CPC Latin America, and CPC Asia.**

Background Desired
Business administration, marketing, and accounting.

How to Apply
Write to: CPC International
            International Plaza
            Englewood Cliffs, NJ   07632

DuPont

Because this foremost manufacturer of nylon and textiles is heavily engaged in the international market, there are many possibilities for those with an international background. Perhaps the most available positions are for those with a heavy finance and accounting background in addition to international relations. With this background you should aim for the Treasurer's Department for work in foreign financial affairs.

Foreign financial analysts in DuPont headquarters work closely with the financial officers in DuPont's foreign subsidiaries to help develop and implement financing plans for overseas investments. They establish cash utilization and dividend policies in light of prevailing economic, political, and exchange conditions. They also review foreign financial statements and forecasts. The foreign and banking staffs likewise are involved with devaluation risks of soft currencies and with assisting in financing arrangements for joint ventures.

Background Desired
Accounting and finance for jobs in the Treasurer's Department; otherwise, marketing, chemistry, science, and data systems.

How to Apply
Write to: EI DuPont deNemours & Company
            Wilmington, DE   19898

Exxon

Divisions and affiliates of Exxon operate in the United States and nearly 100 other countries. The principal business is energy, involving exploration for and production of crude oil and natural gas, manufacturing of petroleum products, and the transportation and sale of all three. Exploration for, mining, and sale of coal and uranium are other concerns of this multinational. Nuclear fuel is also produced. Foreign earnings from exploration and production of petroleum and natural gas account for about 50 percent of total earnings; foreign earnings from refining and marketing petroleum and natural gas represent about 60 percent of the total.

Background Desired

Petroleum engineering, business administration, finance, accounting, marketing, and Middle East studies.

How to Apply

Write to: Exxon
PO Box 1999
Church St. Station
New York, NY   10008

Foreign Credit Insurance Association

The FCIA was created in 1961 to place American exporters on a par with their foreign competitors. It does this by insuring US exports against commercial and political loss, allowing the exporter to offer credit terms, and facilitating the financing of his or her foreign receivables.

FCIA is an association of some fifty of the leading insurance companies in the United States operating in cooperation with the Export-Import Bank (see Chapter Five). The private insurance industry underwrites the commercial credit risks, and Eximbank covers the political risks.

Background Desired

Accounting, finance, business administration, banking, and insurance.

How to Apply

Write to: Foreign Credit Insurance Association
One World Trade Center
New York, NY   10048

General Motors

Although only about 10 percent of its total income is attributable to foreign operations, this organization, because of its size, merits consideration for those seeking an international career. GM's strongest overseas showing is in Europe, although sales in other parts of the world are considerable.

Background Desired

Business administration, finance, marketing, accounting, and personnel.

How to Apply

Write to: General Motors
3044 West Grand Blvd.
Detroit, MI 48202

Gulf Oil

Gulf's international earnings amount to about 60 percent of its total earnings, a percentage similar to that of several other major oil companies. West Africa and the North Sea have been the areas of expansion as far as new explorations are concerned. The former is Gulf's most important foreign producing area outside North America and the Middle East.

Background Desired

Petroleum engineering, finance, accounting, marketing, business administration, West African studies, and Middle East studies.

How to Apply

Write to: Gulf Oil
PO Box 2140
Houston, TX 77001

International Business Machines

IBM is the foremost manufacturer of business machines in the world. It also produces a majority of the world's computer hardware. About half of its gross income comes from its overseas operations: 33 percent from Europe, the Middle East, and Africa; 17 percent from Latin America and the Far East. Non-US operations have experienced a slightly higher rate of increase than the United States in recent years. Its subsidiaries overseas are wholly owned.

Background Desired

Business administration, computer technology, engineering, economics, science, area studies, marketing, and finance.

How to Apply

Write to: IBM World Trade Europe/Middle East/Africa
360 Hamilton Ave.
White Plains, NY 10602
or

IBM World Trade Americas/Far East
Route 9
North Tarrytown, NY   10591

International Telephone and Telegraph

ITT is a multinational as well as a multiindustry company. Its five principal product segments are:

1. *Telecommunications and electronics* ITT is the leading manufacturer and seller of telecommunications equipment outside the United States and second on a worldwide basis. This segment accounts for 33 percent of ITT's total income. The major market for this segment is Europe, which accounts for two-thirds of total volume, followed by the United States, then Latin America, Africa, Middle East, and Far East.
2. *Engineered products* ITT is a principal worldwide manufacturer of pumps, second among Europe's components and semiconductor manufacturers, and among the top ten auto parts suppliers worldwide.
3. *Consumer products and services* Included are Continental Baking, Bobbs–Merrill publishing, Sheraton Hotels, and Scott's lawn-care products.
4. *Natural resources* ITT is the world's leading producer of chemical cellulose pulp.
5. *Insurance and finance* Included is the Hartford Insurance Company.

Background Desired
Business administration, economics, area studies, telecommunications, engineering, marketing, and accounting.

How to Apply
Write to: International Telephone and Telegraph
320 Park Ave.
New York, NY   10022

Eastman Kodak

Foreign photographic sales amount to about 45 percent of Kodak's total sales. Primary manufacturing units in this field are located in England, France, Germany, Mexico, Brazil, Argentina, and Australia. The Asian, African, and Australian regions are growing faster than the Latin American region.

Background Desired

Business administration, marketing, finance, accounting, public relations, science, chemistry, and area studies.

How to Apply

Write to: Eastman Kodak
343 State St.
Rochester, NY   14650

Merck and Company

Merck is a worldwide organization engaged primarily in the business of discovering, producing, and marketing medicines and health products. The company's operations outside the United States are conducted primarily through subsidiaries and have grown over the years. Sales outside the United States, including export sales to overseas markets, amount to about 50 percent of total sales.

Background Desired

Marketing, chemistry, finance, science, accounting, and business administration.

How to Apply

Write to: Merck International Division
126 East Lincoln Ave.
Rahway, NJ   07065

Pan American World Airways

Pan Am's air transport operations serve most areas of the world from a number of US cities but have not been authorized to carry passengers moving solely within the United States. Pan Am has, however, received its first unlimited all-cargo service authority within the United States. It also carries traffic between many of the various countries it serves.

The company's principal subsidiary, **Intercontinental Hotels Corporation**, operates or invests in hotels in forty-eight countries on six continents. Some are wholly or partially owned, some operated under leases, and others under franchise arrangements.

Background Desired

Marketing, finance, accounting, public relations, business administration, air transport, and aeronautical engineering.

How to Apply
Write to: Pan American World Airways
             Pan Am Building
             New York, NY   10017

Pepsi-Cola

In addition to soft drinks, Pepsi is now heavily into snack foods, transportation, and sporting goods. Soft drink sales of Pepsi International exceed the growth rate of the domestic soft drink market. Pepsi snack foods have also made a significant dent in the international market. Latin America has been an area of substantial growth in both drinks and foods, but emphasis in the future is expected to be put on Africa, which the company believes represents a major commercial development potential.

Background Desired
Business administration, economics, accounting, finance, marketing, public relations, and area studies.

How to Apply
Write to: Pepsi-Cola
             Anderson Hill Road
             Purchase, NY   10577

Pfizer

Pfizer is a worldwide research-based company with primary interests in health care products, including pharmaceuticals, medical and dental specialties, and orthopedic devices. It also has a line of animal health products, and seed and poultry genetic operations. It has almost 150 production facilities in over forty countries. About 60 percent of its personnel are engaged in operations outside the United States.

Background Desired
Marketing, business administration, accounting, finance, chemistry, science, and biology.

How to Apply
Write to: Pfizer, Inc.
             235 East 42nd St.
             New York, NY   10017

RJ Reynolds Industries

RJ Reynolds is still primarily a cigarette manufacturing company but it has diversified significantly in other fields as well. **RJ Reynolds Tobacco International** directs RJR's tobacco operations outside the United States. The company manufactures its cigarette brands in more than twenty countries and sells them in more than 140. It manufactures cigarettes in foreign countries either at its own plants or through licensing agreements. In addition, it exports some of RJR's domestic brands.

In 1969 Reynolds acquired **Sea-Land Service**, the world's largest containerized shipping company. Sea-Land ships products door-to-door in the same sealed container by combinations of ship, train, and truck.

Reynolds has also entered the petroleum business with its 1970 acquisition of American Independent Oil Company and its 1976 acquisition of Burmah Oil. Reynolds likewise manufactures and sells food and beverage products—notably Hawaiian Punch and Patio Mexican foods—in the United States and abroad.

Background Desired
Marketing, finance, business administration, and accounting.

How to Apply
Write to: RJ Reynolds Industries
Reynolds Blvd.
Winston Salem, NC 27102

Texaco

Texaco's operations are worldwide, encompassing the production, transport, refining, and marketing of oil and gas products. Texaco has extended its interests into some 135 countries.

Texaco and its subsidiaries and affiliates abroad are staffed largely by nationals of the countries concerned, although some opportunities exist for Americans who wish to work abroad.

Background Desired
Geology, marketing, accounting, engineering, and sometimes language fluency, in German, French, Italian, Spanish, or Portuguese.

How to Apply
Write to: Texaco, Inc.
PO Box 52332
Houston, TX 77052

J. Walter Thompson Co.

This company is the largest advertising agency in the world, employing over 5,000 people in about thirty countries. It offers a full range of creative, marketing, media, research, and related communications services to its clients. Among the latter are many of the large mutinationals. Most of its overseas offices are in Europe, although Central and South America and the Pacific/Asia region are well covered.

Background Desired
Marketing, accounting, business administration, English, languages, design and layout work, and media and public relations.

How to Apply
Write to: J. Walter Thompson
            420 Lexington Ave.
            New York, NY   10017

Toyoda America, Inc.

Toyoda America is a wholly owned American subsidiary of Toyoda Kaisha, Ltd. It imports and exports steel and other metals, textiles, industrial products, bicycles, foodstuffs, and cotton. The company plays such roles as shipping agent, purchasing agent, retailer, distributing agent, marketing research firm, and negotiating agent.

Background Desired
Marketing, trade, finance, accounting, business law, and Japanese studies.

How to Apply
Write to: Toyoda America, Inc.
            One World Trade Center
            New York, NY   10048

Union Carbide

In addition to the manufacture of batteries and antifreeze products, Union Carbide has now diversified into other fields: foamed plastics, electronic materials, biomedical systems, pollution abatement systems, energy, food, and pesticides.

Overseas earnings now represent about one-third of total company earnings. International operations are divided into **Union Carbide Pan**

America, Union Carbide Europe, Union Carbide Eastern, Union Carbide Africa and Middle East, and Union Carbide Canada.

Background Desired
Business administration, marketing, finance, accounting, science and technology, engineering, and area studies.

How to Apply
Write to: Union Carbide
270 Park Ave.
New York, NY   10017

An additional list of companies that ordinarily welcome résumés from those with international training and an accounting–marketing or accounting–finance background follows, as does a list of companies with special interest in trade with Russia and with Eastern European countries.

Increasing opportunities may be available for Chinese language and area specialists as China–US trade develops. Follow the financial pages of newspapers to find out which companies are doing substantial business with China.

If you wish to pinpoint targets in a specific country, refer to the invaluable *Directory of American Firms Operating in Foreign Countries,* Eighth edition, compiled by J. L. Angel (New York World Trade Academy Press, Simon & Schuster, 1975). It lists by country all the American firms with subsidiaries and branches in that country. Finally, refer to the bibliographies for directories of businesses and banks.

Other International Businesses

(Marketing and/or Finance)

Allied Stores Marketing Corporation

American Metal Climax (AMAX)

American Home Products

American Importers Association

American Foreign Insurance Association

American International Underwriters Corporation

American Machine & Foundry

Arabian American Oil Company

Elizabeth Arden

Associated Metals & Minerals

Avon Products

Bache & Company

Bell & Howell

Boyle Midway International

Brazilian Government Trade Bureau

Brunswick International

Burlington Industries

Caltex Petroleum

Cargill

Canada Dry

CBS Records International

Celanese Corporation

Chrysler Corporation

Clairol, Inc.

Colgate Palmolive

Continental Can Company

Continental Grain

Council of the Americas

Crompton & Knowles Corporation

East–West Trade Council

Farrell Lines

Ford Motor Company

Fortune Magazine

Fund for Multinational Management Education

General Cable

General Electric

Gibney International

General Telephone & Electronics International

WR Grace & Company

Frank B. Hall & Company

Walter E. Heller Overseas Corporation

Hertz, Inc.

IBM World Trade

International Basic Economy Corporation

International Economic Policy Association

International Flavors & Fragrance

International Paper Company

International Telephone & Telegraph

Intsel

Intertex

Johnson & Johnson

Journal of Commerce

KLM Royal Dutch Airlines

Koppers, Inc.

Kurt Orban Company

Lehman Brothers

Lever Brothers

Liggett & Myers

Litton Industries

MBA Resources

Merrill, Lynch, Pierce, Fenner & Smith

Metropolitan Life

Mitsubishi International

Mobil Oil Company

National Cash Register

North American Phillips

Olin Matheson

Olivetti Corporation

Owens–Illinois

JC Penney Company, Inc.

Phillip Morris International

Phillips Petroleum

Revlon, Inc.

Richardson–Merrill

Schering Plough

JE Seagram and Sons, Inc.

Sperry Hutchinson

Sterling Products

ER Squibb & Company

Tesoro Petroleum

Towers, Perrin, Forester & Crosby

Trans World Airlines

Uniroyal

US Gypsum

US–Japan Trade Council

Vick International

Webster, Johnson & Stowell (WJS, Inc.)

Westinghouse Electric

Xerox

US Companies with Special Interest in Russian and East European Trade

American Express Company
65 Broadway
New York, NY 10004

Arthur Anderson & Company
1345 Avenue of the Americas
New York, NY 10019

Armco International
345 Park Ave.
New York, NY 10022

Bank of America
Bank of America Center
San Francisco, CA 94120

Brown and Root, Inc.
4100 Clinton Drive
Houston, TX 77020

Caterpillar Tractor Company
100 NE Adams St.
Peoria, IL 61602

Chase Manhattan Bank
One Chase Manhattan Plaza
New York, NY 10005

Chemical Construction Corporation
(CHEMICO)
One Penn Plaza
New York, NY 10001

Citibank
399 Park Ave.
New York, NY 10022

Continental Grain
277 Park Ave.
New York, NY 10017

Cooper Industries
First City National Bank Building
Houston, TX 77002

Dow Chemical Company
Midland, MI 48640

EI DuPont deNemours & Company
DuPont Building
Wilmington, DE 19898

Englehard Minerals & Chemicals
Corporation
299 Park Ave.
New York, NY 10017

General Electric Company
570 Lexington Ave.
New York, NY 10022

General Motors
3044 West Grand Blvd.
Detroit, MI 48202

Hewlett–Packard Company
1501 Page Mill Rd.
Palo Alto, CA 94304

Honeywell, Inc.
2701 4th Ave. South
Minneapolis, MN 55408

IBM
Old Orchard Rd.
Armonk, NY 10504

Ingersoll–Rand Company
200 Chestnut Ridge Rd.
Woodcliff Lake, NJ 07675

International Harvester Company
401 N. Michigan Ave.
Chicago, IL 60611

Manufacturers Hanover Trust
350 Park Avenue
New York, NY 10022

Occidental Petroleum Corporation
10889 Wilshire Blvd.
Los Angeles, CA 90024

Pan American World Airways, Inc.
Pan Am Building
New York, NY 10017

Pepsico, Inc.
Anderson Hill Road
Purchase, NY 10577

Pullman Corporation
200 S. Michigan Ave.
Chicago, IL 60604

Satra Industrial Corporation
475 Park Ave. South
New York, NY 10016

US–USSR Trade & Economic Council
280 Park Ave., 33rd Floor
New York, NY 10017

Business-Servicing Organizations

Don't forget to include in your job hunt organizations that service business in one form or another: (a) the institutes that represent a whole industry, such as **American Petroleum Institute, American Bureau of Metal Statistics, Aerospace Industries Association;** (b) the outfits that provide information and analysis of legislative programs important to business, such as the **Chamber of Commerce;** (c) the organizations that perform research for business with international interests, such as **Business International;** (d) and the organizations that provide briefings for business people and their families going abroad as well as briefings for US ambassadors, such as the **Business Council for International Understanding.**

These organizations are sometimes technically not-for-profit but, with the exception of the Business Council for International Understanding (listed in the chapter on nonprofit organizations), are included here because they are either subsidized by business or at least immediately related to industry.

American Petroleum Institute

The API fosters foreign and domestic trade in American petroleum products and promotes in general the interests of all branches of the petroleum industry.

Background Desired
Economics, statistics, and petroleum engineering or other petroleum background.

How to Apply
Write to: American Petroleum Institute
2101 L St. NW
Washington, DC   20037

American Bureau of Metal Statistics

The bureau collects and publishes statistics on the production, marketing, and consumption of copper, lead, and other nonferrous metals. In general, it aims to aid the worldwide nonferrous metals industries.

Background Desired
Economics, statistics, business administration, and knowledge of the metals industry.

How to Apply

Write to: American Bureau of Metal Statistics
420 Lexington Ave.
New York, NY   10017

Aerospace Industries Association

This association offers guidance to the exporting segment of the aerospace industry. It also provides for an exchange of views between government and industry in order to increase aerospace exports.

Background Desired

Economics, business administration, public relations, trade, and knowledge of the aerospace industry.

How to Apply

Write to: Aerospace Industries Association
1725 De Sales St. NW
Washington, DC   20036

American Management Association (AMA)

The AMA is a membership organization for all types of management development. Through conferences, workshops, and publications, it provides a forum for members to exchange ideas concerning management education. It has many divisions, one of which is the **International Management Division**, geared to executives responsible for overseas operations and coordination with overseas affiliates.

Background Desired

Business administration, economics, management and personnel training, conference and seminar organization, public relations, and work in publishing.

How to Apply

Write to: American Management Association
135 West 50th St.
New York, NY   10020

Chamber of Commerce of the United States

The Chamber of Commerce keeps its members informed of important legislative programs with national and international significance. Among the latter are international economic policy and relations, and international energy and/or environment decisions.

Background Desired
Business administration, economics, Congressional lobbying, and energy and environmental training or experience.

How to Apply
Write to: Chamber of Commerce of the United States
1615 H St. NW
Washington, DC   20036

Business International

BI publishes a wealth of reports based on its own research on problems of interest to internationally oriented business. Among these are: compensation surveys; management monographs; short- and medium-term forecasts for every region of the world as well as for individual country markets; and in-depth research reports on Europe, Africa, the Middle East, Europe, and the Western Hemisphere. Offices are located in New York, Geneva, Hong Kong, and Tokyo.

Background Desired
Economics, business administration, research ability, and area and country studies.

How to Apply
Write to: Business International
One Dag Hammarskjold Plaza
New York, NY   10017

Management Consultants, Public Relations Firms, and Other Business-Oriented Organizations

These kinds of organizations may interest you enough to include them in your job hunt, although an international affairs background may not be sufficient to get you hired.

In the first place, specializations, not necessarily international, may be required. If a management consultant firm, for example, contracts with a foreign government to revise its tax structure, it will form a team of experts to do the job. Experienced economists, taxation specialists, and financial experts will be hired in addition to an international affairs specialist. But in almost all cases these people have to be immediately productive. Because there is no training period, they usually have to arrive on the job with years of experience in their field. Unless needed to service the team, a junior professional without substantial experience is not likely to be considered.

Similarly, in a public relations firm, experienced public relations experts are used. Still, despite this obvious drawback for the neophyte, contact these firms if you have specific motivation for the career they represent. A PhD is generally preferred, unless you have long years of experience.

If you are interested in consulting work, one of the best sources of job openings is a knowledge of consulting firms that are given contracts by US government agencies. A listing of consultants awarded such contracts—with types of projects—is carried frequently in the *Federal Register*, a daily publication of the US Government Printing Office. Additional information is provided in *Consultants and Contractors: A Survey of the Government's Purchase of Outside Services*, prepared by the Subcommittee on Reports, Accounting, and Management of the Committee on Governmental Affairs, US Senate, August 1977. This report can be bought from the Government Printing Office for $4.50.

The following pages include only a few random examples of consulting organizations. For a listing of directories of consultants, refer to the bibliographies.

Louis Berger International

This firm has been involved at one time or another in transportation and urban planning in the Middle East, environmental planning and water resources in the United States, railroads in Africa, information systems in Iran, and agricultural improvements in Central and South America.

Background Desired
Economics, urban and social planning, architecture, economic development, engineering, area studies, and world resources.

How to Apply
Write to: Louis Berger International, Inc.
100 Halsted St.
East Orange, NJ 07019

Cresap, McCormick, and Paget

This management consulting firm, with overseas offices in England, Australia, and Brazil, performs services to corporations, retail enterprises, manufacturers, banks, medical centers, universities, and government. Services include corporate development, marketing functions, management systems, personnel, retailing and consumer services, and health and education services.

Background Desired
Business administration, finance, marketing, accounting, economics, personnel, health, and education.

How to Apply
Write to: Cresap, McCormick, and Paget
245 Park Ave.
New York, NY   10017

William E. Hill and Company

This firm, a wholly owned subsidiary of Dun and Bradstreet Companies, is a general management consulting firm providing services in corporate planning, including acquisitions and mergers, technology planning, marketing services, organization, and compensation. These services are provided for both US and foreign clients.

Background Desired
Business administration, economics, marketing, finance, and accounting.

How to Apply
Write to: William E. Hill and Company
640 Fifth Ave.
New York, NY   10019

Promethean Corporation

This consulting firm provides services mainly to exporters interested in trade with Eastern Europe and Africa. Among the services performed are: expediting transactions ordinarily burdened with red tape and delays; marketing and technical assistance; transportation and insurance; financing; contracts and contacts; and promotion of overseas sales.

Background Desired
African and Eastern Europe studies and languages, marketing, economics, and business administration.

How to Apply
Write to: Promethean Corporation
815 Ritchie Highway
Severna Park, MD   21146

Robert R. Nathan Associates

RRNA specializes in economic consulting. It conducts foreign and domestic development studies and provides counsel to governments, international agencies, businesses, and labor clients. Its work in developing countries includes macro- and microeconomic studies in overall planning, sector studies, and project feasibility studies.

A sampling of RRNA activites includes: development plans for countries in Asia and Latin America; fiscal and monetary advice to many countries; studies on agriculture, transportation, industry, education, health, and labor, primarily in Asia and Latin America; and studies of the impact of European trade preference on Latin American trade.

Background Desired
Economics, economic development, area studies, trade, labor, agriculture, finance, and business administration. A PhD is preferred.

How to Apply
Write to: Robert R. Nathan Associates
1200 18th St. NW
Washington, DC 20036

Carl Byoir and Associates

This is a public relations firm with overseas offices in Frankfurt, Paris, and London, and affiliates in Japan, South Africa, Canada, Australia, and many countries in Europe, the Middle East, and Latin America.

The names of its departments pretty well define the scope of Byoir activities: **Financial Services; Research; Magazine–Book; Consumer Affairs; Graphics; Pictorial News Photo Services; Travel and Tourism; Sports; TV, Radio, Film; Womens' Interests;** and **Editorial Direction.**

Byoir's main function is to present a favorable public image of its clients through all devices and media.

Background Desired
Public relations, marketing, communications, publishing, journalism, editing and writing, research, and languages.

How to Apply
Write to: Carl Byoir and Associates
International Public Relations Consultants
800 Second Ave.
New York, NY 10017

Organization Resources Counselors, Inc.

ORC concentrates its efforts on human relationships in organizations. Drawing on its knowledge of personnel practices of many overseas companies, ORC offers counseling to organizations with large numbers of third-country and foreign national employees. It also conducts seminars and training courses in the United States and abroad dealing with current aspects of international employee relations activities.

Background Desired
International affairs, personnel studies, psychology, and business administration.

How to Apply
Write to: Organization Resources Counselors, Inc.
1270 Avenue of the Americas
New York, NY   10020

International Banking

In recent years international banking has been one of the best sources of jobs for students of international affairs. This may sound surprising, but there is a good explanation for it. Beginning in the 1960s, the international earnings of some banks have grown faster than their domestic earnings, and as this happened, these banks have turned increasingly to schools of international affairs for their young talents.

Is This Trend Likely to Continue?
Opinions vary. According to some economists, the days of large-scale lending to developing countries may be coming to an end. Amounts of loans to these countries by commercial banks are levelling off and the International Monetary Fund seems to be resuming its old role as a major source of such financing. In addition, some banks fear that the loans they earlier made to developing countries may not easily be repaid.

Because of these uncertainties, you should inform yourself about international banking prospects when you start your job hunt. A placement office or instructor in banking subjects of a university might be a good source for this information. Also get copies of the latest annual reports of large banks, such as Citibank and Chase Manhattan, and compare their current and past international earnings.

What Kinds of Banks Offer the Best Chances for International Work?
You should focus your job hunt on the following:

1. *Commercial banks* Citibank, Chase Manhattan, Bank of America, Chemical Bank—they are all heavily involved in international business. Their normal work, of course, is to handle checking accounts for individuals and to make loans to business.

2. *US branches of foreign banks* This is a relatively new field and a growing source of jobs, whether or not commercial banks reduce their international hiring. The increasing number of these banks, such as the Swiss Bank and the Bank of Tokyo, stems in part from legislative changes making it easier for foreign banks to do business in New York, and also from an increase in investments by foreign companies in American manufacturing concerns.

If you are interested in the investment side of banking, include investment banks, such as Goldman Sachs and Salomon Bros., on your job search. These banks provide financing for business by floating their stocks and bonds. They are less visible than other banks because they usually do not deal directly with the public.

Savings banks and savings and loan associations offer fewer opportunities for you because of the lack of international content of most of their work.

Overseas Assignments and Languages

Only in the case of the largest commercial banks—such as Bank of America, Citibank, and Chase Manhattan—is a substantial part of your career likely to be spent overseas. In other cases, you will ordinarily do your international work at US headquarters.

For this reason, language proficiency is particularly valued at the largest banks, where assignments abroad are expected, or at American branches of foreign banks.

Entry-Level Jobs

Your initial assignment in international commercial banking is liable to be full-time academic course work—in the case of the largest institutions—or academic work mixed with on-the-job training in the case of smaller institutions.

In both cases, the thrust of your training will be to acquaint you with procedures and problems in the evaluation of applications for loans. Since credit analysis is the heart of much commercial banking, there will be stress on accounting procedures, problems of finance, and money and banking practices.

When training is over, you may be assigned as a loan investigator or credit analyst, depending on the credentials you bring with you. After some years of creditable performance, you may reasonably expect to become a branch bank manager.

An MBA is not necessarily the best degree to get for international work at a bank. If you have a Masters in international affairs, or the equivalent, from one of the schools mentioned in Chapter One and have taken the accounting–finance courses suggested for business, you will often fare better than the MBA—except at investment banks. These banks still prefer the MBAs, since ordinarily business school graduates will have had more intensive training in finance and investment.

The happy fact is that commercial banks are usually more flexible about the background required of applicants than are businesses. This flexibility extends beyond the conventional accounting-finance courses to include economics and a general international affairs background—depending on the bank.

Which Banks Require What Background?

The flexibility of background requirements often varies in proportion to the size of the bank and the comprehensiveness of its training program. Citibank and Chase Manhattan, which offer extensive training programs, are more relaxed on the academic qualifications of candidates than are the smaller banks with limited training facilities.

In other words, even if you have not taken accounting and finance courses, you may still be given serious consideration by the largest financial institutions. The theory on which these banks operate is that it is easier to teach finance and accounting to applicants who have an international affairs background than it is to teach international affairs to students equipped with the basic technical courses in banking. A few other banks, such as Chemical Bank, Bank of America, and Wells Fargo, will accept an economics background in lieu of banking courses.

Many large banks publicize their interest in finding the best "human being" rather than the graduate with the best technical background. They will send campus recruiters who majored in English or biology, perhaps to deemphasize the importance of conventional accounting and finance studies. Still, when you look at the statistics of those hired by these banks, you will find that the large majority of successful candidates have had courses in finance and accounting.

Smaller banks may be forgiven for requiring that you have technical banking courses before they will interview you. Since they do not have the training facilities of the largest banks, they want you to be fully productive as soon as you come on board.

Note: Many of you who are attracted to international banking because of the availability of jobs may not belong in this career. Before you blithely scramble into position be sure you know what you're doing. And that means, as we have seen, find out—through reading, experimenting, and talking with friends and relatives in banking—what it's like and if it's right for you.

BA—MA—MBA—PhD? A Summary

For international business the optimum degrees, in order of preference, are:

1. MBA, or MA in international affairs with accounting and finance courses (your chances increase if you select your targets as indicated earlier in this chapter)

2. BA (for lower-level jobs)
3. PhD (be prepared to answer the question: "Why are you applying for a business job when you seem to have prepared yourself for teaching or research?")

For international commercial banking they are:

1. MA in international affairs with accounting and finance courses
2. MBA (ranks first for investment banking)
3. BA (as above)
4. PhD (as above)

The rest of this chapter is devoted to a listing of some major banks, primarily commercial, with international interests.

Bank of America

This is the world's largest privately owned banking organization, with more than $50 billion in assets and more than 1,100 offices worldwide. Retail banking—services to the individual—remains the largest area of its business, but the bank increasingly services businesses and institutions. Its **World Banking Division** provides wholesale banking services to large organizations on a global basis.

The bank has built a vast global network of branches, subsidiaries, affiliates, and representatives throughout the world. This network provides the conventional commercial services plus some unusual financing possibilities: from leasing capability in Japan to special centers for money management in London, Singapore, and Panama. It is divided into four geographic departments: **Asia Division; Europe, Middle East, and Africa Division; Latin America Division;** and **North America Division.**

Background Desired
Usually accounting and finance, but economics is also acceptable, and occasionally a background limited to general international studies.

How to Apply
Write to: World Banking Division
              Bank of America
              PO Box 37020
              San Francisco, CA   94137

Bankers Trust

This is the nation's seventh largest bank, with assets of over $20 billion. From its first international offices established in the 1920s in London and

Paris, it now has a network of branches, subsidiaries, and representative offices throughout the world.

Background Desired
Accounting and finance studies and/or economics, plus international affairs.

How to Apply
Write to: International Banking Department
             Bankers Trust Company
             1 Bankers Trust Plaza
             New York, NY   10006

Brown Bros. Harriman and Company

Brown Bros. Harriman has provided a full range of commercial banking services for over 150 years. It is also an investment manager and adviser, corporate finance specialist, securities broker, short-term money investor, foreign exchange adviser, and investment research house.

Its **International Banking Department** helps American corporations with their international expansion plans, aids foreign interests with direct investment in the United States, and provides them with international financial assistance. Though committed to correspondent banking relationships abroad, Brown Bros. Harriman is directly involved in offshore money and capital markets through its London affiliate and a branch office in the British West Indies. In Zurich a wholly owned subsidiary serves investment clients throughout Western Europe.

Background Desired
An MBA, preferably with a specialty in finance.

How to Apply
Write to: Brown Bros. Harriman and Company
             59 Wall St.
             New York, NY   10005

Chase Manhattan

Commercial banking remains a priority with Chase, although its services to corporations and institutions are growing. It has a worldwide network of 107 branches, twenty-two representative offices, and forty-four affiliates in more than 100 countries. Banking relationships have recently been established with the Soviet Union and with the People's Republic of China. In the last few years, Chase's international earnings have more than tripled.

Chase has a prodigious training program, perhaps the most complete in the banking world. Rigorous training in academic subjects pertinent to banking has lasted up to eighteen months. Because of the thoroughness of the work, some students do not finish the program, either by their own choosing or at the request of the bank. Those who do finish the work find themselves desirable commodities on the job market should they wish to leave Chase. Smaller banks without training facilities often try to hire these Chase trainees, who on graduation need no further training to be fully productive.

Background Desired
General international background, plus finance and accounting or economics.

How to Apply
Write to: Chase Manhattan Bank
1 Chase Manhattan Plaza
New York, NY 10015

Chemical Bank

The name "Chemical" comes from the company's original purpose, the manufacture of chemicals in 1824. Since then, Chemical has emerged into the "complete" bank for the consumer. It has expanded internationally until recently its international loans amounted to about 40 percent of total loans.

It has offices in twenty-six countries, and there is a likelihood that additional offices will be established. Latin America is the bank's oldest international market, with the result that today there is a broad market penetration in every major country in the area. Its first European branch, in London, opened in 1960 and the company's business in Western Europe has developed rapidly. Although the bank has emphasized business with multinational companies in Europe, its relationships with indigenous companies in the area have grown. Asia and the Middle East are becoming increasingly important to Chemical; in Africa, its business is conducted primarily through a network of correspondent banks. Its first African office has been opened in the Ivory Coast.

Background Desired
Banking and finance or economics, plus international affairs.

How to Apply
Write to: Chemical Bank
20 Pine St.
New York, NY 10005

Continental Illinois Corporation

CI Corp is a bank holding company and **Continental Bank** is its main subsidiary. The corporation operates 126 units in thirty-nine countries.

Through its **International Banking Department**, Continental acts as a multinational bank, attracting deposits, making loans, and providing other financial services to promote trade and investment. Its network of branches and subsidiaries extends to Europe, Asia, Latin America, Africa, and Australia. Lending officers provide international services to US and foreign customers; they also travel to various parts of the world to sell bank services to corporations and governmental entities. The International Banking Department also operates domestic subsidiaries in New York, Los Angeles, and Houston that specialize in international trade and overseas financing. The New York unit includes one of the major foreign exchange trading operations in the world.

Background Desired
Banking and finance subjects, or economics, plus international affairs.

How to Apply
Write to: International Banking Department
Continental Illinois Corporation
231 South La Salle St.
Chicago, IL   60693

First National City Bank (Citicorp and Citibank)

Citicorp is a holding company, with Citibank as its principal subsidiary. It does business in about 100 countries with more than 300 offices outside the United States.

Citicorp's overseas activities are encompassed by the Consumer Services Group, the International Banking Group, the Merchant Banking Group, and the World Corporation Group.

The **Consumer Services Group** has an Overseas Division that services the financial needs of individuals throughout the world. It focuses on ten key markets: Germany, England, Belgium, Australia, Brazil, Hong Kong, France, Italy, the Philippines, and Puerto Rico.

The **International Banking Group** is responsible for Citibank's overseas branches, representative offices, subsidiaries, and affiliates in fourteen countries that are not the responsibility of other banking groups. It provides a broad range of financial services to corporations, financial institutions, and the public sector in countries outside the United States. The IBG is organized into geographic divisions, each responsible for a group of countries and managed by a division head.

The **Merchant Banking Group International Division** provides international merchant banking services through a network of twenty-two offices, subsidiaries, and affiliates in fourteen countries. Principal international services include loan syndication and the underwriting and trading of international securities.

The **World Corporation Group** provides credit and financial services to 450 of the leading multinational corporations whose global operations require integrated account management. WCG stations account officers in twenty-six countries near each multinational customer's headquarters.

To show the expansion of the company's international activities, Citicorp has changed from basically a New York bank with overseas branches into a global financial services organization. International earnings have grown each year, increasing from $58 million in 1970 to $313 million in 1977. In this latter year, international activities accounted for 82 percent of Citicorp's operating earnings.

Most of Citicorp's overseas loans are in highly developed and industrialized countries. Only a small percentage of loans are in developing countries.

A Citibank career is the closest to a foreign service career outside of the Department of State. The company has branches in as many countries as the Department of State has embassies. Employees in the World Corporation Group and the International Banking Group spend a large part of their careers overseas, receiving frequent changes of assignment. Also like the State Department, area and language specializations, though often respected, are no guarantee of an assignment in a particular part of the world.

Citibank recruits on many US college campuses. It has positions each year for the BA, the MBA, and the MA, especially with a specialization in international affairs. It will interview PhDs in political science, but any PhD candidate for a Citibank job should be prepared to answer the question: "How do we know you are really interested in a banking career when there is nothing in your résumé to suggest such an interest?"

Successful candidates will spend several months in New York headquarters for technical training and briefings on the Citicorp global network. After this initial training, new appointees will be assigned to one of Citibank's overseas regional offices: Mexico City (for Central and South America); Manila (for Asia, Pacific, and Africa); Athens (for the Middle East and North Africa); and London (for Europe, Canada, and Australia). After several months of training in one of these regional centers, an employee will be assigned to a Citicorp bank in that region.

Background Desired
A generalist international background will probably get you an interview, but economic or accounting–finance studies combined with international training will get you a more serious hearing.

How to Apply
Write to: First National City Bank
             399 Park Ave.
             New York, NY   10043

French–American Banking Corporation

This corporation is a wholly owned American subsidiary of the Banque National de Paris. With its $25 billion in assets and about 2,000 branches, agencies, affiliates, and representative offices in sixty countries, the BNP is the largest French and European bank and the fourth largest bank in the world.

It works closely with foreign governments and European and American companies, offering all of them a full range of loan, investment, and correspondent banking services. It focuses particularly on financing foreign trade and is active in the Eurocurrency market.

Background Desired

Banking, finance, accounting, and economics, plus international affairs. An MBA is preferred.

How to Apply

Write to: French–American Banking Corporation
120 Broadway
New York, NY   10005

Goldman Sachs

Goldman Sachs is one of the world's leading international investment banking firms, providing a variety of financing services to corporations, governments, and investors around the world. It has fourteen offices: in the United States, London, Tokyo, and Zurich.

Goldman Sachs raises capital in the United States and overseas for governments, their agencies, and US and foreign corporations. It uses the following major capital markets for international borrowers: the US long-term public bond market; private placement with US institutional investors; the commercial paper market; the international capital market, the largest segment of which is the Eurobond market; and project financing.

Background Desired

Finance, accounting, banking, and economics. An MBA is preferred.

How to Apply

Write to: Goldman Sachs
55 Broad St.
New York, NY   10004

Irving Trust Company

Like many other banks, Irving's international earnings have been increasing until now they represent about 60 percent of the corporation's income.

The **International Banking Group,** which conducts all the bank's overseas business, consists of three divisions and three functional departments:

The **International Corporate Banking Division** develops and serves the international banking needs of multinational and major foreign-based corporations. It is also responsible for Irving branch offices in foreign financial centers.

The **International Correspondent Banking Division** serves as a conduit to US business for foreign banks throughout the world. It is also responsible for representative offices in Europe, Asia, and Latin America.

The **International Operations Division** handles foreign credit activities.

The **Foreign Exchange Trading Department** provides foreign exchange trading and information to customers.

The **International Investments Department** supervises Irving's investments in foreign countries.

The **International Planning Department** examines the bank's opportunities in international markets for new products, services, and capital expansion.

An important aspect of the International Banking Group's work involves international financing, both short- and medium-term, to banks, corporations, and governments. Another is to translate US economic conditions and banking procedures to overseas customers.

Background Desired
Banking and finance and economics, in addition to international studies.

How to Apply
Write to: Irving Trust Company
1 Wall St.
New York, NY 10015

Marine Midland Bank

The bank's international operations produce about one-third of its total operating income. The bank has facilities in Beirut, Bogota, Buenos Aires, Caracas, Frankfurt, Hong Kong, Jakarta, London, Madrid, Manila, Mexico City, Nassau, Panama City, Paris, Rio de Janeiro, Rome, São Paulo, Seoul, Singapore, Sydney, Tehran, and Tokyo. In addition to a broad range of credit services, international activities include money management services covering foreign exchange, Euro-deposit business, and other money market instruments. An international treasury services group provides custom counseling on all corporate money matters.

Background Desired
Banking and finance and economics, plus international affairs.

How to Apply
Write to: Marine Midland Bank
              140 Broadway
              New York, NY   10015

Manufacturers Hanover Corporation

About 50 percent of the operating income of Manufacturers Hanover comes from foreign operations. Only a small percentage of its foreign loans is in less-developed countries, while the major share is centered in industrial countries. The corporation is sanguine about the quality of credits to non-oil-producing developing countries, an attitude attributed to an improvement in the economic health of these countries.

Overseas branches exist in England, Bahrain, Rumania, Egypt, Germany, Hong Kong, the Philippines, Italy, Nassau, Singapore, Japan, and Switzerland. Representative offices are located in Greece, Thailand, Lebanon, Colombia, Argentina, Venezuela, Scotland, Indonesia, Malaysia, Peru, Spain, Mexico, Kenya, Norway, France, Brazil, El Salvador, Australia, and Iran.

Background Desired
Banking and finance, economics, and area studies.

How to Apply
Write to: Manufacturers Hanover Corporation
              350 Park Ave.
              New York, NY   10022

Morgan Guaranty Trust Company

Morgan Guaranty is a wholly owned subsidiary of JP Morgan and Company. The bank is the fifth largest in the United States in terms of assets. It has, however, fewer customers than any other large bank because it is a "corporate" bank—its clients are predominately corporations and institutions. Only a few individuals—in the United States and abroad—with substantial income and assets are serviced. Its offices are in London, Paris, Brussels, Antwerp, Amsterdam, Frankfurt, Düsseldorf, Munich, Zurich, Milan, Rome, Tokyo, Hong Kong, Singapore, and Nassau. It has representative offices in Madrid, Beirut, Sydney, Jakarta, Kuala Lumpur, Manila, São Paolo, and Caracas.

Its **International Banking Division** is organized by area as well as by specialized departments, such as **Foreign Exchange, International Money Management, Commodities and Export,** and **International Currency and Eurocurrency Trading.**

Background Desired
Banking and finance and economics. An MBA is preferred.

How to Apply
Write to: Morgan Guaranty Trust Company
              23 Wall St.
              New York, NY   10015

First National Bank of Boston

The international activities of this bank now account for about one-third of total corporate earnings. Over 3,000 employees work in the bank's international network. Branches, offices, and wholly owned subsidiaries are located in Argentina, Brazil, Panama, Venezuela, Costa Rica, Uruguay, Dominican Republic, Bolivia, Haiti, Nassau, Mexico, England, France, Germany, Spain, Luxembourg, Iran, Japan, Hong Kong, Singapore, and Australia. Most kinds of financial assistance are offered to overseas customers as well as to US clients: export and import financing, project financing, foreign exchange, letters of credit, and money transfer operations.

After an initial training program, candidates are assigned to Boston, New York, or an overseas office.

Background Desired
Banking and finance, economics, and area studies (Latin America).

How to Apply
Write to: First National Bank of Boston
              100 Federal St.
              Boston, MA   02110

              or

              International Divison
              First National Bank of Boston
              767 Fifth Ave.
              New York, NY   10022

Philadelphia National Corporation

The **International Banking Group** of the corporation engages in: foreign banking and international financing activities, including making loans to foreign banks, governments, and multinational corporations; letter-of-credit financing; foreign exchange trading; and related financial services. Besides its head offices in Philadelphia, the group maintains offices in Nassau and Luxembourg, and representative offices in London, Manila, São Paulo, Panama City, Tehran, and Sydney.

The Banking Group includes not only the international division of the Philadelphia National Bank but also two wholly owned subsidiaries of the bank; The **Philadelphia International Bank,** headquartered in New York, which provides international banking services to foreign and multinational clients; and the **Philadelphia International Investment Corporation,** headquartered in Philadelphia, which engages in foreign investment and financing activities. During the mid-1970s, the earnings of the group from international activities have increased markedly until now they represent about one-third of the corporation's total income.

Background Desired
Banking and finance and international relations, with economics.

How to Apply
Write to: Philadelphia National Corporation
              PO Box 7618
              Philadelphia, PA   19101

United California Bank

UCB has a growing **International Division** with more than thirty branches, representative offices, and merchant banking activities in fifteen countries. The international services performed for foreign and multinational corporations include import–export financing, international payment services, and foreign exchange facilities.

Background Desired
Banking and finance, international relations, and economics.

How to Apply
Write to: United California Bank
              630 Fifth Ave.
              New York, NY   10020

Wells Fargo International

Wells Fargo International is a wholly owned subsidiary of Wells Fargo in California. It provides complete international commercial banking facilities in New York. These services include receiving deposits from those living outside the United States and from those in the United States if the funds are used for international purposes. It also handles letters of credit, collections, remittances, dollar clearings, and foreign exchange.

Background Desired
Banking and finance and/or economics, plus international affairs.

How to Apply
Write to: Wells Fargo International
40 Wall St.
New York, NY 10005

Following is a more complete listing of banks, primarily commercial and with international interests, as well as a list of major *foreign* banks located in New York. As indicated earlier, these banks should be a major target for those of you who have international training, language proficiency, and accounting–finance courses.

Other International Banks

Bank of Boston
Bank of Montreal
Bank of New York
Bank of Nova Scotia
Barclay's Bank
Crocker International Bank (California)
Export–Import Bank of the United States
Federal Reserve Bank (New York)
Federal Reserve Bank (Washington)
Fidelity Bank of Philadelphia
First Boston Corporation
Kuhn Loeb

Mellon Bank International
Moody's Investor Service
National Bank of North America
North Carolina National Bank
Republic National Bank of New York
Smith Barney
State Street Bank, Boston, International
Swiss Bank Corporation
United States Trust Company of New York
White Weld & Company
Barron's

Major Foreign Banks in New York

Algemene Bank Nederland N.V.
Allied Irish Banks Ltd.
Argentine Banking Corporation
Atlantic Bank of New York
Baer American Banking Corporation
Banca Commerciale Italiana

Banca Nazionale Del Lavoro
Banco de Bogota Trust Company
Banco de Ponce
Banco di Napoli
Banco di Roma
Banco di Sicilia

Banco do Brasil Sociedade Anonima

Banco Popular de Puerto Rico

Bank Hapoalim, B.M.

Bank Leumi Trust Company of New York

Bank of Montreal Trust Company

Bank of Nova Scotia Trust Company

Bank of Tokyo Trust Company

Banque de L'Union Europeenne

Banque Francaise du Commerce Exterieur

Banque Nationale de Paris

Barclays Bank International, Ltd.

Barclays Bank of New York

Bayerische Hypotheken und Wechsel-Bank, Akt.

Bayerische Vereinsbank (Union Bank of Bavaria)

Berliner Handels-Und Frankfurter Bank

Canadian Bank of Commerce/Trust Company

Chinese American Bank

Credit Commercial de France

Credit Industriel et Commercial

Credit Lyonnaise

Credit Suisse

Credito Italiano

Dai-Ichi Kangyo Bank, Ltd.

Daiwa Bank Trust Company

Deutsche Bank AG

Deutsche Genossenschaftsbank

Dresdener Bank Aktiengesellschaft

European–American Bank and Trust Company

French American Banking Corporation

Fuji Bank and Trust Company

Governor and Company of the Bank of Ireland

Habib Bank, Ltd.

Hongking & Shanghai Banking Corporation

Industrial Bank of Japan

Israel Discount Bank, Ltd.

Israel Discount Trust Company

Korea Exchange Bank

Kredietbank N.V.

Lloyds Bank International, Ltd.

Long-Term Credit Bank of Japan, Ltd.

Mitsubishi Bank, Ltd.

Mitsui Bank, Ltd.

National Bank of Pakistan

National Westminster Bank, Ltd.

Nederlandische Middenstandsbank N.V.

Nippon Credit Bank, Ltd.

Nordic American Banking Corporation

Philippine National Bank

Royal Bank of Scotland, Ltd.

Royal Bank and Trust Company

J. Henry Schroder Bank and Trust Company

Standard Chartered Bank, Ltd.

State Bank of India

Sumitomo Bank, Ltd.

Swiss Bank Corporation

Toronto Dominion Bank and Trust Company

Toyo Trust and Banking Company, Ltd.

UBAF Arab American Bank

UMB Bank and Trust Company

Union Bank of Switzerland

United Americas Bank

United Bank, Ltd.

Westdeutsche Landesbank Girozentrale

Yasuda Trust and Banking Company, Ltd.

CHAPTER NINE

International Communications

The term "communications" in this handbook covers print or newspaper journalism, radio and TV broadcasting, and magazine and book publishing. All three areas have certain features in common. For one thing, they pay considerably less to the beginner than government, the United Nations, business, or banking. Low salaries almost seem to be a test of motivation and dedication, qualities that are essential for most careers in communications. Small salaries may also ward off the dilettante attracted to this field by its apparent glamour, although in reality there is just as much tedium and nitty gritty in a beginning communications career as in many others.

A second feature common to print journalism, broadcasting, and publishing is that you may have to put your international training on the back burner during the initial stages of your career. The reasons for this vary by occupation. In the case of *journalism* and *broadcasting,* international news is covered mainly by the large metropolitan dailies and broadcasting stations. Reporting jobs in these organizations are practically nonexistent for the beginner. If upon graduation you apply to *The New York Times* or NBC, you will likely be advised to get a job on a small town newspaper or broadcasting station and accumulate some experience before trying out for "the big time."

Your initial job in the boondocks may be in obits, sports, or local news, but hardly in international. After a few years you may progress to a small metropolitan paper or station where your international background will still be of peripheral interest to your employer. It is only later—with five years or more experience—that you will be considered for a reporting job with a large metropolitan paper or station. Even then, don't expect immediate recognition of your international background. If you do land a job with the *Times* or the Associated Press, for example, it doesn't mean you will soon be sent abroad as a foreign correspondent or even work in headquarters on international news. These jobs are plums usually reserved for those who have made names for themselves after some years in New York.

The above represents the norm for newspapers and broadcasting. As we have stressed before, there are always exceptions. If your father is the boyhood friend of the managing editor of a large paper, you may be able during your junior year to land a summer job that can blossom into a reporting job when you graduate. Or an even more unlikely event—if you have command of an exotic language at a time when a news service is desperately in need of someone with that language fluency for an overseas office, you may be hired. It would be wise to recognize, however, that the chances of this happening are slim indeed.

In the case of *book publishing,* you may have to put your international training on hold for quite another reason. The international business of most publishers, although growing, is still small. Accordingly, there is usually only limited value placed on your international background. Your chances improve if you apply to the following types of publishers:

1. *Firms that specialize in medical, scientific, and technical books.* These are the best selling books overseas. The international sales of these companies may amount to as much as 40 percent of total sales.

2. *Firms that have foreign subsidiaries.* These are especially good targets if some of the employees come from the United States.

Your entry job will most likely involve selling or assisting in the editing of books for the American market. But even in houses where the international may only amount to a small percentage of total business, there is still international work to be done. Once you are on the payroll—even if it is on a strictly domestic job—you can probably maneuver a transfer to the international division when a vacancy arises.

The largest publishers have an International Sales Manager at headquarters who is responsible for placing books of that house in the bookstores of foreign countries. Also at headquarters, there is likely to be a Subsidiary Rights Department responsible for licensing foreign rights, including translations.

The procedure for marketing books abroad depends on the size of the company. The largest companies employ agents overseas to sell their books or translation rights to foreign publishers. Smaller US publishers without overseas agents may send copies of books and galley proofs to foreign publishers in order to effect sales. The annual Frankfurt and London Book Fairs provide occasions for book publishers of all countries to sell books they control, as well as negotiate translation rights. In addition, there is a Children's Book Fair held every year in Bologna, Italy.

Background Desired

To prepare yourself for a long-range international career in *journalism or broadcasting,* take courses in journalism as well as international affairs. Make them joint specializations. At least one journalism course should be practical, i.e., it should include exercises for covering a story and then submitting your article to a presumed editor a few hours later.

Courses in economics can be most helpful. So few economists can make their science understandable to a wide public that if you can write economics-oriented stories that are informative and enjoyable you may well find yourself a national treasure.

An internship at a local paper, wire service, or broadcasting station will also be extraordinarily illuminating. Besides, it will look very good on your résumé even if the experience does not lead to a job upon graduation.

If you can't find a paid job and you intend to go abroad anyway, contact any of the wire services or major dailies to see if you can become a "stringer." You will not be on the regular payroll, but you can submit stories and articles and get paid for those that are accepted. Chances of being a "stringer" are obviously better if the wire service or newspaper to which you are applying does not have a regular correspondent in the country where you plan to be. This background also adds strength to your résumé.

If qualifications other than the above are needed for journalism and broadcasting, the additional background desired will be noted in individual cases. The background desired for *publishing* will be covered later in the chapter.

Travel Abroad and Languages

If you do land an internationally oriented job in publishing, you will usually work in the United States, with perhaps an occasional short trip abroad. In contrast, foreign correspondents of the wire services and large metropolitan dailies spend the majority of their careers overseas. A tour of duty abroad may last many years, depending on the area of assignment. If you are assigned overseas, language proficiency is, of course, a great asset.

As in the other chapters, we will list only a few random examples of newspapers, broadcasting stations, and publishers.

Print Journalism

United Press International

UPI has six international divisions with headquarters in London (Europe/Africa/Middle East), Hong Kong (Asia, Anzac), Buenos Aires (South America), Mexico City (Mexico and Central America), San Juan (the Caribbean), and Montreal (Canada). It has eighty-one offices abroad with a staff of almost 600 engaged in international operations.

How to Apply

Write to: United Press International
220 East 42nd St.
New York, NY   10017

Associated Press

AP has more than 2,500 staffers in sixty foreign offices and 108 cities in the United States. More than 10,000 newspapers and radio and TV stations in over 110 countries receive AP news and pictures each day. It is the oldest and largest news agency. As Mark Twain once said, "There are only two forces that can carry light to all corners of the globe—the sun in the heavens and the Associated Press down there."

When you apply, you will probably be given a written exam to test your ability to write a story for the newspaper-reading public.

How to Apply

Write to: Associated Press
50 Rockefeller Plaza
New York, NY   10020

The Chicago Tribune

The Chicago Trib has four full-time foreign correspondents: one based in Berlin, one in Moscow, and two in London (one to cover Great Britain; the other, the Middle East). In addition, it uses part-time correspondents and "stringers" for coverage in other parts of the world.

How to Apply

Write to: *Chicago Tribune*
Tribune Tower
435 North Michigan Ave.
Chicago, IL   60611

The Los Angeles Times

The *LA Times* covers all major areas and countries with its nineteen full-time foreign correspondents: Athens, Bangkok, Bonn, Brussels, Buenos Aires, Cairo, Hong Kong, Jerusalem, Johannesburg, London, Mexico City, Moscow, Nairobi, New Delhi, Paris, Rome, Tokyo, Toronto, and the United Nations.

How to Apply

Write to: *Los Angeles Times*
Times Mirror Square
Los Angeles, CA   90053

The New York Times

The *Times* has its own network of foreign correspondents in major foreign capitals and also engages in the worldwide syndication of news and features.

How to Apply

Write to: *New York Times*
229 West 43rd St.
New York, NY   10036

The Washington Post

The *Post* has twelve foreign correspondents based in major capitals. The foreign bureaus are located in London, Paris, Bonn, Addis Ababa, Buenos Aires, Tokyo, Hong Kong, Beirut, Moscow, Cairo, Bangkok, and Jerusalem.

How to Apply

Write to: *Washington Post*
            1515 L St. NW
            Washington, DC   20005

The Christian Science Monitor

The *Monitor* publishes not only daily North American editions, but also a weekly international edition, which is printed in London and distributed worldwide. The *Monitor's* international news bureaus are located in Bonn, Beirut, Hong Kong, Latin America, London, Moscow, Nairobi, Paris, Tokyo, and the United Nations.

How to Apply

Write to: *Christian Science Monitor*
            1 Norway St.
            Boston, MA   02115

The New York Daily News

The *News* has only sporadic international coverage, but from time to time it does announce career openings for degree candidates as well as a limited number of summer internships for undergrads. Among these have been: administrative assistants; sales development (training program in advertising space sales); editorial trainees (trainees rotate through various editorial activities and, usually within eighteen months, receive permanent assignments in one of the paper's divisions); staff accountants.

How to Apply

Write to: *New York Daily News*
            220 East 42nd St.
            New York, NY   10017

Knight-Ridder Newspapers, Inc.

Knight-Ridder publishes over thirty daily newspapers located from coast to coast. Its range is from papers with a half million circulation—*Detroit Free Press, Miami Herald, Philadelphia Inquirer*—to those with less than 25,000—*Boca Raton News, Aberdeen American News*. Knight-Ridder also controls **Poole Broadcasting Company**, which operated several VHF television stations.

How to Apply

Write to: Knight-Ridder Newspapers, Inc.
One Herald Plaza
Miami, FL 33101

Capital Cities Communications

Capital Cities owns newspapers, broadcasting stations, and a publishing house, all operating from coast to coast. Its newspapers include the *Kansas City Star Times* and the *Oakland Press,* among others; its broadcasting includes TV and radio stations; and its **Fairchild Publications** include *Women's Wear Daily,* the *International Medical News Group,* the *Supermarket News,* and the *American Metal Market.*

Background Desired
For the publishing division: business administration, English, and editing.

How to Apply
Write to: Capital Cities Communications
485 Madison Ave.
New York, NY 10022

New England Press Association

The association represents the interests of the community press of New England, whether a small town, large town, city, suburb, or county. Its membership from the six-state area is made up of weekly, semiweekly, triweekly, and daily newspapers.

For the internationally trained student looking for a job, two of the association's services are of special interest:

1. NEPA arranges for newspaper leaders in New England to make study missions abroad in important countries so that on their return they can inform the American public "what people are really like" overseas.

2. NEPA has a placement service, which acts as a clearing house and registration headquarters for newspapers seeking personnel as well as for individuals looking for jobs.

How to Apply
Write to: New England Press Association
Northeastern University
360 Huntington Ave.
Boston, MA 02115

Newspaper Fund

The fund is a foundation that aims to encourage talented young people to enter news careers. Its programs serve the news industry by locating minority-member journalists and new editors, by encouraging excellence in journalism teaching at the high school level, and by providing information about journalism career opportunities. The following programs cover these needs: **Editing Internship Program, Reporting Internship Program, Teacher Fellowship Program, Journalism Teacher of the Year Selection, Urban Journalism Workshops, Urban Writing Competition, Editor-in-Residence Program, Career Advertisement Program,** and **Career Information Program.**

How to Apply

Write to: Newspaper Fund
PO Box 300
Princeton, NJ   08540

National News Council

The NNC is a nonprofit organization that aims to preserve freedom of communication and promote fair news reporting. It receives, investigates, and reports on complaints involving the accuracy and fairness of news stories disseminated by the nation's major print and electronic media. It also reviews attempts to restrict access to information that is of public interest.

How to Apply

Write to: National News Council
1 Lincoln Plaza
New York, NY   10023

Time Magazine

If you are lucky enough to get a reporting job at *Time*, whether through long apprenticeship in the provinces or through some fortuitous event upon graduation, you may not have to wait as long for an international assignment as if you were with a newspaper. Your international background may even be crucial in your hiring, and your apprenticeship at headquarters accordingly relatively short.

In addition to reporting and writing jobs, *Time* has a sizable research staff that may be of interest to you. The magazine's research functions are broken down by geographic area, economics, and other functional subjects. There is some turnover in these jobs because promotion possibilities are limited.

Background Desired

For research: international affairs, area studies, and international economics.

How to Apply

Write to: *Time*
1271 Avenue of the Americas
New York, NY   10022

☆

Newsweek Magazine

Same as for *Time* above.

How to Apply

Write to: *Newsweek*
444 Madison Ave.
New York, NY   10022

☆

Public Relations News

The *News* is geared to management and public relations executives in the United States and abroad. It provides information on all aspects of public relations and keeps its subscribers current with developments in this field.

How to Apply

Write to: Public Relations News
127 East 80th St.
New York, NY   10021

☆

Women's International Network News

WIN's purpose is to establish a worldwide communication system for women of all backgrounds, ages, and nationalities. Its *News* publication is said to carry "all the news that is fit to print by, for, and about women."

Background Desired

Publishing, editorial work, English, and interest in women's periodicals.

How to Apply

Write to: Women's International Network News
187 Grant St.
Lexington, MA   02173

Editor and Publisher

E and P, the weekly newsmagazine of the newspaper industry, is often referred to as the "newspaperman's newspaper." Its coverage includes activities of all departments of US newspapers, including news and editorial, advertising, circulation, business, promotion, personnel, and public relations. *E and P* also publishes the *International Year Book*.

How to Apply

Write to: *Editor and Publisher*
850 Third Ave.
New York, NY   10022

Facts on File

Facts on File publishes a reference work of world happenings that is available at schools and libraries. Weekly updatings of this material are undertaken by a staff of researchers whose functions are broken down into geographic areas.

Background Desired

For research: area studies, international economics, and foreign policy.

How to Apply

Write to: Facts on File
119 West 57th St.
New York, NY   10019

Broadcasting

American Broadcasting Company

ABC has five divisions: the **Radio Network**, the **TV Network**, **Radio Owned and Operated Stations**, **TV Owned and Operated Stations**, and **International**. Each of these divisions has the same purpose: the sale and/or programming of air time.

How to Apply

Write to: American Broadcasting Company
1330 Avenue of the Americas
New York, NY   10019

Columbia Broadcasting System

CBS began as a radio broadcasting service in 1927 and today operates one of the nation's three commercial TV networks, five TV stations, a nation-wide radio network, and fourteen AM and FM radio stations.

Three key CBS businesses are international in scope: recorded music, musical instruments, and publishing. **CBS Records International Division** handles all international record business for CBS; the **International Publishing Division** does the same for CBS publishing; and the international marketing of musical instruments is carried out by various divisions within the **CBS/Columbia Group**. International Publishing was formed to give the domestic divisions of the publishing group a single unified overseas arm. In addition, International Publishing publishes original material. Its overseas operations are concentrated in Latin America, Canada, the United Kingdom, and Australia.

Background Desired
For publishing and records: marketing, business administration, area studies, languages, editing, and music.

How to Apply
Write to: Columbia Broadcasting System
51 West 52nd St.
New York, NY   10019

National Broadcasting Company

The scramble for jobs in NBC parallels that in ABC and CBS. Even those with a Master's degree sometimes start as pages or tour guides and then get in line for higher-level jobs when they open up. The progression is usually from tour guide or page to copy boy or clerical, then to research, and from there to news writing and production. NBC has a division that sells TV shows abroad (marketing is a helpful background for this type of job), and another division that prepares international reports. A third target for the internationally trained student is the NBC office that bids for contracts for installing TV stations abroad (marketing would also be a curriculum asset for this kind of work).

How to Apply
Write to: National Broadcasting Company
30 Rockefeller Plaza
New York, NY   10020

TV Information Office

This office provides reference and information services; publicizes programs of special interest; conducts research on public attitudes toward television; and issues publications and audiovisual materials on the structure and operations of the industry. Financial support comes from commercial and educational TV stations.

Background Desired
Public relations, research ability, publishing, statistics, and poll taking.

How to Apply
Write to: TV Information Office
745 Fifth Ave.
New York, NY   10022

Broadcasting Foundation of America (BFA)

BFA is a nonprofit organization whose purpose is to invite nations through-out the world to share their art, music, cultural, and traditional materials with the American people via taped radio programs. Some fifty countries in Europe, Asia, Africa, South America, and the Middle East participate in BFA's work. In addition to providing these programs to commercial and educational radio stations in the United States, BFA services with its tapes the Armed Forces, secondary schools, colleges, and universities.

Background Desired
Art and cultural studies, music.

How to Apply
Write to: Broadcasting Foundation of America
52 Vanderbilt Ave.
New York, NY   10017

International Radio and Television Society

There are three educational projects under the IRTS banner:

1. **Faculty/Industry Seminar** Here major decisionmakers of broadcasting and government meet with faculty from many universities for the purpose of sharing information on developments in radio and TV.

2. **College Conference** This is the largest of the foundation-funded projects. Panels and seminars are held for college-level Juniors and Seniors to provide them with an inside view of the radio and TV business.

3. **Internship Program** This is a summer program for a selected few students, which acquaints them with the industry through seminars and lectures.

Background Desired
Educational studies, seminar and conference organization, public relations.

How to Apply
Write to: International Radio and Television Society
             420 Lexington Ave.
             New York, NY   10017

Board for International Broadcasting

BIB oversees the operations of **Radio Free Europe** and **Radio Liberty**. The former is beamed to the peoples of Eastern Europe and the latter to the USSR. Together they broadcast almost 1,000 program hours weekly in twenty-two languages. A multilingual staff of some 1,800 is employed, and an estimated daily audience of some 18,000,000 in six countries is reached. RFE/RL also engage in area and audience research.

Background Desired
Eastern European and Russian languages, translating, and research ability.

How to Apply
Write to: Board for International Broadcasting
             1030 15th St. NW
             Washington, DC   20005

Corporation for Public Broadcasting

The corporation is a private organization largely supported by federal funds. Its mission is to help develop an American noncommercial public radio and TV system that will "inform, enlighten, entertain, and enrich the lives of people."

Among its responsibilities are: to stimulate diversity, excellence, and innovation in programs; to advance the technology and application of delivery systems; to safeguard the independence of local licensees; and to act as trustee for funds appropriated by Congress or contributed to CPB by other sources.

CPB is also responsible for determining the potential audience's priority needs and interests.

Background Desired

Research ability, engineering, sampling polls and surveys, and law.

How to Apply

Write to: Corporation for Public Broadcasting
1111 16th St. NW
Washington, DC   20036

Channel 13

Channel 13 is both a producer and broadcaster of TV programs. Its most visible producing partnership, the MacNeil/Lehrer Report, is a staple of national public television. The Dick Cavett Show is a cultural equivalent of the issue-oriented Report. Channel 13 also has an international division that is concerned with international programming and research.

Background Desired

Area studies, research ability, program production and planning.

How to Apply

Write to: Channel 13
356 West 58th St.
New York, NY   10019

American Women in Radio and Television

AWRT is a nonprofit organization of professional women in the broadcast industry and allied fields. The goals of the organization are to provide a medium of communication and exchange of ideas, to promote the advancement of women in broadcasting, and to try to improve the quality of radio and TV.

Among the services provided to members is an **International Broadcasters Program** that hosts foreign women broadcasters who wish to explore US broadcasting systems and techniques. There is also an **International Study Tours Program** that provides opportunities for US women in the industry to study foreign broadcast facilities and advertising methods.

Background Desired

Exchange program experience and public relations.

How to Apply

Write to: American Women in Radio and Televison
1321 Connecticut Ave. NW
Washington, DC   20036

Book Publishing

Many hundreds of firms in the United States are engaged in book publishing, and each year many thousands of books are published. The three major types of publishing are: general or "trade" books, sold in bookstores for the general reader; books for professionals, e.g., doctors or lawyers; and books for schools and colleges.

Types of jobs in book publishing are:

Editorial At the bottom of this ladder is the editorial assistant, who often is 50 percent secretary and 50 percent editor's helper. Typing skills are usually required. The job may sound menial and may often be just that, but it should not be sloughed off if you are really motivated for a publishing career. Promotion can be rapid if your editing skills are of a high order. After that you can become an assistant editor with full-time editorial assistant duties, then associate editor and editor with full responsibility for a manuscript.

Designing This job has responsibility for any artwork required, the selection of all typefaces, and the cover of the book.

Production This covers all arrangements for composition, printing, binding, and packaging.

Marketing This involves not only selling the book but advertising, promotion, research, and supervision of field sales managers.

Training Programs

One or two of the largest publishing houses have training programs of several months duration for a few BA or graduate degree students. If you are lucky enough to be selected for such a program, you will spend a few weeks in each of the following areas: production, sales, subsidiaries (including foreign rights), publicity, book stores, and one of the editorial groups of the company. A background in English literature or the social sciences is considered desirable. Try Doubleday in particular.

Background Desired

Unless otherwise specified, the ideal backgrounds for breaking into publishing are as follows: for editorial jobs—journalism, English, writing, and editing; for design jobs—artwork and designing; for production work—printing and typesetting; and for international work—business administration, marketing, sales, advertising, public relations, and languages (particularly French, German, and Spanish). Special backgrounds desired for individual cases will be noted.

Association for American Publishers

AAP is a confederation of several hundred publishers of books of all types. Its goals are to represent book publishing and educational publishing to the general public and to government, as well as to provide members with information concerning trade conditions, markets, copyright issues, manufacturing processes, taxes, duties, censorship movements, government programs, and other matters of importance to publishers.

How to Apply

Write to: Association for American Publishers
1 Park Ave.
New York, NY   10016

Crowell, Collier, and Macmillan, Inc.

In addition to book publishing, Crowell, Collier is engaged in: (a) home-study schools, some of them international (**British Institute of Engineering Technology, Metropolitan College**); (b) instruction, some of it international (**Berlitz** and the **Cleaver-Hume Language Laboratory**); (c) music publishing; (d) audiovisual materials; (e) retailing of books, some of it international (**Claude Gill Books, Duckett, Ltd.**); and (f) paper converting abroad (**Metropolitan Paper Works**).

Background Desired

Music, marketing, business administration, and educational studies.

How to Apply

Write to: Crowell, Collier, and Macmillan, Inc.
866 3rd Ave.
New York, NY   10022

Fawcett Publications

This organization is one of the largest paperback book publishers in the world; it is also a leader in the consumer magazine field (*Woman's Day, True Magazine*).

How to Apply

Write to: Fawcett Publications
Fawcett Place
Greenwich, CT   06830

Harcourt Brace Jovanovich, Inc.

HBJ is a highly diversified organization. It is composed of five groups: **The University and Scholarly Publishing Group** includes the **Academic Press** (with an office in London) and the **HBJ International Division,** which distributes HBJ books and materials abroad. Publishing houses are also located in Toronto, Montreal, and Australia.

The **Popular Enterprises Group** is comprised of **Sea World,** which manages marine parks in California and Florida. Surveys are being made in Japan and Puerto Rico to determine the feasibility of establishing similar marine parks.

The **School Materials and Assessment Group** includes textbooks, audiovisual materials, psychological tests, and research into school curricula.

The **Periodicals and Insurance Group** includes organizations that publish farm periodicals and sell various kinds of insurance.

The **General Publishing and Broadcasting Group** includes bookstores, a TV station, a consulting firm, a printing company, and United Media International, which publishes newsletters.

Background Desired

Marketing, business administration, finance, area studies, educational studies, public relations.

How to Apply

Write to: Harcourt Brace Jovanovich, Inc.
757 Third Ave.
New York, NY 10017

McGraw-Hill

There are four McGraw-Hill units:

The **Book Company** includes not only books but also films, tapes, records, home-study courses, and school science kits.

The **Publications Company** publishes magazines and newsletters and is involved in opinion research.

The **Informations Systems Company** markets technical information services as well as military specifications in microfilm form.

Standard and Poor's Corporation provides financial information on most large corporations. It also offers computer services, including one that can supply almost instantaneous financial analysis.

Background Desired

For Standard and Poor's: finance, accounting, business administration, and computer programming.

How to Apply

Write to: McGraw-Hill
1221 Avenue of the Americas
New York, NY 10022

National Geographic Society

The **Book Service** and **Special Publications** divisions of the society prepare illustrated books ranging over a broad spectrum of interests, from ancient Greece and Rome to American inventors.

The society's cartographers are well known for the quality of their maps, and the *National Geographic Atlas of the World* is a standard reference work. *The National Geographic Magazine* is perhaps the most popular product of the society.

Background Desired
Geography, area studies, anthropology, cultural studies.

How to Apply
Write to: National Geographic
1145 17th St. NW
Washington, DC   20036

Prentice-Hall, Inc.

Prentice-Hall serves both a domestic and international market with its textbooks for all levels of education. It also produces fiction and nonfiction trade books, legal and business loose-leaf compilations, and tax and business newsletters for the professions.

How to Apply
Write to: Prentice-Hall
Englewood Cliffs, NJ   07632

Unipub

Unipub is a central source for specialized international publications. It began as the US distributor for publications of UN agencies, but its service has continued to expand until now it handles the output of many more organizations that publish works of international interest. Its offerings are particularly comprehensive in the fields of energy, food supply, education, environment, human rights, and economic development.

Unipub also publishes *IBID—International Bibliography, Information, Documentation.* An annotated quarterly journal, *IBID* reports on the entire publishing output of the UN system and other international bodies.

How to Apply
Write to: Unipub
Box 433
Murray Hill Station
New York, NY   10016

Xerox Publishing Division

This organization is composed of five companies operating in various sectors of publishing in the United States and abroad:

1. **RR Bowker Company,** which publishes trade magazines, such as *Publishers Weekly* and *Library Journal.*
2. **University Microfilms International,** which provides microfilm copies of issues of more than 11,000 periodicals, some dating back to the eighteenth century.
3. **Ginn and Company,** which publishes a wide variety of textbooks and programs.
4. **Xerox Education Publications,** which publishes classroom periodicals, such as *Know Your World, Current Events,* and *My Weekly Reader.*
5. **Xerox Learning Systems,** which develops and markets training and professional development programs. It also offers consulting services for developing training programs in individual companies and government agencies.

Background Desired
Educational studies, personnel management, management consulting.

How to Apply
Write to: Xerox Publishing Division
One Pickwick Plaza
Greenwich, CT   06830

RR Bowker Company
1180 Avenue of the Americas
New York, NY   10036

University Microfilms International
300 North Zeeb Road
Ann Arbor, MI   48106

Ginn and Company
191 Spring St.
Lexington, MA   02173

Xerox Educational Publications
245 Long Hill Road
Middletown, CT   06457

or

Xerox Learning Systems
One Pickwick Plaza
Greenwich, CT   06830

Reference Works

Directories and reference works with listings of newspapers, periodicals, and publishers are found in the bibliographies.

CHAPTER TEN

Teaching at Home and Abroad

There are two types of opportunities for those with an international background who want to teach. The first is to teach international subjects at home; the second is to teach American subjects abroad.

If you wish to teach international subjects at home, you have probably specialized in political science, international economics, languages, area studies, or history. Teaching jobs in any of these subjects are difficult to find. If you are aiming at college- or university-level teaching, a doctorate in the discipline of your choice is essential. If you are interested in junior colleges or secondary schools, an MA may be sufficient, although even here a PhD will occasionally be needed. In any case, work through past instructors and any professional associations to get leads to the few job openings that develop in your field.

Special Tips

If you want to teach abroad, you must first be a teacher in the United States—or at least have the necessary credentials. It is rare indeed that you will be hired for an overseas assignment unless you have some teaching experience. Assuming, then, that you have met this requirement, two questions arise: How do I find out about overseas teaching opportunities? and How do I go about applying?

Let's look at procedures first.

When you are being seriously considered for a job, your potential employer will ask for a copy of your dossier. Therefore, even before you start looking for a job, establish your credentials—i.e., arrange to have transcripts and letters of recommendation on file at your college placement office, or in your own possession. It is often acceptable practice to send the material yourself to an overseas school. Since it is easier to let your college take care of these administrative details, however, you will probably thankfully leave this chore in their hands.

There are three main sources of teaching jobs overseas: (1) Department of Defense Overseas Dependents Schools; (2) overseas American elementary and secondary schools assisted by the Department of State; and (3) schools established by American business for the dependents of their employees. There are other sources of jobs, however, and we will discuss these under the all-embracing Other Opportunities.

A tour of duty abroad averages one or two years, depending on the area of assignment. In general, proficiency in the particular foreign language is not required.

Department of Defense Dependents Schools

Overseas dependent schools of the Department of Defense are located in the Azores, Bahamas, Belgium, Bermuda, Cuba, Denmark, England, Germany, Greece, Iceland, Italy, Japan, Korea, Midway Islands, Morocco, Netherlands, Bahrain, Newfoundland, Norway, the Philippines, Scotland, Spain, Taiwan, Turkey, and West Indies.

Background Desired

Among the qualifications for teaching positions, unless otherwise noted below, are: eighteen semester hours in professional teacher education courses, a valid teaching certificate, and at least one year's full-time teaching experience within the past five years (practice, student, and substitute experience do not qualify).

How to Apply

Write to: Office of Overseas Dependents Schools
Department of Defense
2461 Eisenhower Ave.
Alexandria, VA   22331

DOD Dependents Schools
European Region
APO New York   09164

DOD Dependents Schools
Pacific Region
APO San Francisco   96553

or

DOD Dependents Schools
Atlantic Region
Naval Education and Training Program Development Center
Pensacola, FL   32509

Overseas American Schools Assisted by the Department of State

There are over a hundred of these schools, which educate the dependents of US government personnel stationed overseas. These schools have either binational or international student bodies.

How to Apply

Write to: Office of Overseas Schools
Department of State
Washington, DC   20520

Schools Established by American Businesses

These schools are operated by American companies that employ substantial numbers of Americans overseas.

How to Apply

Write to corporate headquarters. Among such companies are:

United Fruit Company
Prudential Center
Boston, MA   02199

Anaconda Company
25 Broadway
New York, NY   10004

Exxon
1251 Avenue of the Americas
New York, NY   10020

Gulf Oil Corporation
Gulf Building
Houston, TX   77001

Orinoco Mining Company
525 William Penn Pl.
Pittsburgh, PA   15230

Firestone Tire and Rubber Company
Akron, OH   44317

Arabian American Oil Company
505 Park Ave.
New York, NY   10022

Texaco, Inc.
135 East 42nd St.
New York, NY   10017

Other Opportunities

Canal Zone Government

Even though American control of the Canal is passing out of existence, presumably the Canal Zone government, an independent agency of the US government, will continue until the twenty-first century to operate schools for its employees' dependents. These schools are on all levels: kindergarten, elementary, junior high school, senior high school, and college.

Background Desired

The Canal Zone government is one of those rare exceptions—it does not require teaching experience except for jobs at the college level.

How to Apply

Write to: Panama Canal Company
US Recruitment Section
Personnel Operating Division
Box 2012
Balboa Heights
Canal Zone

International Schools Services

The ISS provides educational services for American schools overseas. Among these services are recruitment and recommendation of personnel, curricular guidance, liaison between overseas schools and American educational resources, and consultative visits to overseas schools. It is a useful source for lists of available teaching opportunities in all overseas schools, except for Department of Defense schools, which it does not service.

If you wish to take advantage of ISS facilities on your job hunt, you will have to pay a registration fee and subsequently a placement fee if you find an appropriate position with ISS assistance.

How to Apply

Write to: International Schools Services
126 Alexander St.
Princeton, NJ   08540

Peace Corps

The Peace Corps still hires a few teachers with experience for countries in Africa, Asia, and Latin America.

How to Apply

Write to: Peace Corps
Action
812 Connecticut Ave. NW
Washington, DC   20525

Overseas Colleges and Universities

Teaching opportunities with three overseas institutions, two of which are American-related, should be explored by the PhD.

How to Apply

Write to: American University of Beirut
305 East 45th St.
New York, NY   10017

Istanbul Robert Kolej
Yuksek, Okulu
Robert College
Pk 8
Bebek, Istanbul
Turkey

or

American University in Cairo
866 UN Plaza
New York, NY   10017

Specific Locations

If you have special aptitudes for the Middle East, you may wish to explore opportunities with the following:

American–Mideast Educational and Training Services
1717 Massachusetts Ave. NW
Washington, DC   20036

For positions in Greece, Turkey, and Lebanon, write to:

Near East College Association
305 East 45th St.
New York, NY   10017

The African–American Institute has information on teaching jobs in Africa. Write to:

African–American Institute
833 UN PLaza
New York, NY   10017

and ask for its free brochure, *Opportunities in Africa.*
The Hershey Chocolate Corporation finances a program for sending teachers to schools in Nigeria and Ghana. Write to:

Hershey Chocolate Corporation
Hershey, PA   17033

Positions are occasionally available in the Trust Territories to assist native teachers. These jobs are located throughout Micronesia. Write to:

> Trust Territory of the Pacific Islands
> Building 112
> Fort Mason
> San Francisco, CA   94123

Australia may be interested in applications of teachers for the primary and secondary grades. Write to:

> Victoria Teacher Selection Program
> California State University
> Hayward, CA   94542

Exchange of Positions

If you have a teaching position and merely wish to temporarily exchange with an overseas teacher, write to:

> Teacher Exchange Section
> US Office of Education
> Washington, DC   20202

Additional Organizations

For a list of agencies that assist overseas placement, or for specific job opportunities under US government and foreign government programs, write to:

> Information and Reference Division
> Institute of International Education
> 809 UN Plaza
> New York, NY   10017

A booklet with information on agencies and organizations in almost a hundred countries that are concerned in one way or another with recruiting teaching staff may be obtained by writing to:

> National Commission for UNESCO
> UNESCO
> New York, NY   10017

Also, get a copy of *Opportunities Abroad for Teachers*, a booklet put out by the Office of Education that explains the Fulbright program for exchanging teachers. Application procedures, awards, and arrangements with cooperating countries are covered in the booklet. Write to:

> Office of Education
> Department of Health, Education, and Welfare
> Washington, DC 20202

Other booklets you may wish to look at are: *Teaching Abroad*, compiled by Marjorie Beckles and put out by the Institute of International Education (809 UN Plaza, New York, NY 10017) and *Teachers' Guide to Teaching Positions in Foreign Countries*, compiled by H. Dilts and H. Hulleman (Box 514, Ames, IA 50010).

A list of additional contacts for teaching jobs overseas follows:

Teaching Positions

Canada

Department of Education, Edmonton, Alberta

Department of Education, Victoria, British Columbia

Director of Education, Fredericton, New Brunswich

Department of Education, St. Johns, Newfoundland

Department of Education, Halifax, Nova Scotia

Department of Education, 44 Eglinton Avenue, West, Toronto 12, Ontario

Education Division, Department of Indian Affairs and Northern Development, Ottawa, Ontario

Department of Education, Yukon Territorial Government, Box 2703, Whitehorse, Yukon Territory

Europe

Austro-American Institute of Education, Operngasse 4, Wien 1, Austria

Gloria Felix School, Leck-Arlbert, Austria

American International School, Villa Bella Vista, Ave. de Vallauris, Cannes, France

American School of Paris, 41 Rue Pasteur, 92210 Saint-Cloud, France

The American Community School, 129 Aghias Paraskevis St., Ano Halandri, Athens, Greece

The British Institute, Athens, Greece

The Institute of American Studies, 72 Academias St., Athens, Greece

American Community School, Via Spadiri, 2 (High School) and Via Bezzola, 6(Lower School), Rome, Italy

American School of Florence, Via Roti Michelozzi 2, Florence, Italy

LeFleuron, Toree de Cattaia, Via de Michelangelo, Florence, Italy

Miss Barry's American School, Via dei Bardi 30, Florence, Italy

St. Stephen's School, Via Lungro, 1, 00178 Rome, Italy

The American Junior High School in Italy, Ravello, Costiera Amalfitana, Italy

The International School of Milan, Via Caccialepori 22, Milan, Italy

American High School in Luxembourg, American College in Luxembourg, 52 Av. des Bains, Mondorf-les-Bains, Luxembourg

American International School of Rotterdam, Hillegondastraat 21, Rotterdam, Netherlands

American School of The Hague, Doornstraat 6, The Hague, Netherlands

International School of Amsterdam, Meer en Vaart 13, Amsterdam, Netherlands

American High School of Barcelona, Via Augusta 123, Barcelona, Spain

King's College, Cuesta del Segrado Corazon 10, Madrid-16, Spain

American College of Switzerland, 1894 R. Leysin, Switzerland

Franklin College, 6902 Lugano, Switzerland

Le Chateau des Enfants, The American School in Switzerland, CH 6926 Montagnola, Lugano, Switzerland

The International School of Geneva, 62 Route de Chene, 1208 Geneva, Switzerland

United Nations School, 1 Ave. de la Paix, Geneva, Switzerland

International Finishing School, C.u.R. Heyer, 452 Beckum, Westf., West Germany

John F. Kennedy School, Teltanerdamm 87/93, Berlin, West Germany

Munich International School, 8136 Percha-bei-Starnberg, Schloss Buchhof, West Germany

Latin America

Escuela Americana, Apartado Postal 1572, San Salvador, El Salvador

American School, Apartado Postal No. 83, Guatemala, Guatemala

American School, Tegucigalpa, Honduras

American High School, Apartado 1119, Cuernavaca, Morelos, Mexico

American School Foundation, Calle Sur 136 No. 135, Tacubaya, D.F., Mexico

American School Foundation of Monterrey, Rio Missouri Ote 555, Colonia del Valle, Monterrey, N.L., Mexico

Escuela John F. Kennedy, Queretaro, Qro., Mexico

Pan American School of Monterrey, Apartado 474, Monterrey, N.L., Mexico

American-Nicaragua School, Apartado Postal 3670, Managua, Nicaragua

Romey Air Force Base Schools, Puerto Rico, APO New York, 09845

Secretary of Education, Department of Education, Hato Rey, Puerto Rico 00900

Escuela Bella Vista, Apartado 290, Maracaibo, Venezuela

Escuela Campo Alegre, Apartado del Este 60382, Caracas, Venezuela

Director of Personnel Services, Department of Education, Charlotte Amalie, St. Thomas, Virgin Islands 00801

Pacific Area

Director of Education, Department of Education, Pago Pago, American Samoa 96920

Department of Education, Queensland, Brisbane, Queensland, Australia

Education Department, Tasmania, GPO Box 169 B, Hobart, Tasmania, Australia

Education Department, Victoria, Treasury Place, Melbourne, C.2, Victoria, Australia

Education Department, Western Australia, Parliament Place, Perth, Australia

Personnel Director, Department of Education, Agana, Guam   96910

Office of Personnel Services, Department of Education, State of Hawaii, PO Box 2360, Honolulu, Hawaii   96803

Personnel Director, Department of Education, Agana, Guam   96910

CHAPTER ELEVEN

International Law

If you have a background in law and international affairs and wish to put both to use on the job market, you will find yourself in a very strong position indeed. This unusual combination provides you with one of those rare backgrounds that gives you serious consideration in the United Nations, the federal government, nonprofit organizations, businesses, banks, and the communications field, not to mention private practice—in other words, just about everywhere.

Of the two degrees—law and international affairs—you will find the former of paramount importance on the job hunt. You will ordinarily not get a professional job on the legal staff of any organization without a law degree. The addition of an international degree, even though it will not guarantee you work of an international nature, will give you an inside track for such jobs as they develop.

Generally, a law degree takes three years and a Master's of international affairs takes two. It is possible, however, to get both degrees in less time. Columbia University, for example, has a joint program between its Law School and its School of International Affairs that grants the Juris Doctor and the Master of International Affairs in four years.

A World of Opportunities

What exactly are the career possibilities for this combined background?

United Nations

As an American looking for a legal job on the UN Secretariat's legal staff, you will find your chances brighter than those of Americans with only an international affairs degree who are looking for political or economic work. Jobs are few and highly competitive, but a background in public international law will improve your credentials. Because most specialized agencies in the UN structure have their own legal staffs, these should also be included among your targets.

Federal Government

All the foreign-oriented agencies of the US government have Legal Divisions or General Counsel offices that will find your combined background of unusual interest. The State Department even sends recruiters to some law schools in order to interview prospective candidates. Entry into the Department's Legal Adviser's office is by interview, not by written exam.

As for the domestic-oriented agencies, most of the large ones have legal staffs and would welcome your application. Since international work may be less important in these agencies, you may be initially assigned to domestic legal problems, but your international training can eventually be used when a vacancy calling for international know-how develops.

Federal government salaries are good but not as high as in top law firms. Competition for government jobs, accordingly, may be less keen than in the private sector.

Businesses and Banks

The largest of these organizations have their own Legal Division or General Counsel. Others place their legal work in the hands of retained law firms. Where businesses and banks are heavily engaged in the international, your combined background will give you a serious hearing.

Communications

The largest wire services, networks, and publishers either have their own legal staffs or contract for legal services from outside firms. Here again the combined background is a decided plus.

Nonprofit Organizations and Foundations

Only the largest of these organizations in the international field have legal staffs. The majority obtain outside legal help. Put the Ford Foundation first on your list of targets. Here you will find that salaries often approximate those in the private sector.

The **International Legal Center** has a program for sending recent law school grads to Third World areas to help develop their legal structures and institutions. Teaching may also be involved in some assignments. Grants are modest and usually cover only transportation and maintenance. Write to:

> International Legal Center
> 866 UN Plaza
> New York, NY 10017

Private Practice

With your combined background you will ordinarily gravitate to private law firms with special international interests. Consider in particular the fields of maritime law and international patents.

In most of these cases, you will be based in the United States, not abroad. Even in the State Department, though you may make trips overseas to participate in legal negotiations undertaken by embassies, you will spend most of your time in Washington.

One of the most helpful publications for your job hunt is the *Directory of Opportunities in International Law,* Fifth edition, John Bassett Moore Society of International Law, 1977. This pamphlet can be purchased for $5. Checks should be made payable to the John Basset Moore Society of International Law, and sent to the Society at the University of Virginia School of Law, Charlottesville, VA 22901.

Bibliographies

Books of General Interest

Boll, Carl, *Executive Jobs Unlimited* (New York: Macmillan, 1965).

Bolles, Richard N., *What Color Is Your Parachute?* (Berkeley, CA: Ten Speed Press, 1976).

Brown, Newell, *After College ... Junior College ... Military Service ... What?* (New York: Grosset and Dunlap, 1971).

Calvert, Robert, Jr., *Your Future in International Service* (New York: Richard Rosen Press, 1969).

Joint Committee on Printing, *Congressional Directory* (Washington, DC: Government Printing Office).

Elwood, Robert L., ed.-in-chief, *Directory of Opportunities in International Law* (Charlottesville, VA: John Bassett Moore Society of International Law, 1977).

Greco, Ben, *How to Get the Job That's Right for You* (Homewood, IL: Dow Jones-Irwin, 1975).

Gruber, Edward C., ed., *Résumés That Get Jobs, Résumé Service* (New York: ARCO Publishing Co.)

Haldane, Bernard, *Career Satisfaction and Job Success* (New York: American Management Association, 1974).

International Directory for Youth Internships (New York: Foreign Areas Material Center, 1977–78).

Irish, Richard K., *Go Hire Yourself an Employer* (Garden City, NY: Anchor Books, Doubleday, 1973).

Jackson, Tom, *28 Days to a Better Job* (New York: Hawthorne Books, 1977).

Knott, James E., *Career Opportunities in the International Field* (Washington, DC: School of Foreign Service, Georgetown University, 1977).

Liebers, Arthur, *How to Get the Job You Want Overseas* (New York: Pilot Books, 1975).

Mann, Thomas E., *Career Alternatives for Political Scientists, A Guide for Faculty and Graduate Students* (Washington, DC: American Political Science Association, 1977).

Medley, H. Anthony, *Sweaty Palms—The Neglected Art of Being Interviewed* (Belmont, CA: Lifetime Learning Publications, 1978).

Moore, Charles G., *The Career Game* (New York: National Institute of Career Planning, 1976).

Payne, Richard A., *How to Get a Better Job Quicker* (New York: Taplinger Publishing Co., 1972).

Pell, Arthur R., *The College Graduate Guide to Job Finding* (New York: Simon and Schuster, 1973).

Powell, C. Randall, *Career Planning and Placement for the College Graduate of the 70's* (Dubuque, IA: Kendall/Hunt Publishing Co., 1974).

U.S. Government Manual (Washington, DC: Office of the Federal Register, General Services Administration, 1978–79).

Yearbook of International Organizations (Brussels, Belgium: Union of International Associations, 1974).

Washington Information Directory (Washington, DC: Congressional Quarterly, Inc., 1978–79).

Wasson, Donald, *American Agencies Interested in International Affairs* (New York: Praeger Publishers, 1964).

Directories of Nonprofit Organizations

Conservation Directory (Washington, DC: National Wildlife Federation). Annual list of organizations and agencies concerned with the conservation, management, and use of natural resources.

Directory of Organizations Concerned with Environmental Research (State University of New York at Fredonia, 1970). Geographic and subject listing of organizations (governmental, university, and private) throughout the world involved in environmental research.

US Non-Profit Organizations in Development Assistance Abroad (New York: Technical Assistance Information Clearing House, 1978). Comprehensive directory of information on over 400 nonprofit organizations, agencies, missions, and foundations and their work in 124 countries in Africa, East Asia, and the Pacific, Latin America, the Near-East, and South Asia. The alphabetical listing gives programs and objectives, with cross-references by region, country, and organization.

US Voluntary Organizations and World Affairs (New York: Center for War/Peace Studies). Listings of national and community organizations concerned with world affairs, explaining their purposes and activities, addresses, and staff sizes.

Directory of University Research Bureaus and Institutes (Detroit: Gale Research Company). Lists research and development organizations, social and psychological science groups, documentation, operations research, and computer specialists, and federal government laboratories.

Research Centers Directory (Detroit: Gale Research Company). A directory of 4500 research institutes, centers, foundations, laboratories, bureaus, and other nonprofit research facilities in the United States and Canada. Information includes scope of research activities and names of publications.

Foundation Directory, ed. Marianna O. Lewis (New York: The Foundation Center, Columbia University Press).

Technical Assistance Programs of US Non-Profit Organizations (New York: American Council of Voluntary Agencies for Foreign Service). Separate volumes exist for Latin America (1967), Africa (1969), Near East–South Asia (1969), and the Far East (1966).

International Directory for Youth Internships (New York: Foreign Area Materials Center 1977-78).

World Directory of Environmental Research Centers, William K. Wilson (New York: Orix Press, 1974). Distributed by RR Bowker Co., New York.

Directories of Businesses and Banks

General Directories

Standard and Poor's Register of Corporations, Directors, and Executives, two volumes (New York: Standard and Poor's Corporation). Updated annually. Alphabetical list of approximately 34,000 US and Canadian corporations, giving officers, products (if any), sales range, and number of employees. Also, brief information on about 70,000 executives and directors.

Million Dollar Directory (New York: Dun and Bradstreet). Lists about 31,000 US companies with a stated worth of $1 million or more. Gives officers, products (if any), approximate sales, and number of employees. Also, alphabetical listing of officers and directors.

Middle Market Directory (New York: Dun and Bradstreet). Lists approximately 33,000 US companies with a stated worth of $500,000 to $999,999.

Thomas Register of American Manufactures. Eleven volumes updated annually. Volumes one to six list manufacturers by specific product. Volume seven is an alphabetical listing of companies, and includes addresses, branch offices, subsidiaries, products, and estimated capitalization. Volume eight is the index to product categories and also contains a list of leading trade or brand names. Volumes nine to eleven contain catalogs of products.

Moody's Manual (New York: Moody's Investment Service). Updated annually. Has both alphabetical and geographic lists. Gives descriptions of each company and brief histories, and lists plants, products, and officers.

Trade Directories of the World, compiled by U.H.E. Croner (New York: Croner Publications). This annotated list of businesses and trade directories is arranged by continent and by country. Includes an index to "trades and professions" and a country index.

Directories of American Companies with Foreign Subsidiaries

Bureau of International Commerce, Trade Lists (US Department of Commerce). Updated annually. Lists American firms, subsidiaries, and affiliates in each country with brief descriptions and addresses.

Directory of American Firms Operating in Foreign Countries, eighth edition, compiled by Juvenal L. Angel (New York: Simon & Schuster 1975). Lists companies alphabetically, giving name of officer in charge of foreign operations and countries of operation; also lists companies by country of operation.

American Firms: Subsidiaries and Affiliates in Brazil (New York: Brazilian Government Trade Bureau).

Directory of US Firms Operating in Latin America (Washington, DC: Pan American Union). This gives company lists, including the name of each manager, arranged by country.

Directories of Foreign Companies with American Subsidiaries

Directory of Foreign Firms Operating in the United States, compiled by Juvenal L. Angel (New York: Simon & Schuster).

Directory of Japanese Firms and Offices in the US (New York: Japan Trade Center).

American Subsidiaries of German Firms (New York: German–American Chamber of Commerce).

Directories of Companies in Foreign Countries

Major Companies of Europe, ed. J. Love (New York: McGraw-Hill). Description of "Fortune 500" companies of Western Europe.

Current European Directories, G. P. Henderson (Beckenham, Kent, England: CBD Research, Ltd.). An annotated guide, arranged by country in Europe, to general directories of associations and research organizations.

Principal International Businesses (New York: Dun and Bradstreet).

Jane's Major Companies of Europe (London, England: Jane's Yearbooks). Updated annually.

Export–Import Companies

American Register of Exporters and Importers (New York: American Register of Exporters and Importers, Inc.). An especially important volume for those with both international and business qualifications, since export–import firms need both types of background.

Dun and Bradstreet Exporter's Encyclopedia, World Marketing Guide (New York: Dun and Bradstreet International). Updated annually.

Directories of Banking and Finance Industries

Money Market Directory. A directory of 6,000 institutional investors and their portfolio managers.

Polk's Bank Directory.

Security Dealers of North America.

Financial Market Place, Steven E. Goodman.

Investment Companies, (New York: Arthur Weisenberg and Co.).

Moody's Bank and Finance Manual (New York: Moody's Investment Service, Inc.) Two volumes updated annually.

Banks of the World (Frankfurt am Main, Germany: Fritz Knopp Verlag).

International Bankers Directory (New York: Rand-McNally).

Who's Who in Banking: The Directory of the Banking Profession, Second edition (New York: Business Press, Inc.).

Banking Periodicals

The Banker
The Bankers Magazine
Bankers Monthly
Banking—The Journal of the American Bankers Association
Federal Reserve Bulletin
Journal of Commercial Bank Lending

Trade and Professional Associations

Directory of National Trade and Professional Associations of the United States (Washington, DC: Columbia Books). Alphabetical list of 4,300 national trade and professional associations. Gives chief officer, number of members, annual budget, and publications.

Encyclopedia of Associations, (Detroit: Gale Research Co.). Comprehensive list of national associations, with an alphabetical and key-word index. Gives name of chief officer, brief statement of activities, number of members, and publications.

Corporation Records

Annual Reports to Shareholders

10-K Reports to the Securities and Exchange Commission

Proxy Statements

For companies traded over-the-counter, the Marvin Scudder Financial Collection is a valuable source of company history, annual reports, prospectuses, reorganization plans, and miscellaneous financial information.

Histories of Companies

Studies in Enterprise: A Selected Bibliography of American and Canadian Company Histories and Biographies of Businessmen (Boston: Harvard University Graduate School of Business Administration).

American Economic and Business History: A Guide to Information Sources, Robert W. Lovett.

Directories of Consultants

The Consultants and Consulting Organization Directory, eds. Paul Wasserman and Janice McLean (Detroit: Gale Research Co.).

Directory of Consultant Members, American Management Association. Annual.

Directory of Management Consultants and Industrial Services, Los Angeles Chamber of Commerce. Lists consulting firms and business and industrial services.

Directory of Membership and Services, Association of Consulting Management Engineers. Annual.

Directory of Membership and Services, American Management Association. Annual.

Engineering Careers with Consulting Firms, Resource Publications, DR Goldenson and Company. Page profiles describing the activities of the firm, the nature of engineering services, and requirements for positions. Information arranged by specialty and geographic location.

Industrial Research Laboratories of the US, Revised edition. ed. William Buchanan. Bowker Associates.

Who's Who in Consulting: A Reference Guide to Professional Personnel Engaged in Consultation of Business, Industry and Government (Ithaca, NY: Cornell University Graduate School of Business and Public Administration).

Directories of Book Publishers, Newspapers, Periodicals, and Broadcasting Networks

Book Publishers

International Literary Market Place, ed. Peter Found (London and New York: RR Bowker). Updated annually. Contains facts on the worldwide publishing industry, minus the United States.

Literary Market Place With Names and Numbers (New York: RR Bowker). Updated annually. Contains facts on 22,000 firms and individuals in US publishing, listing names, titles, addresses, and phone numbers.

Publisher's International Directory (RR Bowker Company). This directory gives names and addresses of 20,000 active publishers in 144 countries.

Who's Who in Publishing, An International Biographical-Guide (RR Bowker Company). Contains detailed biographical data of 3,500 leading persons in the publishing field.

Editor and Publisher International Yearbook (New York: Editor and Publisher). Updated annually.

Careers in Book Publishing (New York: McGraw-Hill, 1976).

Newspapers, Periodicals

Newspaper International (National Register Publishing Company). Lists newspapers and newsweeklies in over ninety countries. Published annually in January, plus updated supplements.

Standard Periodical Directory. Annual. A subject listing of 53,000 US and Canadian periodicals giving addresses, scope, year founded, frequency, subscription rate, and circulation. Alphabetical index at end.

Ayer's Directory (Philadelphia: NW Ayer & Son). Lists newspapers, magazines, and trade publications.

Ayer's Directory of Newspapers and Periodicals (Philadelphia: NW Ayer & Son).

Editor and Publisher International Yearbook (New York: Editor and Publisher). Encyclopedia of the newspaper industry. Directory of over 8,000 US and Canadian weekly and nondaily newspapers. Directory of newspapers in Latin America, Europe, Asia, Africa, and Australia.

Broadcasting Networks

Broadcasting Yearbook (Washington, DC). Updated annually.

Photo Credits

Index